WITH

D0915208

PRELUDE TO HONGKONG

PRELUDE
TO
HONGKONG

by

AUSTIN COATES

Routledge & Kegan Paul

LONDON

*First published 1966
by Routledge and Kegan Paul Ltd
Broadway House, 68–74 Carter Lane
London, E.C.4*

*Printed in Great Britain by
John Wright & Sons Ltd
Bristol*

TO

J. M. BRAGA

IN GRATITUDE AND FRIENDSHIP

CONTENTS

ILLUSTRATIONS

Illustrations 6, 9 and 10 are reproduced by permission
of F. Lewis Publishers, Limited, and first appeared in
George Chinnery (1774–1852) Artist of the China Coast, by
Henry and Sidney Berry Hill (1963).

INTRODUCTION

As THE TOURIST BROCHURE unambiguously states, the British first occupied Hongkong in 1841 during the Opium War. In fact, the acquisition of Hongkong and the conflict that went with it—one of the most extraordinary encounters in the history of any two nations—cannot be seen in isolation, being the outcome of a historical process of which the development from origins takes us back at least two hundred years prior to 1841, and if the experience of the Portuguese, who were the pioneer Europeans on the China coast, is included, well back over a further hundred years.

For the greater part of this long period Hongkong was a nameless island, not an issue between anyone, not even known to any save the handful of Chinese villagers who lived on it and the minor Chinese district officials in whose area it lay, a region of innumerable and similarly nameless islands. The scene of history lay between two places: Canton, the largest city of South China, in those days considerably larger than any city in Europe; and the tiny Portuguese enclave of Macao, eighty-three miles south of Canton at the mouth of the Pearl River.

The Portuguese entered the picture with their first voyage to China in 1513. Against many obstacles, of which the most important was Chinese official unwillingness, they persisted in their attempts to do trade with China, and in 1557, by an agreement with the local Chinese authorities, were permitted to erect permanent buildings at Macao, which in the space of a few years became—and for several decades remained—a

Introduction

city of great riches, for many years unique in being entirely unfortified, linked by close commercial ties with Canton.

The region in which these two places are situated lies just within the tropics, with hot and humid summers of heavy rainfall, winters cool, dry and pleasant, and a spring usually overcast with cloud amid which fall gentle showers. The coastal region is subject to typhoons occurring mainly in late summer, between July and October.

It is a land of rivers, with in those days few means of communication other than by boat, the riverine areas being flat, interrupted here and there by starkly rising isolated hills. The principal occupations of the Chinese inhabitants were farming and fishing, the largest crop being rice grown by wet cultivation. The trees native to the region are pine, camphor and Chinese banyan, and the area was famous for its fruit orchards of laichees, lung-ngan, loquat, pomelo, bananas, plums and pears, and for its winter oranges of many varieties including the tangerine, of which this is the original home. To these native fruits the Portuguese had introduced from South America a number of others, including papaya, guava, custard apples and the pineapple. They had also introduced the peanut, in the oil of which two-thirds of all Chinese food is cooked.

Among the delicacies of the river were prawns, crabs and oysters, and pond fishing was a specialized occupation. Along the Pearl River were numerous villages constructed on stilts over the water. Distinct from the land-based fishermen-farmers was a separate race of fishermen who lived entirely in their boats. These were outcasts, forbidden to reside ashore, to have their children educated or to wear shoes. Many among them were pirates, their favourite haunt being the scattered rocky islands off the mouth of the Pearl River.

But although a land of great plenty, the area was regarded by the Chinese Government as the outer fringe of civilization, a remote place more than a thousand miles away from the sophisticated splendours of Peking. Chinese civilization, many thousand years old, had grown up far to the north, in the basin of the Yellow River, whence it had gradually expanded among tribes and clans which adopted Chinese ways, names and language, and were soon indistinguishable from other Chinese.

x

Introduction

Since the year 221 B.C. China, hitherto more a cultural than a political entity, had been unified under a central imperial government, and it was at this time that Kwangtung province, in which our scene lies, came within the orbit of Chinese control, Canton becoming a garrison city connected with the north by a canal waterway, one of the great engineering feats of ancient times. Not till about a thousand years later did Kwangtung become a place of distinctively Chinese habitation, due to southward migration and pressure of population further north. At the time our story begins the region had been under full Chinese control for about six hundred years.

Of the two cities with which we are to be concerned Macao, though much the smaller, is in relation to the matters to be observed the more important, in that it was Portuguese tenure of Macao, often precarious, which enabled the West to maintain continuous relations with China from 1557 onwards. Portuguese endurance in Macao was the foot by means of which, through centuries of difficulty, the door of China was prevented from closing entirely. The opening it made was narrow. It was hard to squeeze through. But without it there would have been no entry whatever.

Let us therefore approach as every foreign traveller in early times had to—via Macao—being rowed ashore in ship's barge towards the Praia Grande, that elegant crescent of Latin architecture facing the waterfront, beyond which rise the low domes and towers of seminaries and churches, the whole creating that uniquely unexpected European view which is Macao's greeting to every visitor from the sea.

I

JOHN WEDDELL'S VOYAGE
TO CHINA

I: THE CITY OF THE NAME OF GOD

ON 27TH JUNE 1637 four English ships under the command of Captain John Weddell anchored among the rocky grass-covered islands just south of Macao. As chief factor, or commercial officer, of the voyage came Peter Mundy, one of the most travelled Englishmen living, whose diary enables us to have an unusually clear impression of what took place on this, the first English trading voyage to China.

In response to a salute fired by Weddell's ships a boat was sent out from Macao warning the English not to approach further without the permission of the Portuguese Captain-General. On the second day Peter Mundy was sent in Weddell's barge to deliver a letter from King Charles I, together with one from Weddell. Accompanying Mundy ashore were John Mountney, accountant, and Thomas Robinson, secretary and interpreter, who spoke Portuguese, the *lingua franca* of Eastern trade. The Captain-General, Dom Domingos da Camara Noronha, received them briefly in the company of the members of Macao's local ruling body, the Senate. Robinson presented the letters. After being told that replies would be delivered to them on board next day, the Englishmen withdrew.

Before returning to their ships they were invited to lunch at the Jesuit seminary, headquarters of the far-flung Jesuit mission in the Far East. The invitation was a gesture of thanks to the

English for having brought several Jesuits with them from Malacca. After lunch they were taken to see the architectural marvel of the city, the Jesuit church of São Paulo.

Today and for more than a hundred years what visitor to Macao has failed to be impressed by the remains of this once magnificent church? All that is now to be seen is a great carved stone façade, its windows like sightless eyes, standing stark against the sky at the head of a magnificent sweep of ascending steps. Of the church itself, destroyed by fire in 1835, nothing survives. Yet even thus, gaping and churchless, São Paulo remains one of the unforgettable landmarks of Christian Asia.

Peter Mundy saw it two years after the stone façade had been added, erected with the help of the Jesuits' Japanese students and converts. Externally majestic and austere, within the church was sumptuous. 'The rooffe is of the fairest Arche that yett I ever saw to my remembrance,' wrote Mundy, 'of excellentt worckemanshippe, Carved in wood, curiously guilt and painted with exquisite collours.' It was a baroque extravaganza executed by the people who above all others excel in the carving and painting of wood.

Of Macao itself Peter Mundy wrote that it was 'built on rising hills, some gardens and trees among their houses making a pretty prospect somewhat resembling Goa, although not so big; their houses double-tiled, and that plastered over again, for prevention of hurricanes or violent winds that happen some years, called by the Chinese typhoons, which is also the reason (as they say) they build no high towers nor steeples to their churches'.[1]

In the entire city, which by this time had been established for eighty years, there was only one woman from Portugal. The wives of the earliest Portuguese settlers had been Malay and Japanese, who brought with them many of their own customs. Macao women, their Muslim traditions not quite extinguished, still veiled themselves with light shawls in public. The richer women travelled in norimons, Japanese litters, though the sedan chair was just coming into vogue. In the street women wore Malay sarongs of splendid colours and designs, and high

[1] For convenience some of the quotations in this chapter are in modernized spelling.

cork-soled shoes, but at home they no longer concealed themselves from strangers; shawl and sarong were discarded to be
replaced by a Japanese kimono. In all, the influence of Japan
was very noticeable, Macao having risen to prominence on its
control of trade between Japan and China.

Despite Macao's prosperous appearance, however, the English
quickly perceived that the Portuguese position there was not as
sound as might have been supposed. While being allowed by the
Chinese to stay in Macao, the Portuguese were subjected to
numerous vexations. Their Japan fleet, which sailed annually
for Nagasaki, was ready to depart, but the goods purchased by
Macao merchants at the spring trade fair at Canton had not yet
arrived, having been 'embargoed or detained for a great sum
of money which the Chinese demand of the Portuguese for
building a vessel bigger than they have leave or warrant for.
On divers other occasions they devise ways and means to extort
moneys from them, as for killing, wronging or abusing a China-
man, there being a great many that live together in the town
with them and near about them, having a Mandarin or Judge
of their own to decide their differences'.

In other words, there was something odd about Portugal's
tenure. Macao was not, like Goa and Malacca, an area in which
Portuguese writ ran undisputed.

II: A RECONNAISSANCE IN THE PEARL RIVER

The following day came the Captain-General's reply. Pleading
lack of orders from higher authority (the Portuguese Viceroy at
Goa), Domingos da Camara regretted that he was unable to
give the English any assistance other than to provide for the
fleet anything urgently needed. Weddell's ships were still not
allowed into the harbour. Watchboats were sent out bringing
them food twice a day but preventing anyone from approaching.

During these days of inaction, which the English used to
careen their ships, a Chinese official with a suitable entourage
came to make a report to Canton on the nature of their business.
'Hee was apparelled in a gowne or coate of blacke Sarsanette or
tiffany, and under thatt other garmentts with strange attire on
his head. Hee had carried before him a broad board written

3

with China Characters, itt seemes the badge of his Authority and Commission.' After a few more days a more important officer 'came in a bigge vessell with a kettle Drumme and a broad brasse pan, on both of which the[y] beatt, keeping tyme together. They had allsoe on their vessell certaine Flagges and streamers'.

When after a day or so Macao's goods came down from Canton the English saw that the Portuguese had no intention of dealing with them till after their own fleet had safely left for Japan. Portuguese pleasure boats sailed or rowed round them in a holiday atmosphere for all save the English; but none came too near, and as Peter Mundy remarked with a wink in his Protestant eye, 'China stuffes, not any to bee broughtt us on paine off excommunication'.

It will be seen that the Portuguese were installed at the mouth of the river somewhat in the capacity of a filter, without passing through which no outsider could make contact with the Chinese. It was in fact for precisely this reason that the Portuguese had been allowed to settle in Macao, originally to keep the lower parts of the Pearl River free of pirates, but also with the idea that seafaring foreigners would probably prove the most appropriate people to keep other seafaring foreigners away.

The English were not of course aware of this curious situation. As they saw it the Portuguese were trying to keep them out for reasons of self-interest. After a fortnight Weddell decided to try the chances of bypassing Macao and establishing direct connexion with Canton. Robinson and Mountney were sent in the fleet's pinnace and barge 'to seeke For speech and trade with the Chineses' up the Pearl River.

They sailed up the great estuary—between fifteen and twenty miles wide—to the narrow entry of the river proper called Hu Mên, or Tiger Gate—in European tradition the Bocca Tigris—and from there up-river, making themselves understood by dumb signs. Some way up they were met by a fleet of junks commanded by an officer of the approximate rank of Commodore, among whose crews were some Africans, runaway slaves from Macao, who could speak some Portuguese and who acted as interpreters.

The Commodore, after a hostile opening, became more friendly and circumspect when he discovered that the English had reached so far with no pilot. He agreed that provided they left the pinnace and went the rest of the way in a small junk, the officers might go further up towards Canton. It was not lost on the English that the reason for ordering that they tranship was not the shallowness of the river but the fear inspired by the pinnace, although the junks were armed equally and carried three times the number of men.

In the junk they came to the First Bar, about thirteen miles below Canton. Here they were informed by customs officials that no application to trade could be made unless routed through the proper channels—the mandarins in the Macao area—but that if they would peacefully re-enter their ships and depart every assistance would be given them in obtaining a trade licence. Optimistically Robinson and Mountney returned to Weddell with this information.

But Weddell, a weather-beaten sea dog as tough as they come, was not a man to be taken in by a civil service answer. To apply in Macao meant the application being interfered with by the Portuguese, who in a special mission from the Senate during the pinnace's absence had explained to him that the Chinese would allow no one else to trade in the river. Gentler methods, as Weddell saw it, had failed. What was required was sterner stuff.

On 29th July Captain Weddell sailed with all his ships up the Pearl River.

III: IN THE BOCCA TIGRIS

In narrating what follows I would have liked to confine our sights to our own countrymen, in order to give as full an impression as possible of what they themselves experienced. This, however, would defeat our purpose, in that we would end by sailing away from China with them, as baffled and perplexed, as ignorant of the situation into which they had stepped, as they were themselves. Accordingly I propose that we should occasionally lift the veil surrounding them and look into the world which from them was hidden. Let us do so now.

By any standards, those of yesterday or today, China was admirably ruled. The largest country in the world, with the largest population, its government was superior to any that had

B   5

hitherto been evolved in any part of the globe; and when one considers the immensity of the task of ruling China, then as now, the state of justice, peace and order which prevailed, without the country being in any sense a slave state, is little short of miraculous.

In the prime position of responsibility for all this were the mandarins,[1] the civil service, the heads of which were directly responsible to the Emperor. Appointed by competitive examination in the Chinese classics, the members of the civil service were a *corps d'élite* of intellect. The mandarinate was in fact the archetype of all other civil services, and particularly of our own, the gradual development of which owed more than is immediately visible to ideas becoming current in Europe at the end of the seventeenth century as a result of a growing knowledge of China and her institutions.

By this time, along the swift channels of information available to the Chinese civil service, word had come from Canton to all concerned that dangerous, unidentified foreigners had reached Macao and might attempt to enter the river. The mandarinate's foremost consideration, for reasons which will in due course become apparent, was that the greatest care must be taken to avoid any disturbance that might have to be reported to Peking. If the foreigners could be removed by empty blandishments this would be the most satisfactory outcome, causing the minimum disturbance. If force had to be used it should only be in a situation wherein success was certain. The barbarians were extremely able when it came to fighting, and force would only succeed if applied by subterfuge. A direct engagement should be avoided at all costs.

As for the Portuguese in Macao, their difficulty was that in Chinese eyes the English resembled the Dutch, of whom the Chinese had formed a very bad opinion. Red-haired, with penetrating blue eyes, the Dutch had from their first appearance on the China coast created a frightening impression, becoming immediately classed as red barbarians, a species new to Chinese

---

[1] Mandarin: a Chinese civil servant. Used originally by the Portuguese, this word appears to bear no reference to any Chinese appellation or title. It is said to be a corruption of the Malay word *Mentri* (meaning a minister or officer) as pronounced by a Chinese of former times: man-da-li.

experience. When two years before Weddell's visit an English ship, the *London*, under charter to the Portuguese, had called at Macao, the English crew had been identified as red barbarians and the city severely fined by the mandarins for negligence in allowing them in. Weddell's up-river intrusion would mean another mass fine. Chinese and Portuguese were thus united in their desire to be rid of the English as soon and as quietly as possible. This the English did not understand. To the end they attributed their troubles to Portuguese scheming in protection of their monopoly position, which the English believed to be a hoax, but which was not. The Portuguese were indeed the only foreigners who were in practice allowed to trade with China from the sea.

Disregarding two Chinese warnings to stop, the English sailed on, passing two Chinese fleets with watchful care. From the second of these, consisting of forty well-armed junks of great size, an officer was sent to speak with them. Courteous and seemingly understanding, he promised Weddell that if he would wait, permission to go up to Canton would be speedily obtained. Sailing a short distance further, the English entered the Bocca Tigris and anchored beneath a disused fort at its mouth—known in European tradition as Anunghoi Fort—where they decided to await permission to proceed.

Many junks and smaller boats were about, but evidently on orders none would come near them; and when they went ashore to procure food they were menaced by soldiers at the fort. Hastily retiring to their ships, the English displayed 'bloudy ensignes' instead of white, 'the King's collours' instead of the flag of St. George, and made other warlike preparations.

Which were understood. A messenger was sent down with an interpreter, begging Captain Weddell to wait six days, when permission would certainly be received to go up. At the same time the English noted with concern that the fort was being invested with cannon and men.

Next day, with a white flag before them, another party went ashore to purchase food. The white flag meant nothing (white is the colour associated in China with funerals) and their landing was resisted. Nevertheless they pushed ashore, bought what they wanted, and with a crowd of country people gaping and chatting around them inspected a village.

They were offered some simple hospitality.

'The people there gave us a certaine Drinke called Chaa, which is only water with a kind of herbe boyled in itt. It must bee Drancke warme and is accompted wholesome.'

As Peter Mundy penned those words that night in his cabin he had little idea of the part that 'Chaa' was destined to play in the future relations between Europe and China, that the brew that had passed his lips would alter the social life of nations, providing the lure which was to bring foreigners ever more imperatively to pound upon China's doors.

It may seem strange that the Cantonese word *cha*, while passing into Indian languages, did not pass into English except as a slang word picked up two centuries later by British soldiers in India. The reason is that when tea-drinking was first introduced into Europe, in the second half of the seventeenth century, the French and the British were in touch with the great tea-producing province of Fukien, where the same Chinese word *cha* is pronounced *teh*. The French thus introduced *thé* into Europe, the English their own native version, *tea*, originally pronounced much the same as in French.[1]

IV: PAULO NORETTE

The six days of waiting having passed, the Chinese politely proceeded to ask for another four. This was too much for John Weddell. The barge was sent to take soundings further up.

As she moved, the fort opened fire. Up went the bloody ensign again, the English ships returning the fire. One shot from the fort hit the flagship, doing slight damage, but apart from this the Chinese fire was ineffectual. The fort cannons were in fixed positions, so no proper aim could be taken, and due to faulty gunpowder several balls just dropped out of the mouths of the cannon and fell in the grass below the fort's wall.

Irritated by the treatment they had received, the English did not let the inferiority of their opponents restrain them, but continued firing until the Chinese, having fired each of their guns once, evacuated the fort without even recharging them. The English then landed, occupied the deserted structure,

---

[1] viz. Alexander Pope: *The Rape of the Lock*,

'Here thou, great ANNA! whom three Realms obey,
Dost sometimes counsel take—and sometimes tea'.

hoisted the King's colours, and before returning to their ships partly dismantled the place, taking some of the more service-able guns.

Another facet which was to puzzle decade after decade of Europeans had appeared. Here was this vast nation, peaceful, prosperous and obviously extremely well governed. Was this the only kind of army they had to protect so great an empire? How was it possible? A few ceremonial guns, a scared bunch of ill-accoutred soldiers, a navy which was frightened of a small English pinnace. What did it mean? Beneath the whole of the pre-1842 period ran this unanswered riddle. Was China mili-tarily weak or strong?

Weddell was still undecided about his next move when the situation unexpectedly changed for the better with the arrival of an envoy from Canton, a Chinese official speaking Portu-guese. Brought up in Macao, he was one of that intriguing group of men who figure prominently in the early relations of Chinese and Europeans: the Chinese who, in Macao, Manila or one of the other European settlements, became a Christian of sorts, having been either adopted by a Christian family as a child or else converted as a boy, with a European godfather to make him his heir. Many such Chinese, dissatisfied with themselves or over-ambitious, later deserted their Christian surroundings to go back among their own people, where with duplicity for which they were uniquely adapted they became intermediaries in a dangerous but profitable intercourse between men of the two races.

No description of this one survives, yet we see him clearly. He is obviously Chinese, yet his youthful association with foreigners has changed something in his expression. There is a brightness, a sharpness in his eyes; he senses our humour and emotions; we feel he has broken from his ancestors' non-Christian ways and deserves our help and sympathy. He has great charm of manner, a little feminine perhaps, and in Western attire could easily be mistaken for a Eurasian. We cannot help being amused by his subtle understanding of his own people's weaknesses and shortcomings.

But he has given up his Western ways, grown his hair in Chinese fashion, and in official headgear and longcoat, with a wisp of beard and a fingernail or two carefully preserved, it needs only a flicker of the mind for the bright, intelligent look to be replaced by suave concealment, observing yet withdrawn, remote yet calculating. We realize then how tellingly he can inform his Chinese friends of our own weaknesses and short-comings.

He had two names, of course. His Chinese name is not found in Western accounts; his European name is not found in Chinese accounts. It is an element of the situation.

To Weddell and his compatriots he introduced himself as Paulo Norette. He hated the Portuguese and (having discovered the English were Protestants) the Catholic priests. They had taught him all kinds of falsehood about Christianity, he said, thereafter treating him so wretchedly that he had run away in despair to Canton, although his poor wife and children were still in Macao. Now that he was a government official, on very close terms with the highest executives—the English had met the Commodore, had they not? as a matter of fact, he resided in the Commodore's house in Canton—he would be only too happy to make sure the English received a licence to trade and so ruin those vile Catholics who had brought such misery to himself and hundreds of his fellow-countrymen.

Everyone was delighted. 'Now there appeared some hopes of setting a trade in these parts', wrote Peter Mundy in his account of the day. Norette would go and get permission from higher officials a little way up-river for a delegation of the English to present a petition for a licence in Canton.

Next day he returned with permission for a delegation given. Mountney, Robinson and one other, taking several fine presents with them, embarked in Norette's junk and reached Canton in the evening of the following day. After having a petition drawn up for them in Chinese, in the afternoon they were conducted ashore to the Commodore's palace, a large establish-ment with interior courts guarded by soldiers. In an inner hall they knelt before the Commodore in the abject posture adopted by ordinary Chinese when approaching a high official, and presented their petition, it being taken from their hands by Paulo Norette, who with yet more ceremonies handed it to his superior. The merchants then returned to their junk and were brought down-river again. By travelling that night and all next day they reached Weddell at midnight.

V: THE CHINESE SYSTEM OF OFFICIAL PERQUISITES

In introducing Norette I have taken the liberty of giving a broad hint about him, a hint which the English, new to the East, had no means of arriving at. Let us again draw back the curtain and look at what lay concealed behind it.

Who was Norette?

He claimed to be an official, and was certainly able to organize things in official quarters with remarkable address. Had the English known more of China they would have detected, even at his very first interview with Weddell, a flaw in his story.

His wife and children were at Macao.

Extracted and set apart from the other facts, this one alone showed plainly that whatever Norette was he was not an official. What official would be trusted who kept his wife and children in the settlement of the Western Ocean barbarians? Besides—he admitted it—he had formerly been an interpreter in Portuguese pay. His dislike of the Portuguese, his dissociation from the past, would not be sufficient for the immense traditions of China's bureaucracy while wife and children were still in Macao.

What was he then?

The Macao Senate later claimed that Norette was employed by them as an interpreter at the last trade fair in Canton, but that having swindled Macao merchants out of 80,000 taels of silver he was afraid to return there to his wife, and had accordingly pleaded with the Canton authorities to be allowed to stay where he was.

Supposing this to be the truth—and it is the most precise information we have about him—what was he doing posing as an official in the presence of so important a person as the Commodore, the Commander-in-Chief of the Pearl River defences?

Let us examine the timings. Robinson and Mountney reached Canton at about 7 p.m. on 17th August 1637. At 3 p.m. the following day they were received by the Commodore. In the entire history of China what foreigner, unless he was an intimate friend, can claim to have been received by a high official in less than twenty-four hours from his arrival? Such things happen only to ambassadors, and even then only rarely. An interview with a high officer is a matter of days, weeks, months of waiting, obtaining introductions, giving discreet presents or expensive dinners, writing obeisant letters. Unless there were some special motive the Commodore would never have received the English so soon.

The question reverses itself. What was the Commodore up to, having dealings with a man like Paulo Norette?

In pulling up this, we bare the roots. The Macao trade, China's only legitimate maritime foreign trade, was financially very rewarding. The chief beneficiary was the revenue, but in China there were no fixed salaries for civil servants, officials being entitled to draw their living costs, declaring to their superiors what they had drawn, from the revenues of their provinces or prefectures. Obviously, with minor adjustments in revenue returns, greater sums than those declared could be purloined. Altogether it is not surprising that most men who succeeded in passing the classical examinations for the civil service ended by making their families rich.

Every so often corruption such as this would be discovered by the Court and vigorously punished; but this was only when one of the Censors memorialized the Emperor or when corruption became so flagrant that it was evident even from Peking that returns were abnormally low. At every level of the hierarchy of government men were taking to themselves money which should or could have been going somewhere else, cheating the revenue and frequently each other as well. The extent of it was such that suppression was virtually impossible, added to which was the difficulty, as will be seen in due course, that in a sense even the Emperor himself was involved in it.

Naturally the officers dealing with Portuguese trade were in a particularly fortunate position; and everyone directly concerned, from the Governor of Kwangtung and Kwangsi down to the minor mandarins who preyed directly upon Macao, improved himself on it financially, though probably none more thoroughly than the Marine Superintendent of Canton. Head of a large department, responsible directly to the Governor, this mandarin controlled customs, tonnage dues and the overall supervision of maritime commerce. As the greatest beneficiary from it—he and his personal staff probably alone knew the real extent of it and the degree to which it could be milked—he stood to lose by anything damaging it, and to this extent could be called an ally of the Portuguese.

The English, however, sailing up the Pearl River, had by chance encountered in the Commodore a man who because of his military–naval status had no share in the foreign trade perquisites, which were reserved to the civil authorities. The Commodore, who had to pay for the upkeep of a large palace in Canton, maintain his ships and pay their crews, saw in the English an interesting opportunity. Learning that the newcomers wished to obtain a licence to trade—in other words they were not pirates, but wanted a legal footing similar to the Portuguese—a line of action quickly presented itself to him. As he had been the first to encounter the English, their petition should be presented to none other than himself, who would thereupon take it to the Marine Superintendent. This was irregular, but it could be done, and would provide the means whereby the Commodore could ease himself in on the foreign trade perquisites.

One drawback was that the only men who could talk to the foreigners were runaway African slaves, the use of whom as intermediaries might lead the English to suspect an irregularity. When he first interviewed Robinson and Mountney therefore the Commodore did not make any definite overtures, and rather than risk an engagement with them he reluctantly let them go up to the First Bar. There unfortunately the customs officials— the Marine Superintendent's men—told the English to go back and apply from Macao. Thinking he had lost his party, the Commodore returned to Canton.

But then the unexpected happened. Instead of doing what they were told the red foreigners had re-entered the river in greater numbers. As soon as their ships were sighted heading up-river there was consternation in Macao, and the news travelled rapidly to Canton. Under the Commodore's orders

Anunghoi Fort was manned and an effort made to prevent the barbarians coming any nearer. The English accounts are full of assertions that the Portuguese were responsible for warning the Canton officials to keep them out; but such assertions betray a lack of understanding of the situation. Canton needed no Portuguese persuasion. The Marine Superintendent and all the vested interests inside the government stood to lose by any upset in the nicely adjusted squeeze arrangements.

Again chance played into the Commodore's hands. The officer in charge of his forty-junk fleet had the good sense to send a messenger over to the English ships asking them to go no further up. He also discovered that they were still only after a trade licence, which fact was reported to the Commodore, from whose point of view it clinched the decision to act.

It was here that Paulo Norette came in as the much-needed interpreter, evidently introduced by one of the Commodore's friends with merchant acquaintances hoping to benefit if the Commodore's venture proved successful. The formal presentation of the English petition at the Commodore's palace was that officer's method of conferring regularity on irregularity. It was also intended to give weight and significance to the occasion in the Englishmen's minds, establishing clearly that the Commodore was their patron and making it seem inconceivable to them that there was anything questionable in his proceeding.

Up to this point everything worked well. The English were entirely convinced. Peter Mundy referred to that well-mannered charlatan Norette as 'Our Mandareene', and to the end of their lives none of them knew what Norette's position was or whose game he was playing.

The Commodore now approached the Marine Superintendent with the Englishmen's petition. This was a pretty miserable document, drawn up in a hurry and not well composed. It might have been tolerantly received even so, had not Norette, in his eagerness to ingratiate himself with the Canton authorities, included in it several references to himself, including some self-complimentary remarks about his honesty in business. How the Commodore was so misguided as to allow this to pass we do not know. Possibly, trusting the plausible Norette, he did not trouble to read the petition before sending it on. He was in a hurry too. The English had already seized some guns, and they might do some more damage if their demands were not satisfied.

The Marine Superintendent spotted the peculiarity. One can almost hear him saying to his secretary, after the Commodore's man had gone:

'These red barbarians: are they not illiterate?'

'Yes, Your Honour.'

'Then who wrote this for them?'

'I will find out, Your Honour.'

Within an hour or so the Marine Superintendent knew the exact circumstances: a third-rate calligraphist engaged, the text dictated by a Macao interpreter who had petitioned to remain in Canton—yes, the one mentioned as being an honest go-between. . . .

The Superintendent weighed up the position. The petition had to be refused, adamantly. These red people and their Chinese hirelings would throw the whole trade into disorder. Caution was needed, though, in one respect. The Commodore had sent the petition, and by its rejection he must not be made to lose face. Loss of face would prompt him to revenge, which the Marine Superintendent, about whom the Commodore clearly knew something which the Governor should not be told, could not afford to risk.

With great tact the Marine Superintendent therefore drafted the rejection as coming jointly from himself and the Commodore. After recounting the facts concerning the English intrusion into the river, he gave his orders:

'And I command as far as I may, and for this purpose I despatch the Officer who bears this sentence, who will forthwith give this order to the ships of the red-haired barbarians, and upon receiving this our order they shall instantly weigh anchor and put out to the open sea. For you have shown great daring in attempting to trade by force with us, we having forbidden it; and in so doing you appear to me to be like puppies and goats who have no learning and no reason.'

At this point one can feel him hesitate. Should he mention the interpreter? Better not. He would concentrate on the three red-heads who had had the temerity to enter Canton. With the same perfect tact he continued:

'One or two of your men, like men without sense, have pressed this business upon me and the Commander-in-Chief that we should consider what you are doing; therefore I warn you that should you have the great boldness to harm so much as a blade of grass or a piece of wood, I promise you that my soldiers shall make an end of you, and not a shred of your sails shall remain.'

The completed document was sent round to the Commodore. No more than the briefest covering minute was necessary; the document itself told all—too much. As a last touch of finesse the Marine Superintendent suggested that it would be more suitable and convenient for the Commodore to arrange for its transmission to the barbarians. The Commodore could not refuse to do this without revealing himself, the Superintendent calculated.

The Commodore was not the first naval officer to learn that politics need handling by an expert.

VI: THREATS IN THE CHINESE SYSTEM OF GOVERNMENT

Another aspect of relations with China, in this case an aspect which was one day to be of the gravest importance, has become apparent. The Marine Superintendent's order, while impeccable as a document within the frame of Chinese government (in all that concerned a colleague, the Commodore), is from the foreign point of view brash and insulting. Above all, it uses threatening language.

As will already have become apparent, the constant aim of the mandarinate was to maintain peace and order with the least possible use of force. Threats and unrestrained insults in official pronouncements were integral to this system of government. They were meant to be taken not so much literally as they were to indicate the degree of importance attached to a problem and the extremes to which authority was prepared to go, probably by indirect methods quite unconnected with force, to deal with it. You had to read between the lines and determine what was minimally required of you, thereafter taking measures to avoid even this if you could. It was a defined system of great antiquity. Even more significant, it had behind it well over a thousand years of successful application.

Reducing the matter to its simplest form, a threat in a Chinese official pronouncement, grave though it might be, did not bear the same aspect of challenge as a threat does in Europe. It was an indication of severity, not a direct engagement of strength. As we proceed, we shall see in steadily darkening colours the effects of this basic difference of understanding between China and the West.

VII: NORETTE'S DUPLICITY

Paulo Norette, the only suitable person available to translate the Marine Superintendent's order to the English, was at the same time the only person who knew the effects which threats and insults produce on men of Weddell's kind. Norette realized that his mission was dangerous, and, making great play of the danger, he allowed himself to be prevailed upon to make the trip alone. For 'Our Mandareene' was both resourceful and daring, and he knew he stood to gain greatly if, unbeknown to the Commodore, he could make some trade for his own merchant friends.

When he reached the English ships Norette was all smiles. Posting the notice up, as ordered, in Weddell's flagship, he proceeded to 'translate' it. Provided the English were willing to pay the normal duties, he told them, the authorities had given them permission to buy and sell whatever they liked, to establish a fortified settlement at the river mouth, and to transact all their affairs through himself, whom he imposingly described as the Assistant Sub-Prefect.

He asked that three men accompany him to Canton, bringing with them money and their goods for sale. Also, not forgetting the Commodore, who had done him a good turn, he made the English restore all the captured guns to the fort. This impressed them with his authority.

As always with Norette, everything was well organized. The three Englishmen, Robinson, Mountney and his younger brother, came alongside the wharves of Canton at night, landed wearing Chinese attire, and were taken by litter to a large house in the suburbs in which Cantonese merchants visited them and did some brisk business. Their host, one of Norette's merchant friends, would not allow them out of the house, and precautions were taken lest they be seen from the street. The doubts this gave them about Norette were allayed by the evidence of his ability to do what he said he would. After a few days Robinson and Norette came down to Weddell with the first consignment for export, two junks full of sugar. Carpenters also came down to crate it, now making the English fleet noticeably active.

When, as was inevitable, it was reported to the Marine Superintendent that his threats to the English had been in-effective and that the ships were still well within the Bocca Tigris, he did nothing directly, merely intimating to the Senate of Macao that unless they saw to it that the English departed they might expect the worst, a message the Senate well under-stood.

The Captain-General, thoroughly aroused, sent three junks 'well provided with Portuguese, mestiços and slaves armed . . . they alleging they came so for their defence, there being many outlaws and sea-robbers among all those islands and creeks'. Sailing into the Bocca they presented Captain Weddell a reasoned petition, pointing out the seriousness of his disregard of Chinese orders, and begging him in the name of friendship to spare the citizens of Macao the consequences and leave.

Weddell was particularly confident at this moment. The trade had started at last; the Assistant Sub-Prefect was their friend, and so too the Commodore. Escaped slaves, coming to him with tales of Portuguese machinations in Canton aimed at bringing about his expulsion, increased his feeling that the Portuguese had misused him. These sentiments dictated his reply to the Captain-General.

'Having received your offensive letters,' he wrote, '. . . we were much astonished to find that you consider us so despicable and of no importance, since you appear to think that your letters, full of groundless threats, will induce us to abandon an undertaking so profitable and so certain. . . . This land . . . is not yours, but the King of China's. Why then should we wait for licence from the King of Castile[1] or his petty Viceroys in these parts?

'We have no leisure at present, because of other occupations, to answer your vulgar letters more at length. . . . We are occupied in matters of greater importance.'

With this the Portuguese were dismissed.

VIII: CHINESE SECURITY FORCES IN ACTION

Norette was with Weddell when the Portuguese deputation reached him, and if the true situation still remained hidden from the English, it was as clear as a bell to Norette. A deputation of Portuguese being allowed up the Pearl River—they were normally only allowed to use the smaller delta approaches to Canton—meant Chinese acquiescence in the trip, which in turn meant that the great administrative wheels were turning, that the game was nearly up, and that if any more money was to be made it must be made quickly. Concealing his anxiety, he took charge of another sum of Weddell's investable capital and, encouraging him to send up the whole of the remainder with Robinson, left for Canton. Robinson followed next day.

Weddell's interview with the Portuguese took place on 6th September; on the 7th Norette left, Robinson on the 8th. Norette got through safely, but by the time Robinson neared the city three clear days had allowed time for observers to report the failure of the Portuguese mission and for offensive action to be put in hand. If the red-heads were illiterate, there was at least one language they would understand.

In the middle of the 9th–10th night, on the ebb tide, a fleet of dark junks was sighted by the pinnace. Thinking they might carry cargo for them the watch let them pass, but as they approached the first of the three larger English vessels someone on guard fired a warning shot and at the same instant two of the junks burst into flames. One after another were ignited. In the brilliant light it could be seen they were chained together, drifting straight for the fleet, rockets and other explosives shooting out of them in all directions, half-naked Chinese men diving out of them into the water.

---

[1] Between 1580 and 1640 Spain and Portugal were under the same (Spanish) king.

The warning shot was fired not a second too soon. The crews awoke, cut their cables, hoisted sail, and in their boats with great daring managed to sail near the firejunks and tow them away just sufficiently for their own ships to clear the main channel, allowing the flaming, hissing mass to drift slowly past, amid 'crackling of the burnt bamboos, whizzing of the rockets'.

The fleet was safe, but the English were shaken by the experience. As Peter Mundy noted, 'Now began we to mistrust the dealing of Norette and to fear the safety of our merchants at Canton.'

They had every reason to fear. The Marine Superintendent's patience was exhausted. The same evening Robinson, nearing Canton, was arrested and transferred to a government junk, his merchandise being seized and removed. From the crew of Robinson's junk the authorities finally managed to discover where the other traders were, and that Norette was involved.

This last discovery embarrassed the Marine Superintendent when he heard of it, suggesting as it did that the Commodore was also involved. As we have seen, he did not dare let his confrère lose face. The illegal trade had to be stopped however, and if the Commodore was in it the simplest course, rather than come into the open and risk his enmity, was to leave the English traders unharmed but organize something to let the Commodore know without words that his activities had been found out. The owner of the house in the suburbs was led out with chains round his neck to prison, his son also, and the rest of the people living in the house were thrown out. The house having been cleared of food and fuel, the English were left locked inside, with guards at the gate.

Needless to say, the Commodore was quickly apprised of this and that an illicit trade had been conducted by his own associates behind his back. Quite as angry as his confrère the Marine Superintendent, the Commodore recommended the sternest measures. The Superintendent agreed. Complacently he ordered that Norette be arrested and mercilessly beaten; and in the words of the voyage's chronicle the officers of the law thereupon 'soe bebosted that poore dogge, that they have scarce left him worth his skin'. For this time there was no fear for the Commodore's face. It was saved by Norette's behind.

IX: WEDDELL'S ATROCITIES

Meanwhile, in the Bocca Tigris, the merchants not returning from Canton, the 'best course was held to do all spoil we could unto the Chinese, that complaint might come to the higher powers, and that they might understand the reason of it as being for the detention of our merchants and company's estate in their hands'. For several days the English stayed in the area, seizing junks and raiding villages for livestock and provisions. One village they set fire to; in another they killed several Chinese. Finally they blew up Anunghoi Fort.

All this having failed to procure the release of their compatriots, they once more allowed themselves to be influenced by African slaves, who this time warned them that a vast fleet was being assembled against them by the Chinese, and that if they were to remain it were better near the ocean. Acting on this advice, they sailed down into the estuary as far as Lintin Island.

In doing so, however, Weddell had another idea in mind. The season was beginning to change. As some time on the autumn wind the Japan fleet would be returning to Macao. Anchoring within commanding distance of the route the fleet was most likely to take, Weddell once more addressed the Captain-General of Macao, blaming him for everything and demanding the freeing of the merchants, restoration of the cargo seized, and compensation for the voyage's losses. The letter ended with a good deal of high-flown stuff, including a hint that Macao's action might cause a rupture of the peace between Great Britain and Spain.

The outcome was typically Portuguese. Instead of sending a long reply, Domingos da Camara Noronha wrote only a brief note of acknowledgment, adding '. . . as all that your Worship states shows clearly that the information you have received against us is contrary to the truth, we have requested the Reverend Father Bartolomeu de Reboredo of the Society of Jesus, whom you brought from Malacca in your ships, and therefore your very good friend, to go and inform you in a friendly way of what really occurred, with which, if your Worship is satisfied, we shall much rejoice'.

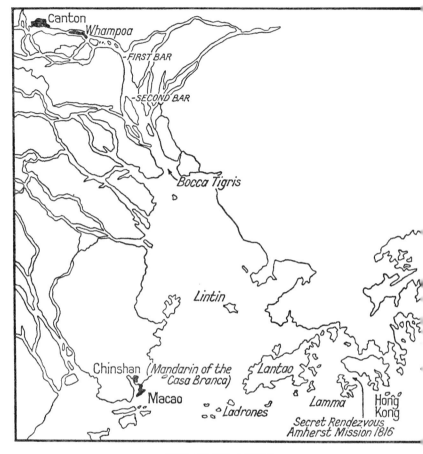

THE PEARL RIVER

Weddell was taken aback. Unable to bluster or rant at his learned former passenger, he was reduced to listening while Father de Reboredo dealt with Weddell's letter point by point, explaining the truth and ending by saying suavely that if the English merchants were to be released, only the influence of the Portuguese could effect this. Among foreigners the Chinese would listen to no others.

If Weddell was unconvinced by the father's explanations, none of which seemed to him to make much sense, he nevertheless appreciated that if he wished to see his men again alive he had better heed the warning. With self-control which in a man of his temper was an achievement he penned a humble answer to the Captain-General asking forgiveness, pleading the ignorance of a foreigner, and begging His Excellency to do him the favour of treating with the Chinese on the English behalf. He also asked that he be allowed to do some trade in Macao 'as compensation for the heavy costs of this voyage'.

Father de Reboredo returned to the city, and the following day Weddell was invited ashore to sign a trade agreement. The English captain's response was to refuse to leave his ships until two Portuguese of quality were first surrendered as hostages. By way of answer the Captain-General simply sent another envoy to repeat his invitation. When Weddell, with considerable misgiving, set out for the city, he found a civic reception organized for him. Guns fired salutes, the principal citizens met him on the quay, and a banquet was given at which the English dined off silver dishes and drank Portuguese wine from silver goblets to the accompaniment of 'indifferent good Musick of the voice, harpe and guitterne'. Within three days a Portuguese deputation left for Canton in an attempt to rescue the merchants, while Peter Mundy, established ashore in a fine rented house, carried out 'a limmitted trade'.

X: WEDDELL'S SUBSEQUENT HUMILITY AND DEPARTURE

In Canton, far from requiring the pleadings of any deputation sent to liberate them, the Englishmen, with the help of their friend the Commodore, had already been liberated and done some profitable trade. It appears as if, provided the English finished their business and left at once, the Marine Superintendent deemed it wise to turn a blind eye on the Commodore making some money just for once. He himself had other ideas, as became apparent the following year when he imposed on Macao the largest mass fine in the city's history.

The Portuguese rescue mission, who between fear of the Marine Superintendent and the expectations of their own Captain-General and Senate were in a cleft stick, were unable to 'protect' the English until the latter were under sail in the river, their junk laden and their trade complete. Keeping their own vessel close to them, the Portuguese waited till they were away from the city, when by yelling threats in Chinese to the English junk they scared the crew into lowering sail and allowing themselves to be towed downstream by the Portuguese craft.

Thus if the Portuguese mission was a failure it was made not to appear so. To the relief of John Weddell and in view of a large crowd of proud Portuguese spectators, the English entered Macao harbour in the wake of their liberators. Only when they were near enough to see three scowling English faces did Weddell and his men deduce that appearances did not tell the whole tale.

But even when Weddell heard of their success he was not disposed to alter his resolve, which was to complete what trade they could and depart. The document falsely interpreted by Norette had been correctly translated to him by the Jesuits. The uncompromising demand to leave the country, when associated with Norette's promises, the Commodore's assistance, and the querulous attitude of the Portuguese, made Weddell realize how little he understood of China.

Upon the orders of the mandarinate he signed a formal submission stating that he and his men had disobeyed the laws of China, and that if they ever did so again they were prepared to submit themselves to whatever punishments the Chinese or the city of Macao might inflict. Considering the damage Weddell had done to Chinese lives and property this was very lenient treatment (for which the Portuguese later paid in terms of cash), but to Weddell it was a public humiliation, the more so as he was obliged to present the document with obeisances to the mandarin authorized to receive it, who entered Macao in a chair borne shoulder-high by two bearers, accompanied by the usual strident music and flags, and with a parasol carried over his head.

Like many men with highly combustible tempers, Weddell had become damp of spirit, like a fire on which water is thrown. Having expended his bombast he became sullen and unenterprising, anxious only to clear up the business and go.

But the tribulations of the voyage were not over. In November the Japan fleet returned in gloom and lamentation, bringing great numbers of Portuguese refugees fleeing from the Christian persecution which was then at its height in that country. Many of the refugees came to Weddell, begging him to carry them on westwards, their beseechings being so piteous that contrary to the Captain-General's wishes he gave berths to some of them. A day or so later Peter Mundy called at the Captain-General's residence from which, before Mundy was even up the front steps, Domingos da Camara burst forth in the vilest of tempers, raging at Mundy with foul language, asking him whether he thought he was in London or in the King of Spain's dominions. Too furious even to explain the reason for his anger, he told Mundy to leave Macao at once, and that if a single Englishman were found in the place in the morning he would be hanged. He then walked back into the residence, leaving Mundy still speechless on the steps.[1]

That night Mundy's trading house was surrounded by a crowd of the Captain-General's servants, armed, carrying flares, and evidently ordered to thrust the English out to the ships. Mundy and his colleagues kept their heads, telling their assailants they proposed to stay two more days, clear up all their obligations, and leave. With this the servants were persuaded to depart.

Two days later, on 27th December, exactly six months after their arrival, the English fleet sailed, having in Peter Mundy's words been expelled 'outt off the Citty and Country, even by Fire and sword as one May well say'.

The voyage was not a success—much of the capital was still uninvested when they left—and greater disasters lay ahead. With the decline in Weddell's initiative and self-confidence morale in the fleet sank into personal rivalries and bickering. By transhipping twice Peter Mundy managed to reach Dover. He was one of the few who did. At Achin, in northern Sumatra, the fleet separated, and thereafter all was lost. Robinson died on Madagascar; John Weddell and the Mountneys were last heard of at Cannanore in South India. Their ships never returned to England. It is presumed they were lost with all hands somewhere in the Arabian Sea.

[1] The Captain-General's motive here was to keep every able-bodied man in Macao. With the closing down of the Japan trade Macao would cease to be of use to the Chinese, and might shortly have to defend itself against them.

XI: CHINESE ASSESSMENT OF WEDDELL'S VOYAGE

Thus ended the first British trading voyage to China. Though commercially insignificant it is important due to the conclusions about the British which were drawn from it by Chinese official-dom, of which the most salient was that red barbarians were particularly dangerous, but that by threats they could be con-trolled. For this, in Chinese official documents, was the story—how a heavily armed English fleet had intruded into the Pearl River, how by stern threatening the English had been tamed, and how they submissively departed. The Chinese knew nothing of the fact that this submission was due to Weddell's change of mood. They only saw that their age-old methods of dealing with unruly barbarian tribes had succeeded and were justified. No government had at its disposal records more comprehensive than those of Imperial China. No country had more respect for precedent. It was the unchanging mandarin belief in the efficacy of threats, drawn from records and experiences such as this, that was ultimately to bring China to the humiliations of the nineteenth century.

In examining the Weddell voyage one sees a number of the elements which were to confuse matters in the future, how on the English side for every moderate, level-headed Mundy there was an irascible Weddell, a lack of uniformity which the Chinese were to find baffling; and how on the Chinese side a contra-diction existed between the eagerness of local merchants to trade with foreigners and the official unwillingness of the mandarins to permit such trade—though once it started they were all too eager to milk it—a contradiction which the Westerners found equally baffling. Above all one sees the total void in understanding which lay between the Chinese and the foreigners, the mental no-man's-land which had somehow to be traversed if orderly international relations were to be set afoot. Basic to this was the fact that Europeans looked upon China as a foreign nation like any other, to be dealt with as other nations were dealt with, while to the Chinese their country was like none other, being unique and superior, the sole point and centre of human civilization, beyond the frontiers of which existed nothing that was either interesting or desirable. This mental no-man's-land would have been of less significance had the nations on either side of it known of its existence. The strangeness of the situation is that for a very long time neither side did, and by the time the Europeans did begin to realize how the Chinese saw themselves in relation to the rest of the world, and thus to glimpse an understanding of how the Chinese should be negotiated with, it was already too late to prevent China being prised open by force.

II

THE FRENCH IN THE LEAD

I: THE DUTCH EMBASSY TO PEKING

IN THE THIRTY-EIGHT YEARS following Weddell's visit—until 1675—the number of English voyages to China can be counted on the fingers, and no voyage was remunerative. Macao, deprived of her Japan trade and thus no longer of use to the Chinese, clung on somehow, only saved from extinction by Jesuit influence in Peking. In 1673, when the East India Company's ship *Return* put in to Macao, the English found the city dreadfully impoverished. They stayed there eight months doing cash trade, which was all the Portuguese would allow. Desperate for commerce the Macao authorities, demanding ridiculous prices for small quantities of Chinese goods, prevented the English from dealing direct with Chinese merchants, and anxious to drain the last shilling out of them, so long delayed issuing a clearance permit that the English finally had to pretend their crew were on the verge of mutiny, making this their excuse to be gone. Throughout this period there was a growing view among the English in the East that trade with China was unprofitable and pointless.

Far away in Europe, though, interest in China was increasing, receiving a great impetus from the Dutch embassy to Peking in 1656 and the decision, unusual in those days when matters concerned with trade and geography were so often kept secret, to permit an account of the mission to be published. Admirably printed, with maps and illustrations, this extensive Dutch description of China, the first of its kind ever to be laid before the

28

European public, aroused the greatest interest and was translated into a number of languages.

The Dutch had gone to Peking in an attempt to negotiate an agreement with the Emperor, persuading him to permit them to trade with his country. In the first place they found that due to long isolation from other lands the Chinese had practically no geographical knowledge of anything beyond the frontiers of China. Only with some difficulty did the envoys manage to persuade the mandarins that Holland did in fact exist and that the members of the mission were not just wandering sea-marauders. Above all, they discovered curious and inexplicable difficulties in opening any kind of negotiation with the Emperor of China or his mandarins.

At this point we must take another look behind the scenes. China's mysterious concept of her own centrality, the origins of which are lost in a remote pre-history, had under the Ming and Ch'ing dynasties become a highly evolved cosmological system in which Peking figured as the centre of the universe, the point of harmonious balance between Heaven and Earth, with the Emperor of China as the Son of Heaven, the supreme master of all that was noteworthy and desirable in material existence, and who in his person, by his innate virtue and practice of virtue, and by the performance of certain important ceremonies connected with agriculture, conducted in rigid accordance with astronomical conditions, maintained the balance of Heaven and Earth as made manifest in good weather, plenty, peace and content throughout the immense kingdom.

In this concept of the universe there was no such thing as an embassy from a foreign country in the sense that this was understood in other lands. All beyond the confines of China, which was alone civilized—indeed China was synonymous with civilization—were tribal barbarians. Naturally such people did not negotiate with the Son of Heaven. No one negotiated with the Son of Heaven, and for anyone to have suggested that they might—as the Dutch politely tried to—was not merely an unheard-of presumption (patiently to be borne because barbarians knew no better): in that it ran counter to Chinese cosmological concepts it was a totally unreal proposition. Reversing the situation, it would have been like an oriental delegation who spoke no European language visiting the Pope and telling him he should alter the wording of the Lord's Prayer.

Among the outer barbarians, however, were certain tribes—and it was into this category that the Dutch were permitted to fit once they had established their *bona fides*—who showed themselves dimly aware of the blessings of civilization by sending from time to time deputations bearing gifts in testimony of their humble regard, gifts which symbolically ranked as tribute and by means of which such tribes—Siam, Burma, Nepal, the Indo-Chinese countries and Central Asian states—were vouchsafed the honour of maintaining contacts with the civilized world. For the countries concerned these contacts were useful in numerous ways, not least in prestige gained among their neighbours. In other words, China's attitude to outer people was not without a basis of reality, but it had become over-lacquered and *précieux*.

It was praiseworthy of barbarian rulers to send envoys to the Son of Heaven, signifying as it did their wish to become more civilized, and a visit to China was improving for them. They were thus treated with every benevolence. Magnanimous rules existed for the proper conduct of barbarian missions. While in the Celestial Kingdom they were provided with all their needs. They were escorted splendidly to Peking, where imperial officers received on behalf of the Emperor their rude gifts. They then had the unspeakable honour of an audience of the Son of Heaven.

This was a very highly regulated ceremonial, almost of a religious nature due to its cosmological overtones, at which at the moment of dawn the Emperor showed himself in silence on his throne, placed in the position of the most favourable geomantic influence in the Hall of the Blending of Heaven and Earth inside the Great Within, the largest royal palace in the world, while before him the barbarian envoys prostrated themselves in the kowtow (knocking head) ceremony, kneeling on the ground and touching their foreheads to the dust nine times.

After this, having presented their chieftain's humble letter to the Lord of the World, they were invited to breakfast. In a day or so the Emperor's letter of reply was received, together with superb presents, and the mission started home.

The Dutch went through the whole of this, even the kowtow, which symbolized their tributary status; but without results. Their petition to trade was met by an exquisitely worded written reply giving them permission to send one ship every eight years, Holland being so far away. In their published account they explained as much as they could understand of their experiences, but they did not fully grasp the fact that an embassy to China was a ceremonial and nothing more. When they met with so little success in the mission's real purpose, they ascribed this to their belief that the Jesuits, who had worked themselves into holding important appointments in the cosmological system, on the Board of Astronomy for example, and on the Boards of Rites and Mathematics, had been scheming against them in the commercial interests of Catholic Macao. In sum, to Europeans reading the Dutch account it still appeared that negotiation with Peking was possible, provided one went about it the right way.

On no European nation did the Dutch account and the new knowledge it revealed about China have a greater impression than on the France of Louis XIV, which from about 1664 onwards began a determined incursion into Eastern seas. The story of Western endeavour in the Far East begins with the Portuguese as the dominating influence, from 1511 to around 1600. There follows the Dutch period, from 1600 onwards, during which the Portuguese were virtually ousted. Now comes the French period, lasting from 1685 to 1763, during which the first of the bolts locking China from the rest of the world were cautiously slid open. Furthermore it was due to French initiative, and in the wake of French ships, that the people already known to the Chinese—rightly, as it turned out—to be the most dangerous of all the barbarians were enabled to establish themselves. The French opened the way for the British.

II: THE OPENING OF CHINA'S PORTS TO FOREIGN TRADE

A feature of the French endeavour, in which missionary interests were in the beginning equally if not more important than commercial ones, is that profiting by Dutch experience the French appreciated that to send ships to China's ports in an attempt to do some illicit trade was all but useless, the key to the situation lying in Peking and in the only Europeans allowed to reside there, the Jesuits.

The Jesuit mission in China had from its earliest days been cosmopolitan in character. The first priest to reach Peking, Matteo Ricci, was Italian, and after him came men of various nationalities, all of whom reached China under the papal arrangement known in Portuguese as the *padroado*, or patronage, under which missionaries to the East only sailed in Portuguese ships with the prior approval of the King of Portugal, with the inevitable outcome that a fair percentage of them were Portuguese. Though cosmopolitan, the Jesuits in Peking were thus in a sense a Portuguese mission, and had up to this time certainly borne a distinct temporal loyalty to Portugal and to the interests of Macao.

It so chanced that at the very moment when the French were becoming interested in the Far East the head of the Jesuit mission in Peking was a Belgian with markedly francophile leanings, Father Ferdinand Verbiest, who had become dissatisfied with the workings of the *padroado*, considering that Portuguese priests were not sufficiently in touch with the intellectual changes taking place in Europe, and that the interests of Christianity in China would be better served by having in Peking more priests from France.

In 1676 Verbiest was appointed to one of the highest posts in China, President of the Board of Astronomy, with close personal dealings with the Emperor, on whom he had a great influence. In private letters to the Jesuits in Paris Verbiest urged the sending of more French priests to Peking, bypassing Lisbon and the *padroado*. The concomitant of this was of course non-Portuguese ships to bring the priests in, and permission for such ships to enter Chinese ports avoiding Macao, where the Portuguese would certainly prevent French priests from reaching Peking. In 1685, when the first two French Jesuits were already on their way from France, the Emperor K'ang Hsi declared the ports of China open to foreign shipping.

III: THE MOTIVES BEHIND THIS

There is a great deal that is unknown concerning the motives which dictated this unusual step, and while not suggesting for a moment that the Emperor had French Jesuits in mind when he authorized it, the fact that the edict appeared when it did, and that Verbiest was an extremely powerful personage to whom K'ang Hsi listened on numerous subjects, cannot be without significance. The Emperor was young and gifted, one of the greatest rulers China ever had. Tutored as a boy by Verbiest's predecessor, Father Adam Schall von Bell, he was singularly broad-minded in his attitude to Europeans. Not long after the opening of the ports K'ang Hsi promulgated another unusual edict. This (1692) formally tolerated Christianity, raising it to the status of one of the recognized religions of China. These two edicts, whichever way one looks at them, reveal confidence in respect of Europeans. This is perhaps about as near as one can come to interpreting the motives underlying the port edict.

Concurrently one cannot escape the sensation that K'ang Hsi did not regard the opening of the ports as being of much importance, certainly nowhere near the importance it subsequently proved to be. To glimpse this we must take a look at basic Chinese attitudes in regard to commerce and the sea.

Commerce, in the Chinese classic concept of life, was one of the lowest forms of human undertaking, unbefitting to educated people; and of all kinds of commerce, that with comers from the sea was the lowest of the low, the Chinese view being that the sea was a dangerous element frequented only by pirates and smugglers. Notable among these in the past had been the despised Japanese, the dwarf robbers as the Chinese called them; but for more than forty years now Japan had been withdrawn in her own isolation and her pirates were no longer a problem. For centuries the coasts of China had been considered the least desirable part of the Central Flowery Kingdom, the least important of the country's frontiers, demanding only such minor attention as was required to cope with inveterate bandits and sea-robbers. This throughout was one of the fundamental attitudes which made it so hard for the Chinese to believe that the Europeans or their trade were of any real significance. Nothing good ever came from the sea.

Linking this with the port edict and Verbiest's influence, it may perhaps be validly said that K'ang Hsi opened the ports expecting neither very much of good nor very much of bad to come of it. His subsequent indecision on the subject, when the effects of the edict came to be felt, is not inconsistent with this view. As for Verbiest, his motives are clearer. His aim was that French Jesuits should reach China without Portuguese obstruction, which the first of them did the following year, and that French intellect should replace Portuguese in Peking, which it rapidly proceeded to do. Insofar as trade entered his thoughts it was French trade—in French ships carrying French priests—while to the Emperor surely the edict was a minor departure from precedent, comparatively unimportant amid the greater realities of governing China, protecting her land frontiers—the only frontiers that mattered in Chinese eyes— from the attacks of nomadic tribes, and quelling uprisings in the outer provinces. Actually, as can now be seen looking back across the past, the port edict was the secret point of weakness in the dam, through which a drop of water oozes that is destined to lead to a devastation.

IV: THE BEGINNING OF SEASONAL BRITISH VOYAGES TO CHINA

As was usual in those days with Chinese imperial edicts, it was two years or so before the effects of the 1685 promulgation became noticeable in far-away Canton and Macao, and several years more before the foreigners realized that some kind of change had taken place, the latter situation being occasioned by the fact that neither side could read the other's writing.

The extension of French influence in the East had already underlined to the English Company the need for a firm base in China, lest the French sail in before them. From 1675 the English had been trading at Amoy during the time when that port was controlled by pirates from Taiwan operating in the name of the defunct Ming dynasty, which had been superseded by the Ch'ing[1] in 1644. Amoy had the advantage of being near the chief silk- and tea-producing area of China. Silk had been in demand from the very beginning of the European connexion. The interest in tea was new, small quantities of it taking

[1] The Ch'ing was a Manchu dynasty which conquered China in 1644 and ruled till 1912.

34

holdspace formerly given to porcelain, pearls and rhubarb. But as the new dynasty brought Fukien province under its control conditions of trade, all of it illegal, became more restricted, and in 1683 Amoy had to be abandoned altogether. Not till the last decade of the century did the East India Company become aware that in some unexplained way conditions of trade with China had eased and that the Pearl River, the nearest and preferred point of contact, was open to foreigners. In 1699 the Company sent their ship *Macclesfield* to try again in that area.

The English were not particularly sanguine of success. Ten years before, in 1689, they had been involved in an unpleasant incident in Macao on the occasion of the visit of their ship *Defence*. It seems as if certain Portuguese persuaded the Chinese customs officers that as the English were notorious (which ever since Weddell's voyage they were) for disobeying orders, special measures should be taken against them. In excess of their powers, the Chinese demanded the surrender of the *Defence's* mast.

Since the supercargoes, as the trading officers were called by this time, were allowed to go directly to Canton by longboat—a noticeable improvement on former voyages—no immediate objection was made to the mast's removal. But the master of the *Defence*, William Heath, had a temper similar to that of Weddell, and as argument proceeded over tonnage dues and other minor matters over which on every China voyage endless time was wasted, Heath lost his temper and sent ashore to the island of Taipa just south of Macao a small raiding party with orders to take the mast back by force.

The men found the mast, overwhelmed a Chinese guard and made off with it to their longboat. Before they could embark the Chinese started stoning them on the beach. Others joined the stone-throwers, shouting angrily and drawing more onlookers. With volleys of stones coming effectively from several sides some of the English were hurt. To cover their withdrawal the sailors opened fire on the menacing crowd.

At the first shot a Chinese was killed, and in the moment of shock that followed, while dozens of them dashed back for shelter and the hail of stones stopped, the sailors made off with the mast as fast as they could to rejoin the *Defence*. Alerted by the disturbance, a Chinese ship in the anchorage opened a cannonade on them, while on shore armed men of the Chinese watch force joined in the firing. The gunnery was inferior and the longboat got away without much difficulty, but other personnel of the voyage, including the ship's doctor, were still ashore in the village. Hearing the shots they came hurrying down to the quay to find the longboat gone and themselves the victims of the crowd's anger. From the longboat the sailors saw the doctor 'miserably cut downe'[1], the rest being seized and savagely beaten.

When the crowd had finished with him the doctor was still just alive. They dragged him to the Taipa watch house and chained him to the dead body of the Chinese the sailors had shot. No one being allowed to tend his wounds, he was soon as dead as his companion.

Again like Weddell, Heath switched suddenly from bluster to tameness. Without even waiting for the supercargoes to return from Canton he gave orders for departure. A sum of money was left with a friendly Chinese merchant with the prayer that he use it to obtain the release of the Englishmen held in custody. The *Defence* sailed without them.

It was to be expected, on the voyage of the *Macclesfield* ten years later, that this incident would be remembered and used by the mandarins to make things difficult. Ten years are less than a day when China chooses to remember something. To the surprise of the English not a word was said about it. Under the new edict these were apparently trivia which China chose not to remember. I repeat, chose not to remember; for the past was not forgotten. Heath had confirmed a long-held Chinese view.

After tonnage dues had been determined at Macao, the *Macclesfield* went up-river as far as Whampoa, the port of Canton, the supercargoes proceeding by junk to the city, where they were allowed to rent a house for the whole of the summer and autumn. The French having preceded them in Canton by a year turned out to be an advantage, making it easier for the English to negotiate with the Chinese authorities.

[1] East India Company records, quoted by H. B. Morse: *Chronicles*.

36

The French in the Lead

The voyage of the *Macclesfield* marks the beginning of regular East India Company trade with China, and was the first remunerative voyage to China made by a British ship. The principal commodity sold in Canton was English woollen cloth. Silk, raw and woven, was the principal purchase, lesser items being gold, pepper (a re-export from Indonesia), tea, quicksilver, porcelain and bric-à-brac—which included three hundred tea-tables in nests of six inlaid with mother-of-pearl, and one hundred thousand fans.

The *Macclesfield* sailed southward in 1700, and every year thereafter the East India Company sent one or more ships to China, trading as occasion offered at Canton, Amoy, Foochow and Ningpo.

V: CHINESE ECONOMIC THEORY ON MEN AND SILVER

Why was it that China had hitherto so insistently prevented foreign trade, and exactly what did the new edict concede? We have already seen why the Chinese disliked people coming from the sea, that the majority if not all of such people were pirates and smugglers, undesirables whose activities no sensible government would countenance. Why, in addition to preventing foreigners from coming in, did the Chinese also prevent their own people going out to trade in other lands? For this was another cardinal Chinese law, that no Chinese men or ships were allowed to leave the country.

A couple of centuries earlier, during the Ming dynasty, there had been an unusually expansive phase in China's history during which vast Chinese fleets had sailed as far afield as Ceylon and Arabia. In 1431, with a restoration of more conservative policies, this period of great voyages abruptly came to an end. There were a number of reasons for this, of which only one need be mentioned. This concerned the very high rate of Chinese emigration (to such places as Luzon, Siam and Malacca) during the years when older restrictions were removed, permitting Chinese to travel abroad. The more conservative mandarins regarded with alarm this tendency to emigrate, and the first thing they did on regaining power was to put a stop to it. With effect from 1431 no Chinese residing abroad were allowed

37

to return to China, and no more Chinese were allowed to leave.

Since this question of preventing emigration is to be of some importance, it may be convenient at this early juncture to have an idea of the reasoning which lay behind it. If one can conceivably use the word in the same breath as anything to do with Imperial China, the reason was economic, based on extremely odd economic ideas, as unreal as was the Chinese cosmology with which they were inescapably entangled.

Basically, in the undesirable barbarian wastes lying beyond the frontiers of China there was nothing to eat—except perhaps roots and the meat of wild animals. This meant that if Chinese were allowed to go to such places and settle there, rice would have to be sent to them, and also money with which to buy many other necessities—for outside China there were no houses, no proper wearing apparel, not even bowls and chopsticks. Emigration and settlement abroad would thus mean a continual drain of rice and silver to support the emigrants in their difficult life. This argument became a constant of great importance in Chinese economic theory. Men, silver and rice must never be allowed to leave the country.

The suggestion has already been made that K'ang Hsi's edict opening the ports was a minor deviation from precedent. That it was seen only as a minor deviation becomes clearer when it is explained that on what was in Chinese theory the major point involved the edict made no deviation of any kind. Though foreigners might come, Chinese were still not allowed to leave, on pain of death.

VI: PORT DISORDERS

What possibly no one had quite reckoned on was the reaction of ordinary Chinese people to the opportunities which the opening of the ports provided. Chinese enthusiasm and determination to cash in on the foreign trade by fair means or foul knew no bounds, while language difficulties and different trading methods made the Europeans from the beginning a prey to every kind of Chinese petty crook imaginable. Norettes flourished by the dozen; Chinese merchants posing as mandarins exacted non-existent taxes; tricksters posing as merchants absconded with cargoes and loans; foreign sailors were jeered at and stoned by Cantonese mobs. At every port Europeans called at conditions of peace and order deteriorated sharply.

Adding to the disorders were the differences among the Europeans themselves. The French and the English were not the only people to avail themselves of the new conditions. Dutchmen, Spaniards, Danes and Swedes came as well. Though semblances of goodwill might exist between supercargoes of these various nations, when their seamen encountered each other ashore it was a different matter. European seamen in their own countries were a continual nuisance to the authorities. Let loose in far-off Chinese cities, among seamen of other nations traditionally at enmity, with order maintained by a Chinese watch force trained to watch but totally incompetent when force was needed, every trading season was an almighty hullabaloo, with fist-fights, murders and brawls so extensive they were often like small wars. Nor was it only the seamen who were to blame. Among the ships' officers were plenty of Weddells and Heaths of all nationalities. full of strutting arrogance. When officers were involved the fights were some-times worse—better led and organized.

Chinese of the lower orders aggravated the situation by pandering to the sailors, running brothels, drinking and gamb-ling houses for them, soaking them in cheap potent Chinese liquors and robbing them (a favourite trick) when they passed out.

To obtain the right perspective it must be reckoned that there were probably not more than twelve ships of all nations coming to China each year, and they were divided among five or six ports. The commotion caused seems on these figures surprising until one also reckons that ships in those days stayed in port between six and eight months—of continuous com-motion. The mandarins, who had never seen anything like it, sent disturbing reports to Peking.

The Emperor reacted—in fact the prevailing attitude of the dynasty towards the matter during the ensuing seventy years may thus be characterized—with prolonged indecision, at the root of which lay the fact that, despite the port disorders, increased foreign trade had resulted in a rise in revenue and in the Emperor's personal income. The measures taken to deal with the situation were thus a series of compromises aimed at restricting the Europeans, because they were dangerous, while keeping the trade with them going, because it was beneficial. Unsupported as the Europeans were by their own armies and navies, such compromises were for the Chinese a practical possibility, and for a very long time remained so.

Foremost among the problems at the ports was the widespread tendency of Chinese traders to go bankrupt, arousing European creditors to such fury that they frequently invaded and looted shops, promoting ugly scenes of popular hostility. This stemmed from the fact that Chinese business traditionally operates on very small amounts of capital, sometimes even on no capital at all. One puff of an ill wind and many an apparently secure structure collapses. Which, in the boom atmosphere of those days in the ports, was what was happening all the time. Furthermore, Europeans anxious to trade were making an already insecure basis of operation still more precarious by loaning money to Chinese merchants to get them started. Even the best of these often ran into misfortunes of one kind or another, leaving them with the all-too-easy avenue of absconding into the teeming anonymity of Chinese cities where no one would ever find them, their European creditors in most cases not even knowing what their names were.

To deal with this problem an attempt was made at Canton in 1702 to channel all foreign trade through a single Chinese broker responsible to the Europeans for the fulfilment of undertakings and to the Chinese authorities for the foreign trade revenue. The position required more capital than even the wealthiest and steadiest Cantonese merchant could afford, and in 1704, as a result of strong European complaints, the broker was allowed to farm out some of his responsibilities to others, each of whom paid the government for the privilege.

In the years that followed, Canton emerged as the port most favoured by Europeans and the volume of its trade rose. As it did so, European dissatisfaction with the restricting broker system grew. In 1715 the British, who were the most vociferous with complaints, demanded freedom to transact business with whomever they wished, failing which they would shift their trade to Amoy. They also asked the Customs Commissioner, the mandarin in charge of foreign trade, to protect them from the insults and abuses of the people. There was no immediate reaction to these demands.

But the dissatisfaction about foreign trade was two-sided. In the last years of his life the great Emperor K'ang Hsi, who had been more permissive in his attitude to Europeans than any former ruler of China, manifested increasing disillusion in regard to them. Quarrels within the Catholic Church caused a lessening of the Emperor's interest in missionaries, while on the trade side not only were conditions in the ports chaotic, but Chinese were once more emigrating—in small numbers, but it was a danger sign, the one thing that must at all costs be prevented. In an endeavour to rid the ports of foreigners while still conserving the financial advantages of their coming to China, the Emperor in 1719 unexpectedly suggested to the Portuguese that foreign trade should in future be conducted entirely and exclusively through Macao.

VII: MACAO'S GOLDEN OPPORTUNITY

Since the ending of the Japan trade, around 1640, Macao had been going through the darkest period in its history. As a Portuguese settlement it had been clinging on by the skin of its teeth. When K'ang Hsi opened the ports of China to foreign trade Macao's reaction was one of resentment and suspicion. The Macao Portuguese mainly saw in the edict a means of depriving them of their ancient monopoly rights. They saw too the newly powerful nations of Europe coming in ships greatly superior to their own, themselves rendered of no account.

In a modest way conditions at Macao had improved with the coming of more Europeans. A seasonal pattern had started, foreign ships arriving with the hot humid south wind of summer, departing with the cool dry north wind of winter. Each summer and autumn Macao filled up with European visitors, waiting either for their ships to be measured at Taipa or for departure permits to be issued. From such a situation there were pickings to be made. By Portuguese law no foreigner could take residence or transact business in Macao, but by allowing visitors to reside in Portuguese homes as lodgers and to do business using the names of Portuguese firms quite a number of Macao people improved themselves financially.

More important still, the War of the Spanish Succession, in which Portugal and Holland were co-members of the Grand Alliance, put an end to the rivalry which had reduced the Portuguese empire in the East to a poverty-stricken remnant of what it had once been. Dutch ships now called regularly at Taipa, while Macao vessels were able to sail without fear of Dutch attack to Timor and India. The Macao shipyards active once more, the city got itself into a new stride, not in inter-continental commerce, for which the Portuguese lacked re-sources, but in what was called the country trade—trade within Eastern waters, in particular with India. Early patrons of the rising British settlement of Calcutta, the Portuguese dealt prin-cipally in spices, cotton and opium, exporting from China silk, tea and porcelain.

All the more surprising does it seem, in these steadily im-proving conditions, that the Senate of Macao considered the Emperor's momentous offer—and declined it.

Why?

In whatever part of the world the Portuguese have been, something of the same kind of situation has always arisen when proposals have been made to allow other Europeans to trade in their territory: that for every far-sighted Portuguese who has boldly advocated such a measure as a means to progress and wealth there has always been a majority opinion which has feared that to allow others in freely would end by the Portu-guese themselves, with their limited manpower and resources, being swamped by those others, a fear of the territories losing their Portuguese identity. In every Portuguese possession at one time or another the same debate has been engaged with the same invariable outcome. In 1719 it was engaged in Macao.

In this debate the senators' minds absorbed a vision of the Chinese Customs Commissioner's head office being transferred from Canton to Macao and becoming the most important building in the place, superior to seminary and palace; they saw the petty sub-prefect of Chinshan, the Mandarin of the

Casa Branca[1] as they called him, with his secretaries and flunkeys, consolidating his control over the city. The vision they unfortunately did not absorb was of suburbs spread all over the hillsides of Lappa and into the fields beyond the city wall, the inner and outer harbours filled with the ships of a dozen nations, and the senators themselves so rich as entrepreneurs that the Mandarin of the Casa Branca no longer figured as a person of any consequence.

To give the Portuguese their due there were many among them who disagreed strongly with the Senate's decision. The Portuguese Viceroy at Goa, Dom Luis de Meneses, Conde de Ericeira, was staggered when the news reached him. Urgently he addressed the Jesuits at Peking, begging them to approach the Emperor with a plea that the offer stand and be reconsidered. But it was too late. The golden opportunity had passed.

VIII: THE HOPPO AND THE CO-HONG

Very shortly after this, in 1720, the system of trading through government-appointed brokers at Canton was discontinued. In its place the Kwangtung Customs Commissioner—in Chinese he was the Yüeh Hai Kwan Pu, known to foreigners as the Hoppo—set up a corporation of Chinese merchants, a trade panel known to foreigners as the Co-Hong, through which all foreign business was to be transacted. The number of merchants on the Co-Hong was limited, and when a vacancy occurred it was put out to tender, going in theory to the merchant who bid highest, though in practice to the one who gave the nicest present to the Hoppo.

The Co-Hong system was a slight improvement, and it enabled Canton to maintain its position as the port most favoured by foreigners. But while the system canalized foreign trade, it also systematized the exactions made from it, and in due course came to be as violently criticized as had the broker system, again mainly by the British. Though the original idea

---

[1] Macao lay in the juridical area of the prefecture of Heungshan (contemporary Chungshan), in the sub-prefecture of Chinshan just north of Macao. The sub-prefect's residence, just visible from Macao's inner harbour, was originally painted white, whence the name, the Mandarin of the Casa Branca (White House).

was that each member of the Co-Hong would operate his own business independently, inevitably the group of Chinese merchants became in all but name a guild. Since the Co-Hong enjoyed monopoly rights in Canton the prices its members charged for goods were arbitrary, usually far above Chinese market values. From these immense profits the mandarins took their squeeze, sometimes on such a scale as to send prices up even higher. The post of Hoppo of Canton gradually became one of the most valuable and desirable in China, keenly sought after and in the personal gift of the Emperor.

This brings out a peculiarly important aspect of the Emperor's indecision in regard to foreign trade. He was himself one of the largest personal beneficiaries from it. Just as at Canton the Hoppo appointed members of the Co-Hong by tender, so in Peking, on a larger scale, posts such as that of Hoppo were in a sense put out to tender by the Emperor, the successful tenderer being the one who gave the largest present, which went into the Emperor's privy purse. As the volume of trade rose, so did the value of such appointments to the incumbents in the shape of squeeze; so too the monetary value of the gifts the Emperor expected to receive.

IX: THE STEP-BY-STEP SYSTEM

With an increase in the size and strength of European ships and a consequent decline in the dangers of sea travel, something of the original seasonal nature of communication with China— arriving on the summer wind, departing with the winter— imperceptibly diminished. It became the tendency for the annual departure from China to be made as near as possible to the end of winter, trade insisting that the captains run it fine before the prevailing wind changed. Naturally with other ships arriving on the first summer winds a situation arose wherein there was practically no season of the year when there were not some foreign ships on some part of the China coast. This brought to the fore one of the key questions of the pre-1842 period—the problem of foreign residence in China.

It has already been noticed how European traders were quietly entrenching themselves in Macao as lodgers using the names of Portuguese firms. From 1720 onwards leading Canton merchants who were not on the Co-Hong, and who were thus deprived of a share in foreign trade, started taking subsidiary houses in Macao, where while ships were being measured for dues at Taipa a good deal of business could be done avoiding the Co-Hong monopoly. By equally strict Chinese and Portuguese laws Chinese were forbidden to own property in Macao or reside there, but by giving presents to the right people silence was obtained.

From the European viewpoint this development added to the advantages of being a Macao lodger, but in that this illicit trade was only on a minor scale it hardly touched the main issue, which was to obtain rights of permanent residence in Canton.

As arrangements stood, a section of the Canton waterfront opposite the garden island of Honam was reserved on Chinese authority for the use of Europeans during the trading season— or more properly for what had formerly been the trading season but was gradually ceasing to be so. The height of this season, such as it was, had come to be during the cooler months, roughly from September to April. Though not allowed to own land or buildings, the larger national companies, French, English, Dutch, etc., rented premises in the reserved area from the Co-Hong merchants, renovated old houses and built new ones in foreign style with all European requirements. What with early arrivals and late departures, the Europeans were on the way to becoming virtual residents of the city.

Chinese rules governing the trade were framed on the assumption, more or less valid in earlier days, that at the end of each season barbarians sailed away to their own lands. Whenever Europeans mentioned to the Hong merchants that it would be convenient to leave representatives at Canton during the summer to look after their companies' affairs and prepare for the next season's buying and selling, the merchants quickly changed the subject. Such a request was inadmissible, and they themselves would be risking their heads if they raised the matter with the Hoppo. Foreigners were not in so many words prevented from passing the summer in China (although the mandarin view was that the sooner Canton was rid of them each year the better); Chinese cosmological theory did not include the possibility that they might wish to stay. How could they stay? They had to take their merchandise home and see their families.

But in China what will be denied by outright request can often be taken bit by bit without even the trouble of asking. Step-by-step is a fundamental Chinese system. Gradually, by a series of little *faits accomplis*, without putting anyone in the embarrassing position of having to grant or refuse, much can be accomplished.

Among the traders in Canton the first to realize the effectiveness of this method were the French. In 1729, without drawing attention to the matter, the Compagnie de la Chine left a few men behind for the summer. After a few days their presence was of course noticed in official quarters. The little *faits accomplis* are always noticed, but when they are sufficiently little nothing is done. The French were not formally accosted for their misdemeanour, the mandarins always avoiding direct dealings with foreigners wherever possible. Instead the Co-Hong merchants were blamed. They were deeply apologetic. The last French ship had had to sail at short notice, they explained, and it would be difficult for the Frenchmen to stay at Macao because that too was contrary to the laws. With small excuses and the presentation of moderate gifts no more was said. In 1731 the East India Company, not to be outdone, also left a representative behind during the off-season. The Dutch did the same.

In the English case that quality of behaviour which in our public life others find so hard to understand—ponderous rectitude—intervened. The local officers of the East India Company were reminded by their superiors in London that they must obey the laws of China. After two seasons the off-season representative was withdrawn. It did not affect the main issue, however. The French and the Dutch remained. A small inroad had been made.

X: CHINESE UNCERTAINTY AND PORTUGUESE CAUTION

Indeed rectitude was a difficult attitude to accommodate on the China coast, for there had entered into the atmosphere a quality of make-believe in much that concerned authority, nowhere more plainly demonstrated than in the interesting counterplay of laws and bribes.

A severe Portuguese law, for example, was passed in 1711 to prevent Chinese from acquiring property in Macao and building houses there; yet Chinese business men, as it needed only a glance round the city to observe, formed an important section of the population and were building houses. Later came a law against European lodgers; yet curiously none of the lodgers departed. In 1729 the Emperor Yung Chêng, K'ang Hsi's successor, laid an interdict on the import of opium to China; yet consignments of it arrived in every foreign ship. In Calcutta the East India Company passed a regulation that none of their ships were to carry the drug—the order was posted up at the start of each voyage—yet every East Indiaman carried some, in the sections of the hold reserved for the private trade of Company servants. In 1719, by the renewal of an old Chinese rescript, Chinese were forbidden to emigrate in foreign ships; yet many carried them. And so on.

The Emperor Yung Chêng was a great deal less favourable to Europeans than his father had been. From his reign onwards there began in China the spasmodic series of repressions of Christianity which by the end of the century had eliminated the religion entirely. On the other main question concerning Europeans—trade with them—Yung Chêng manifested the same indecision, and for the same reasons, as his father had. Still with the idea of somehow reaching a compromise in the matter, in 1733 he reverted to his father's original intention by suggesting informally to the Portuguese that no foreign trade should be conducted except through Macao.

The Senate, with the city internally in a much better state, was ready to accept the offer. This time opposition came from the Bishop of Macao, who disapproved of Macao's cosmopolitan crowd of bachelor lodgers, in particular to the large Protestant element among them, and to what he considered the corrupting influence Europeans in general were having on the city's morals. The Bishop was supported at a distance by a Viceroy, Dom Pedro Mascarenhas, who held similar views about foreigners but for different reasons. This combined opposition proving insurmountable, for the second time a negative answer was returned to Peking.

Within two years the Emperor died, and it was some time before his son and successor, the Emperor Ch'ien Lung, could give his attention to commercial affairs.

XI: ANSON IN THE PEARL RIVER

In the meantime there occurred an event which, though in many another country it would have left no historical mark whatever, wears in the mysterious context of an intrusion into the Chinese cosmology the distinctive guise of a landmark, being the first of a series of warnings to the Chinese concerning the power and mettle of the outside people they were dealing with—warnings which in some cases the mandarins did not understand, but which in this instance they deliberately under-rated. In 1742 China received her first visit of a warship of the Royal Navy.

Great Britain was at the time at war with Spain—the War of Jenkins' Ear—in the course of which a naval squadron under the command of Captain George Anson was sent round the foot of South America to damage Spanish interests in the Pacific. A main aim of the voyage was to seize the galleon which sailed annually from Acapulco, on the Pacific coast of Mexico, to Manila in the Philippines, carrying bullion and cargo reputed to be the most valuable in the world. Learning of Anson's movements, the Spaniards sent no galleon to Manila in 1742; and at the end of a year, after a voyage of many disasters in which all but the flagship, H.M.S. *Centurion*, was lost, Anson reached Macao, where his intention was to careen, effect repairs and take on supplies of fresh food. On arrival he addressed the Governor and Captain-General of Macao, requesting information on the procedure for approaching the Canton authorities for the facilities of the port.

Though initially Anson was unaware of this, his arrival put the Portuguese Governor in an extremely awkward position. H.M.S. *Centurion*, albeit in need of repairs, was for the Chinese going to be a formidable eye-opener on European naval power, and in particular of the power of the British, whom the mandarins regarded as the most difficult of all Europeans to deal with, the barbarian tribe which above all others it was essential to keep in check. If the Portuguese did anything to assist Anson they were liable to be blamed by the mandarins for the warship's presence, with serious consequences to Macao in the shape of fines and other vexations. In his reply therefore the Governor advised Anson to careen at Taipa, where the Chinese would probably take no notice, and warned him that if he went up-river he would have to pay tonnage dues like any merchantman.

By European custom at this date warships in foreign ports were not required to pay dues, and this being the first naval voyage to China Anson was aware that by his actions he would be setting a precedent. On no account was he going to pay dues. Taking the Governor's reply to mean that Macao could supply him with provisionings, he unintentionally plunged the Portuguese into further embarrassment by going ashore to call on the Governor and give him some idea of what was required. The Governor explained that before he could issue anything to the English the authority of the Governor of Kwangtung would have to be obtained. Anson replied coolly that in that case he would go to Canton himself and see the Governor. Hiring a small Chinese boat, he warned the Chinese officials who tried to prevent his departure that if they did not issue the necessary permit immediately he would sail up in *Centurion*. The permit was rapidly issued.

Residing at the East India Company's house in Canton—it was a combined residence, office, warehouse and bank—Anson next found that the only way to approach the Governor, or indeed any mandarin, was through the Co-Hong merchants. These friendly people apologetically explained that it was too dangerous for them to ask for an interview for Captain Anson lest they be mistaken as standing security for *Centurion*.

Security was one of the characteristically Chinese methods of keeping some sort of order in the ports. Long ingrained in Chinese commercial practice, it had since 1720 been extended into the foreign trade system. Every ship, together with her crew, every foreign merchant staying ashore, and most of the Chinese employed in connexion with the trade, had to be secured (guaranteed) by a responsible person, which in the case of foreigners and their ships meant by a member of the Co-Hong. The least misdemeanour committed by anyone so secured and the security could be either fined, imprisoned or banished to the outer provinces. It was one of the main methods by which the mandarins controlled foreigners while as far as possible avoiding direct dealings with them.

Whenever Hong merchants approached officialdom about foreign ships it was to secure them. Thus the danger if any of them petitioned about Anson. Responsibility for the warship would promptly be fixed on the petitioner, the punishment for having allowed it into Chinese waters being certain banishment.

In addition, of course—though this was not explained—had Anson raised the question of dues he would have found himself up against the baffling complexities of the Chinese cosmology, in that to be exempted from dues was another inadmissible request. According to Chinese theory all barbarian ships were cargo carriers. There was no such thing as a foreign ship used solely for war, and therefore no rules on the subject.

While not greatly impressed by the Hong merchants' arguments, Anson conceded that there was a difficulty. Returning to Taipa, he had a Chinese letter sent to the Governor of Kwangtung saying he wished to leave the coast early and asking for assistance in refitting his ship. This, as he calculated, produced a sigh of official relief, evidenced by prompt cooperation. A mandarin of some seniority and great affability came aboard *Centurion*, lunched with the officers, drank well though without the least sign of intoxication—one of the social arts of China with which the English were impressed—and put everything in hand for refitting and replenishment.

The work completed, Anson left the coast in April 1743.

XII: CHINESE IMPRESSIONS OF ANSON

Not for England, however.

Three months later he re-entered the river towing the Spanish treasure ship for the 1743 season, master of several hundred Spanish prisoners and a booty of £400,000, one of the richest prizes ever taken in war.

Appreciating the embarrassment his presence would cause to the Portuguese, he sailed straight into the Bocca Tigris. Anung-hoi Fort was in the same neglected condition as in Weddell's day. Not a gun was fired as, ignoring Chinese orders, Anson sailed in past the fort as far as Tiger Island. There, as on his previous visit, he asked for provisions.

The mandarin reaction was entirely in character. On his first visit Anson had been sized up correctly in relation to the rest of the English, specially in contrast with English merchant captains, of whom the mandarins knew all too much. Here, as they saw it, was a barbarian of some distinction, the first red-faced one of any consequence to come to the Celestial Empire, a quiet-spoken, reasonable man of whom certain standards of decency might be expected. They now saw that behind a deceptive outward appearance he was more dangerous than any barbarian seen in China within living memory, a pirate on a terrifying scale. To describe fully what the Chinese, with their mistrust of the sea and their detestation of piracy, thought of Anson's seizure of the Spanish ship would be all but impossible. Bearing in mind that even in England the seizure was considered spectacular, a national event, let it suffice to say that to the weird, unreal mandarinate of China it appeared horrific.

The cool, forbearing, considerate, entirely gentlemanly naval officer continued to behave as England and his own social class in England would have expected him to behave and, curiously enough, never was the intellectual gulf between China and the West more discernible and absolute. For with Anson's voyage another extraordinary facet of the situation saw the light: that the Chinese found it easier to comprehend a Weddell than they did an educated English gentleman of the new Europe. Unnoticed, and for unanalysable reasons, the poles had moved even further apart.

In everything that Anson proceeded to do he unconsciously helped in the consolidation of the dastardly opinion the Chinese were forming of him. Yin Kuang-jen, the provincial mandarin sent to negotiate with him, made the reprovisioning of *Centurion* conditional upon the payment of tonnage dues and the release of the Spanish prisoners. Anson, only too anxious to be rid of the prisoners, deliberately withheld consent to their release, using this as a bargaining point in the (to him) more important issue of paying dues. Yin thus left with the impression that he had only with great difficulty been able to persuade this calm, urbane, but abominable commodore to perform the meagre act of clemency of liberating the prisoners after all the harm he had done them. This was the view Yin expressed in writing to his superiors. The fact that Spanish officers ashore on parole spoke well of Anson did not diminish the impression created by this quite innocent bargaining.

In September, still without provisions, Anson went up to Canton by barge. For two more months he waited while the Co-Hong merchants promised to arrange for provisions and British traders begged him not to upset their own prospects by any hasty action. And thus he might have stayed for many more months had not a serious fire broken out in the city, in the suppression of which the British sailors from Anson's barge played a conspicuous part. Without their help in demolishing structures in the route of the fire—a measure no Chinese official would ever take the responsibility of authorizing—the greater part of Canton would have been destroyed.

The fire saved the situation. Tonnage dues were overlooked; Anson was courteously received by the Governor and complimented; the Spanish prisoners were released; *Centurion* was reprovisioned; and, expressive of mandarin sentiment, Yin Kuang-jen was promoted for the expert manner in which, it was held, he had persuaded the terrible barbarian to perform at least one civilized act.

After selling the captured galleon at Macao, Anson sailed south, returning to England safely after a voyage round the world. But as H.M.S. *Centurion* left the Pearl River a fleet of Chinese war junks followed her—at a safe distance—and Anunghoi Fort was bravely manned. Parading on its ramparts was a particularly arresting figure, a splendidly armed Chinese warrior wearing what appeared to be a coat of mail. Taking a careful look at him through a glass, to their astonishment the English discovered that his shining breastplate was made of silver paper.

1. The ruined church of São Paulo, Macao.
'. . . one of the unforgettable landmarks of
Christian Asia . . .'

(A) Woman in sarong, with shawl, dressed for going out;

(B) In kimono at home.

2. Macao sketches from Peter Mundy's diary, 1637.

(A) A Japanese, of whom there were usually quite a number in Macao, visitor and resident;

(B) A Chinese 'making his Salutation'.

Uttering their exclamations of incredulity, the English did not realize—had no means of realizing—that they had beheld what was from the mandarin viewpoint the crux of the matter: the actions taken by themselves in the Anson affair and which would form the body of their written report to Peking. Nor did the mandarins realize, when that report was composed and sent, the damage they were doing to their own country and its future. A dangerous red barbarian in a heavily armed ship had threateningly attempted to enter the Pearl River, the Emperor was informed; but terrified by the might of Chinese arms he had been driven away.

The Chinese report on Anson's visit, which could have been written in such a way as to apprise the Emperor of growing British power, merely perpetuated, in its unwillingness to put forward displeasing facts, the myth that in the final issue Chinese armed might was superior to European, and that by threatening them with it even the most dangerous red barbarians could be tamed and brought to heel.

The mandarin report on Weddell's voyage is understandable. The English were in those days a new phenomenon, and Weddell had in fact signed a humiliating submission. Concerning Anson's voyage the mandarin report provokes only a strange pity for those who were responsible for it. The English were no longer a phenomenon, Anson had signed nothing, and a number of mandarins, intelligent and observant, had seen for themselves, and properly evaluated, the power of the British warship and the quality of her officers and men. Yet though much of this was correctly reported to the Emperor, the real significance of it was concealed from him by the absurd ending statement that Anson had been thrust out by force, which even the soldier in the silver-paper breastplate could have told the Emperor was not true.

The Anson voyage and the account of it published in 1748 by Richard Walter, chaplain of H.M.S. *Centurion,* bring out the profound change which had come over Europeans in their attitude to Asia's old empires and kingdoms since the point at which we began.

In those early days of European contact with China, as Peter Mundy's diary shows, there was no question of Europeans thinking themselves superior to Chinese or anyone else in the East. The civilization of Asia at that time was in general more advanced than that of Europe, and in no country was this more trenchantly exemplified than in China.

'This country may be said to excel in these particulars', wrote Peter Mundy: 'antiquity, largeness, richness, healthiness, plentifulness. For arts and manner of government I think no kingdom in the world comparable to it, considered altogether.'

It was the opinion of a widely travelled and exceedingly observant man, and it expresses what was in those days a general European reaction. A hundred years later Englishmen found little or nothing to commend in China, which they considered badly governed and backward. The published account of Anson's voyage authoritatively enunciates an entirely different attitude toward the Chinese, critical and intolerant, describing their corruption, cowardice, greed and arrogance, ridiculing their so-called armed forces and condemning the venality of their courts.

The truth is of course that while Europe had been steadily rising, China was standing still. The Portuguese Discoveries, lowering the prices of Europe's luxuries, materially enriching the lives of ordinary people, may be said to have started the change. In an age of geographical and scientific discovery Europe loosed herself from the shackles of medieval Christianity, which was for us what the Confucian cosmology was to the Chinese.

When Louis XIV reigned at Versailles, East and West were well matched. Given good interpreters Louis XIV and K'ang Hsi would have found much in common. But once the rich, the educated and the purposeful in Europe grew accustomed to raised standards of living, and once the struggle of the Reformation was replaced by the intellectual freedom and opportunity its accomplishment created, the oriental etiquettes Jesuits had so painstakingly studied fell gently from the

marvellous to the quaint, while the tyrannies of Eastern poten-
tates and officials were no longer impressive.

For in Canton, despite the comparative comfort in which the
traders lived and the fact that they themselves were not directly
exposed to the caprice, the greed and the injustice of the Hoppo
and his mandarins, it was tyranny of a singularly distasteful
kind that confronted the foreigners, tyranny directed against
those Chinese associated with them, the Chinese they knew and
liked. The predominant tone of daily life in the foreign factories,
as they were called, on the Canton waterfront was cast of
frustration, threats, intimidation and a sense of insecurity. One
moment a cargo would be withheld or seized; another moment
the factory servants would be ordered from outside to leave;
sometimes the linguists, the latter-day Norettes who were the
indispensable interpreters, would be arrested and flogged; or
a friendly Co-Hong merchant would be sent to prison in chains
and unwarrantably fined. It was not a pleasant experience to
learn that your linguist had been whipped to death for a misdemeanour allegedly committed by you yourself, that there
was no redress of any kind, and that the same thing might
happen again tomorrow. It did not make for respect of Chinese
civilization.

The British suffered it with a great deal less ease than the
rest of the foreigners, yet it is interesting to observe how even
the British, knowing themselves beyond the range of their
country's protection, had adapted themselves remarkably to
their strange conditions and found Anson's arrival with the
captured galleon only a degree less embarrassing than the
Portuguese and the Co-Hong did. Though turbulent, argumen-
tative and condemnatory of the Chinese, they had not yet
begun to think of warships as the answer.

Down in Macao another aspect of the changed European
outlook could be observed in the distinction created between
European and Eurasian. When Peter Mundy stayed in Macao
at least 80 per cent of all the Portuguese he met, men and
women, were of partly Asian descent, intermarriage with
Christian Malays, Japanese and Chinese having been encour-
aged from the first day of the settlement's foundation. Yet in
Mundy's diary there is no feeling of race difference, still less of

racial inequality between himself and the Macao Portuguese he describes.

A hundred years later this had entirely altered. In mid-eighteenth-century Macao the European expatriates formed a superior caste which no longer mixed on terms of equality with Portuguese and others of mixed race, while even among the expatriates the British, by their social aloofness and disinclination to learn other people's languages, had come to form a super-caste of their own.

A newcomer, taking a cursory look round Macao, would be impressed by the well-maintained offices sporting Portuguese company names, suggesting that Portuguese were prominent in Far Eastern commerce. But on going inside one of them he would find all the important people were Europeans, with only a Macao Portuguese or two as clerks. The gentleman whose grandiose name was displayed outside, and who had originally allowed a European to trade through his firm, had long since been supplanted, his former modest business extinguished and himself seldom seen in the office, of which he was merely the landlord.

Inquiring deeper, our newcomer might find that this strange cuckoo-in-the-nest situation had started some years ago when the European rented a couple of rooms in the landlord's private house, and that the same development had taken place there as in the office. After a time the lodger had rented more rooms to accommodate newly arrived compatriots, the landlord descending with his family to the ground floor, sometimes to the basement. There the kindly landlady, lighting candles and placing flowers before her statue of Our Lady, subsided, perplexed by her boisterous lodgers, into being the supervisor of their servants.

III

PERMANENT RESIDENCE
AND JUSTICE

IN CONCENTRATING ON the peculiarly detached existence of the China coast, so remote, so specialized in experience, we have without being conscious of it reached the age of Dupleix and Clive, the age in which France and Great Britain fought each other in a war of global dimensions for what was in effect the mastery of the modern world.

The only sign of the Seven Years' War which China actually saw was an ugly deterioration in the relations between French and British sailors in Canton and Whampoa, where fights and brawls were on such an alarming scale that in 1756 the Chinese designated separate islands for the exercise of the sailors of the two nations, the British to walk on Danes' Island, the French on French Island. But Canton felt a tremor, and even Peking took note, when in 1762, in answer to Spain's entry into the war on the French side, the British stormed Manila and for two years put the Philippines under East India Company administration. It was another of those historic warnings, and this time a genuine attempt was made by the mandarins to evaluate it, the main obstacle being their continued lack of knowledge of the outside world. They did at any rate conclude from the seizure of the Philippines that the British were now the most powerful as well as the most troublesome of the foreigners, though as these continued to be regarded as tribal

57

barbarians the weight attached to this conclusion was insufficient.

The Seven Years' War coincides with the time when the Emperor Chi'en Lung, then in the twentieth year of his reign, turned his attention to foreign commerce and its problems. The measures he inaugurated, though so far as Canton was concerned they did little more than formalize by law the existing trade arrangements evolved by experience, nonetheless constitute a landmark in the story of China's relations with the West. After the long preceding period of indecision these relations were now defined and laid down by imperial decree in the form they were to maintain until the entire system was broken apart in the Opium War. The first hints that an overhaul of the trade system was in the offing were received in Canton in 1755; an imperial edict on the subject was given in 1757; and the entire new scheme was in operation by the season of 1760.

Ch'ien Lung's principal aim was to suppress lawlessness in the ports. Of these Canton, the most frequented by foreigners, had evolved the best trading system. Canton was also providentially the port most distant from Peking. Under the edict the ports of China were closed once more, with the exception of Canton, and by inference Macao. Since this closure order might imply discrimination between provinces and give rise to public complaint (for every coastal province wanted foreign trade), the levies and dues from overseas trade were lifted out of provincial into imperial revenue.

The post of Hoppo at Canton was already about the most lucrative in the civil service. As will at once be apparent, the new system gave it an even higher valuation, the Hoppo being from now on responsible personally to the Emperor for the entire foreign trade of China. Four years as Hoppo, and good management, were all that was needed to amass a fortune. In view of its vast perquisites the post was henceforward reserved to men close to the Emperor, who continued to tender it out to the highest bidder, the sums of money the Emperor thus obtained for himself being on a scale greater than ever before. The Hoppo furthermore had immense prestige. Able politely to command the services of the Kwangtung provincial governor and the commander-in-chief as if they were subordinate to him, he was really a law unto himself, with full military and police powers, although he tactfully kept out of provincial affairs. That such an officer should rank more or less senior to the administrative head of government in Kwangtung province shows the importance attached by this time to barbarian trade.

The rules governing foreigners were a codified version of restrictions already in force, set out in Eight Regulations. All ships were to remove their armament before entering port. No opportunity was to be given to foreigners to become permanently resident. Business must be wound up at the end of the season, all debts paid, no credit held over till the next season. All trade was to be conducted through the Co-Hong. No loans were to be made to private Canton shopkeepers.

So far so good. But we now descend from the sublime to the ridiculous. No foreign women were to come to Canton. The humour of this, as well as the significance of it, lies in the fact that what to European eyes would seem a minor regulation was actually regarded by the Chinese as of prime importance. The Europeans were to discover that though every other regulation could be disobeyed with comparative impunity (and was disobeyed from the first day the rules were promulgated), on the subject of women the Chinese were adamant. As long as no women came, Canton could be cleared of foreigners each year. Once women were allowed in, the place would become another Macao.

No Chinese were to be employed at the European factories as servants. This regulation was based on the theory that it was undignified for citizens of the Celestial Kingdom to work for barbarians. It disregarded the reality that ordinary Chinese welcomed the opportunity to work for Europeans, and that large numbers of Cantonese benefited greatly from such employment. Needless to say, not a single servant was dismissed as a result of this regulation.

No foreigner was allowed to ride in a sedan chair (for reasons similar to the foregoing). Merchants were to remain within their factory premises, taking walks only at restricted places and times. Sailors were only allowed ashore similarly. No European was permitted to enter the Chinese city of Canton.

By the solemnity of their introduction and the ease with which they could be ignored, the Eight Regulations, where Canton was concerned, far from regularizing and controlling matters, merely codified, albeit invertedly, a dozen different avenues for petty squeeze as 'penalties' for disobedience.

II: PERMANENT RESIDENCE AT MACAO

As soon as it became apparent that the Chinese intended to prevent permanent foreign residence in Canton—which being interpreted means that a few Europeans might stay behind each year, but illegally and thus subject to heavy bribes—most of the foreign community turned to Macao as an alternative permanent base in China.

From the moment that Ch'ien Lung's new edict was in the wind the Senate of Macao had been active. Rightly suspecting that the edict would mean stricter measures to clear Canton of foreigners after each season, and realizing the harm done to Macao by its own restrictions on foreign residence, the Senate successfully petitioned their Governor and the Viceroy at Goa, and in 1757, for once overriding the objections of the ecclesiastical authorities, the decree against tenants and lodgers was rescinded. Shortly after this, due to further representations by the Senate, national companies were enabled to transact business in Macao under their own names, although still not being allowed to own land and buildings.

These timely measures by the Senate saved Macao from the unpleasant sequel which could have developed of foreigners more or less installing themselves by force, and they opened the way to an era of prosperity for the Portuguese settlement, which from that time forth took on an international flavour, Macao becoming in effect the outpost of all Europe in China. After the 1761 season the French and Dutch Companies moved into rented Macao houses, the Danes and the Swedes a season or two later. The British, heavily engaged elsewhere, took no advantage of the new conditions until 1770 when in the conclaves of the East India Company in London and Calcutta, commercial considerations for once outweighing moral rectitude, supercargoes were allowed to remain behind between seasons.

In 1773 the Company moved into the first of the four large adjacent houses it came to own on the Praia Grande, next to the Governor's Palace.[1] Individual supercargoes rented private houses of their own; lodgers completed their mastery of the houses they had long occupied; and within a few years there was hardly a house on the Ridge which did not ring with English voices.

Pidgin English had long since replaced Portuguese as the *lingua franca* of trade. It was an extraordinary concoction, almost a language of its own, with a large vocabulary of jargon based on English, Cantonese, Portuguese and Hindi, and with almost no grammatical construction. Much of it was incomprehensible to a newcomer from England, and it contributed strongly to the air of make-believe, giving an unearthly character and atmosphere to every situation in which Europeans and Chinese were involved, in which the roughest merchant captains and the sternest and most authoritative supercargoes were reduced to conducting their negotiations with Chinese in what sounded like finely shaded baby-talk.

III: THE INTERDEPENDENCE OF COMPANY AND COUNTRY TRADE

The British emerged from the Seven Years' War as the leading European power in the East, and in Canton the number of British ships coming each year rose significantly above the numbers sent by other nations. The French and Dutch still sent their regular three or four ships a year, and there were still the Danes, the Swedes and the Spaniards; but within a few years of the peace of 1763 the total number of British ships at Canton more than doubled the number sent by all the rest put together.

This last statement, however, conceals as much as it reveals. Of these British ships less than half were owned by the East India Company. The rest belonged to private British traders based on Macao, Calcutta and elsewhere, operating as the Portuguese did in the country trade.

---

[1] No trace of the great East India Company house survives. Part of the site is now occupied by the Pousada de Macau and by the *travessa* between it and the Governor's Palace. The Company houses extended up the hill as far as the church of São Lourenço.

Under its Royal Charter the East India Company held the monopoly of British trade in Eastern seas and was empowered to prevent other British ships from trafficking in the East. Since quite early times there had been interlopers on the Company's monopoly. Weddell was really an interloper, despite the rights accorded to his managing company by King Charles I; and during the Cromwellian period, when the East India Company's resources were at a low ebb, interlopers were edging in throughout Asia.

As the British settlements in India grew and prospered, the number of Britons in the East rose and it became increasingly difficult to prevent, for example, men leaving Company service and going into trade on their own, or new interlopers obtaining a footing through the Portuguese settlements in India, using Portuguese company names as was done at Macao. Individual British traders were among the first of Macao's lodgers, and by the middle of the eighteenth century had firmly entrenched themselves in the country trade, in which they held the principal interests. They were an unruly collection, far more short-tempered with the Chinese and liable to resort to force than the Company ever was, and the Company regarded with grave concern both the country traders themselves and their own inability to control them.

Needless to say, to the mandarins, accustomed as they were to the other Europeans who traded solely through their national companies with (the important mandarin point) one head man responsible for all of the same nationality, the distinction between Company and country which existed among the British was considered baffling when it was not condemned as a hypocritical deception. And needless to add, the bulk of the mandarins' difficulties were with the country traders.

Around the time when the Company finally decided to take up permanent residence in Macao it was also decided, as a measure of controlling the country traders, to regularize their position by licences issued at Fort William, Calcutta. Control of East India Company affairs in China was from 1773 vested in a Select Committee of Supercargoes resident in Macao and migrating annually to Canton for the trading season. By regulations promulgated in Calcutta the Company gave the Select

Committee authority to issue orders to country traders in China and instructions to see that all British subjects, Company and country, obeyed the Eight Regulations. What the country traders thought of this is succinctly expressed in the fact that where Company men referred to the Select Committee as 'the Committee', among country traders they were known as 'the Select'.

Underlying these arrangements, which at first appear to demonstrate considerable weakness on the part of so powerful an organization as the East India Company, lay the difficulty of financing the China trade. It will be remembered that when regular British trade first started with China, with the voyage of the *Macclesfield* in 1700, the principal export from China was silk, with porcelain and tea figuring as lesser items. Since that date Europe had been at work developing and adapting various skills originally learnt from China, resulting in a considerable change in the priorities of demand for goods from the Far East. Italian and French silk had to some extent replaced the Chinese import, while ladies of fashion who once sipped tea from Kiangsi or Kwangtung cups now used Sèvres or Rockingham. Even tea would have been planted in Europe—there actually were tea plantations in the Azores—had the bush not required special weather conditions which the West could not offer. Thus, as tea-drinking became more and more popular in the West, tea came to hold pride of place in the Company's holds. It even became the sole cargo in many a prosperous voyage from the East.

From the East India Company's viewpoint the most difficult problem of the China trade was what to sell in China to finance purchases of tea. Though no longer more advanced in civilization than the countries of Europe, China yet remained what she always had been, a highly self-sufficient country, which at that time did not actually *need* anything from Europe. More than that, China did not particularly *want* anything from Europe. But Europe urgently wanted China tea.

The other European nations in the tea trade paid the Chinese in silver. The Spaniards in fact paid in such quantities that the Spanish or Mexican silver dollar became for many years the standard currency of foreign trade at Canton. This method of payment, one would have thought, must have been a ruinous drain on the resources of countries such as Denmark and Sweden. But here it has to be explained that the bulk of the tea shipped to Europe in Danish and Swedish holds was smuggled into Britain, whose exorbitant taxes on tea made smuggling a highly profitable business, by means of which silver could be recouped. They did not therefore have the same problem as the British, which was to find some product saleable to the Chinese in sufficient value and quantity to finance the tea trade.

For years the British did their utmost to interest the Chinese in woollen goods, Britain's greatest export, but with very poor response. Quilted coats of silk or cotton waste are more resistant to the harsh dry cold of China's winter, and with tradition included, woollen clothes found little favour. Other British exports were lead and tin from Cornwall.

But if European goods did not interest the Chinese, various Asian products did, notably Indian cotton, pepper and opium, commodities handled exclusively on the network of the country trade, which to the East India Company was a closed book which they would in any case have considered it beneath themselves to open.

The country traders sold their cotton and opium at Canton in exchange for silver. Their problem then was how to remit their earnings home to Britain, the export of silver being absolutely forbidden by the Chinese, a prohibition which unlike so many others was, for reasons already explained, rigidly enforced. This problem the Company conveniently solved for the country traders by taking their silver and in return issuing them bills payable in London. With silver in hand, the Company then paid for the year's tea. Company and country were thus mutually interdependent. One could not carry on without the other.

While cotton remained at the top of the list of country goods this was innocent enough. But as, during the latter years of the eighteenth century, opium imports rose and sales of cotton slowly fell off, the trade assumed a sinister character. Without it, however, the Company could not have supplied Britain with tea.

IV: OPIUM

Opium, a drug consisting of the dried juice of the purple-flowering poppy, hardly figures at all in European trading records until the early 1600s, when a rewarding trade in it developed in Dutch holds between Bengal and the early Dutch stations in Java. Bengal was the principal producer of opium. Originally brought to China by Buddhist priests and doctors from Tibet around the first century A.D., it was used as a medicine to reduce pain, a property of opium which even in these days of scientific drugs enables it to maintain a justifiable place. Its use led to China cultivating her own opium poppies in Yunnan province, where they still flourish. The taking of opium as a drug, long practised in India, did not find favour with the Chinese until the practice was introduced of smoking it.

While the early Portuguese in Asia were takers of snuff, the Dutch were smokers of tobacco. In the Dutch stations in Java in the first decades of the seventeenth century the custom developed of smoking tobacco mixed with a small pinch of opium and arsenic. From there, for the local Chinese who copied the custom, it was but a step to the smoking of opium by itself, a habit which Chinese traders introduced from Java to Taiwan, thence to the mainland of China, where it rapidly acquired popularity. Amounts reaching China from outside were at first slight, the principal carriers being smugglers from Taiwan; but after the port edict of 1685 most ships coming from India and the South Seas carried opium among their other cargoes. As its availability rose in China, so did the demand for it.

The degrading effects of opium on human beings addicted to it were not so very long in becoming apparent to the Chinese authorities, as witness Yung Chêng's edict of 1729 forbidding the import of it. If Chinese today could be persuaded to view the question dispassionately, this moment in history should surely be viewed as the saddest and most telling in view of what was to come. In 1729 the mandarins could have prevented the import of opium without the least difficulty. The foreigners expected they would do so. The East India Company complied rapidly with its regulation forbidding the carrying of opium in

Company ships. But that was as far as it went. The mandarins assessed the wording of the edict, judged it to be not of major importance, and took no serious measures to enforce it, merely using it as another convenient avenue for petty squeeze. Prohibitions under the edict were publicly affixed in the usual places; the Company's regulation was affixed in all ships sailing from Calcutta. This done, the opium trade continued as usual, one side concealing the drug, the other side pretending not to find it.

Meanwhile, as the volume of the tea trade rose and its dependence on opium increased, yet another factor was contributing to the gathering impossibility of suppressing the trade while conditions remained as restricted as they were at Canton. In India the East India Company, from being simply a trading organization with a few coastal settlements, was turning into a government administering extensive territories which, part of a decaying empire, were in urgent need of up-to-date transport, military protection, a workable fiscal system and a civil service. Opium, of which the yearly Bengal crop was purchased by the Company under a monopoly and sold by auction in Calcutta, had by the 1760s become indispensable to the revenue needed to maintain the British Indian administration. Company officials were aware in Calcutta that the drug was contraband in China, but their responsibilities were to India, not China. With a disregard for China which may be condemned from this far-distant point in time, but with a regard for India which was very real and immediate, they assumed the attitude that provided the crop was sold each year and not shipped to China in Company ships, they were not concerned where it went or how, or who bought it.

Thus began the opium trade which was to be the bedevilment of Europe's connexions with China. Due to a mass of Chinese literature on the subject, much of it distorted as to historical accuracy, the overwhelming proportion of the Chinese people today, both inside China and without, believe that opium was forced upon them by foreigners in order to undermine their morale, break their strength, and humble them into obedience to foreign will. The bringing of opium to China, they repeatedly insist, was carefully plotted and planned, dastardly in its cleverness as a means of humiliating the Chinese people.

In fact the opium trade began by sheer accident, due to a curious Dutch social habit which within a handful of years had died out and been forgotten, coupled with the extraordinary and utterly unpredictable Chinese taste for the drug when smoked in a pipe, and the consequent insatiable demand for it. On this if we are honest, and quite regardless of whether we are Chinese or not, we can only recognize that we are discussing the inexplicable. It was not the Dutch, after all, who started filling their pipes with a little more opium and a little less tobacco, and not even in India, the mother country of opium, did the drug ever become a social problem of such vast proportions as it did in China. To this there is no answer. The cynical indifference of the East India Company in Calcutta is displeasing and typical of that age, but to expect them to have behaved in any other manner in those circumstances is to ask for the impossible. Far from opium being forced upon the Chinese, the foreigners found demand for it so keen that in most seasons they could not bring enough.

V: CHINESE JUSTICE—THE SCOTT MURDER CASE

Once the foreign community became resident in Macao—and thus in all but name residents of China—and once their numbers began to mount, as they did from the time the country trade was licensed, the other major problem of the pre-1842 period loomed into importance—the problem of justice.

Chinese criminal law was more rudimentary than English. Trials for criminal offenders were seldom held if a magistrate was satisfied from reports received that the person arrested was guilty. In cases of homicide the law was a life for a life, murder and manslaughter being equally punishable by death. For the solace of the convicted man's family one was a less disgraceful death than the other; but that was all. There was no such thing as a court of appeal.

To give it its due, the system was not as lacking in justice as it appeared to the Europeans of those days. Sentences of death in many instances had to be confirmed in Peking, and no magistrate would run the risk of recommending a man for death unjustly, in that if the deceased man's family later complained through the Censors to the Emperor it generally meant the magistrate's disgrace and dismissal without much further inquiry.[1]

Macao was supposed to be under Portuguese law; but in serious criminal cases the Mandarin of the Casa Branca usually intervened to enforce Chinese sentences, which consisted of various horrible forms of death depending on the offence committed. When there was no interference the Portuguese inflicted their own sentences on Portuguese criminals. Where a Chinese was involved he was handed over to the Casa Branca after investigation.

Instances certain to bring formal Chinese intervention were when a Chinese was killed by a Portuguese, resulting in a summary order to the Governor of Macao to put the accused Portuguese to death. The alternative being to have food supplies cut off, governors usually consented, regardless of the finer points of a case and despite the severest orders from Goa not to obey. Such executions took place publicly in Macao under the supervision of Chinese officers sent for the purpose with an armed escort. The executioners were Chinese or African, and the executions were usually mishandled; either the hanging rope was insecurely tied or else it was too weak and snapped. Violent and dreadful scenes often accompanied the executions, as when in 1744 after the first failure to end the life of a victim probably innocent, priests tried to rush him out of the hands of the Chinese in charge. The Chinese resisted, the Cantonese crowd yelled for death, and the fellow was finally hanged.

Against this must be seen criminal justice in the lands the European traders came from. England was slightly more advanced than the rest—for example, it was forbidden in England to torture a prisoner to make him give evidence. But there were

---

[1] One of the reasons for the summary nature of justice in China was the difficulty of obtaining information from clans, the members of which traditionally stand together in refusing to give each other away. At a judicial hearing on European lines no one would tell the truth, and there would thus be a serious risk of the wrong person being condemned. The Chinese alternative was for the magistrate simply to order the clan head to surrender a man. Few clan heads would risk the odium incurred among their own people if an innocent man was surrendered, and there was therefore a fair likelihood of the real culprit being sent for punishment.

3. *Above   Admiral Lord Anson, who commanded the first ship of the Royal Navy to visit China. Portrait by Sir Joshua Reynolds, 1755.*

4. *Right   Lord Macartney, Ambassador to China, 1793. Engraving by John Hall, from the portrait by Thomas Hickey.*

5. *The Foreign Factories at Canton, circa 1825.*
Artist unknown.

nearly two hundred offences punishable in England by death. One could swing for stealing a sheep or a horse, or for pickpocketing, however insignificant or valueless the article stolen. The law was such a mass of contradictions that with the aid of lawyers murderers went unpunished while others were hanged for stealing five shillings. Executions and floggings were popular spectacles; by accident men were often flogged to death. European continental countries provided other forms of capital punishment such as breaking on the wheel, strangulation and burning alive. At an important continental trial a prisoner had little chance of defending himself.

With such a background it may seem strange that Europeans should have complained of Chinese justice. Injustice, however, is brought home more quickly when seen inflicted by men of another race or nation. Cruelties which in Europe were familiar, in China appeared in a new and unexpectedly lurid light.

The East India Company had scarcely moved into their first Macao house, in 1773, when the situation presented itself in its most serious form. A Chinese was murdered in Macao, suspicion of crime resting on a Briton, Francis Scott. Without public inquiry the Mandarin of the Casa Branca, informing the Macao authorities that he had proof of Scott's guilt, ordered him to be surrendered for strangulation.

Aware of the danger of alienating British goodwill—Macao at this time was very anxious to attract foreigners—the Senate did their utmost to see justice done by Christian standards. They first refused to surrender Scott without trial. Threats poured from the Casa Branca, but the Senate, taking no notice, proceeded to try Scott in a proper manner.

Whether he was guilty or innocent will never be known. At the trial no one would come forward to give evidence against him. That there was no evidence to give is unlikely in a small place like Macao where nearly every human action is observed by somebody. It is more probable that, as Macao saw it, this was a Christian life in danger of being surrendered to a heathen death. Furthermore, the accused was a visitor, a guest of the city's hospitality.

The case having been dismissed for want of evidence, the Senate replied to the Casa Branca refusing to surrender Scott. The Cantonese population was promptly ordered to leave and

F   69

the city deprived of food. The effectiveness of this was that Macao, though it had wells, produced no food of any kind, not even eggs. After several days, when people realized the Chinese were out for blood, a general meeting was held to decide what to do. The Senate was for holding on. The case for surrender was put by the Church. In grim terms the Vicar-General described the people's sufferings, all due to one man, a possible criminal for whom the city bore no responsibility. In a tense and solemn scene the Senate finally yielded. Scott was surrendered to the Chinese and executed. Within a few hours the barrier gate north of Macao was opened, and profit-eager Cantonese hawkers and cultivators were hastening in with pork and vegetables.

VI: THE COMPANY'S DIFFICULTIES WITH COUNTRY TRADERS

For the Select Committee, the most cautious and conservative element among the British, the Scott case was a disturbing revelation of their own powerlessness and insecurity, and of the meagreness of the protection afforded by living in a possession which the Portuguese, though they claimed to own it, could hardly be said to control. For the more ebullient country traders, coming from the growing British possession in India where they were accustomed to giving orders to Asiatics and having them accepted in silence, the entire set-up on the China coast was insufferable, the main target of their criticism being the Select, whose insistence on obeying Chinese orders by ensuring that Canton was cleared of all Britishers at the end of each season struck the country traders as being utterly absurd. If they had their own way they would stay and be damned. They were sure the Chinese would do nothing about it.

In fact, one country trader named George Smith had already proved this as early as 1764, when in a one-man revolt against Company authority he refused to budge from Canton when ordered, and defied the Company to make him. The supercargoes had threatened, reasoned and cajoled with him, but he had his own way. This was before the Select came into existence with their tighter grip on affairs at Canton, but it showed there were limits to the lengths the Company would go in controlling the country traders, due to the Company's peculiar financial dependence on them.

Each year the Select's endeavours to clear Canton met with more opposition and truculence. From the Company's private empire in India quite a number of Asiatic citizens had joined the British in the country trade in cotton and opium. Armenians and Parsis mainly, there were so many of them and they had such peculiar names that the Select soon lost count of them and concentrated on the British, all of whom grudgingly obeyed with the exception of old George Smith, on whom orders, arguments and threats produced no effect whatever. On one occasion, when the Select were particularly insistent with him, he had the glorious impertinence to return his year's credit bills to them with a demand for cash, knowing well that the Committee, having paid out most of their bullion to buy tea, would be unable to pay. When they asked for deferment he insisted on their giving him interest at 50 per cent above the normal rate, and finally sent back nine sets of bills to be rewritten because they were dated on a Sunday.

Then a new kind of misdemeanour started. The French had in 1776 appointed a Consul at Canton. The mandarins did not recognize the gentleman as such, consuls being unknown in the Chinese theory of human existence, but in accordance with the system of little *faits accomplis* the Consul hoisted his flag and stayed. Three seasons later John Reid, a Scot with past experience in the Company's Marine Service in Bengal, when called upon to leave Canton, sent over to the British factory his Austrian citizenship papers and a commission as Consul for the Imperial Majesty of Vienna. The Select, with the immense correctitude of the Honourable Company—a quality John Reid understood—considered these impressive documents and decided it would be improper to interfere. Reid chuckled, and the Canton summer scene was brightened by the flags of France and Austria fluttering from two consular houses.

VII: SINGSONGS, CONSULS AND FLAGSTAFFS

One of the most important aspects of the make-believe which now entered a more pronounced phase was that every mandarin

71

connected with foreign trade had to be given toys at Chinese New Year. This was essential. No one could say how serious might be the consequences if some mandarin in a key post did not get a toy.

The toys were not actually presented by the barbarians; that would have been unseemly. They were handed over in consignments to the Hong merchants, who apportioned them with the *sagesse* for which they were distinguished. In pidgin they were called singsongs, most of them were made in England, and the principal agent for them was James Cox, whose London office was, appropriately enough, in Shoe Lane. His wares included every sort of little mechanical device, musical boxes, intriguing clocks, perfume bottles with flowers that opened and closed their petals, snuff boxes with birds that popped up from inside when the box was opened and sang a little song.

The singsong business was so harmless—and so important —that when James Henry Cox succeeded his father as head of the firm and came to China in 1782 to sell off his remaining stock, the Select gave him permission to stay in Canton between seasons. Finding there that quite a number of the Hong merchants had gone bankrupt, Cox had difficulty in selling his wares for silver and was obliged to barter for goods. Very innocently, and with permission, another private trader had broken through Company barriers. Had they known what the future would bring Cox's modest firm the East India Company would never have let him leave Shoe Lane, for this little *fait accompli*, as will be seen in due course, was the first tremor of an earthquake.

In 1787, to make quite sure there was no difficulty with the Company, the flag of Prussia was hoisted in front of Cox's premises. The Prussian Consul was Cox's new partner Daniel Beale, who had managed to persuade the Prussian Envoy in London to appoint him. The firm's singsong business had now been strengthened by a line in Alaskan furs.

Trouble struck nonetheless, and from an unusual quarter. Private British traders in Calcutta complained to the Governor-General that Cox was doing so well in Canton selling opium for Company servants that he was putting others out of business. This was of course perfectly true. Singsongs and Alaskan furs were, as it were, merely the visible side of Cox and Beale's. Like everything else in Canton it was actually floating on the invisible tide of opium. The East India Company did not trade in opium, but every single one of its officers did; many of them were making a lot of money out of it. Nevertheless, when the fact was bruited in public it called for a stern attitude. Cox, the Council at Fort William decided, was leading Company servants away from the proper path of duty. (It will be observed that the Council's moral sense had by this time become somewhat muddled.) He was forced to leave China.

It would be interesting to know how they actually got him out, for in this matter numerous stratagems were resorted to. With old George Smith they waited till he took a week's holiday in Macao and served a deportation order on him there. Not even that succeeded. George Smith appealed to the Governor of Macao for protection, and under the flag of Portugal he stayed, the Governor being much diverted by the opportunity to show the lordly East India Company the limits of its authority.

Anyway, however it was done, Cox left—for a time. The firm of Cox and Beale survived, thanks to Prussia, under the management of Daniel Beale and his brother Thomas, who came out as Secretary to the Consulate. Naturally, a Consulate needed a Secretary; no one could quibble about that.

A vogue for naturalization set in. Within a year or so David Reid, brother of the John Reid who began it, arrived as a Danish military officer; Charles Schneider was appointed Vice-Consul for the Supreme Republic of Genoa; Cox returned as a Swede, but flew Swedish or Prussian colours as occasion demanded; and there was one Dickerson whose movements were not interfered with since it was rumoured he had protection from Poland.

Several of the foreign houses on the Canton waterfront were thus consular establishments. All had unusually high flagstaffs, on which the colours of an imposing collection of European nations were solemnly hoisted at dawn and lowered at dusk each day. In summer the consular corps descended variously upon Macao, depending on the amount of consular work detaining them in Canton. At Macao more flags were hoisted and lowered and guns fired. The Portuguese were touchy about ships saluting the Fort of Barra on entering Macao harbour, failure to do so being interpreted as non-recognition of Portuguese sovereignty, a grave mistake for a consul to make and one which was noisily avoided.

VIII: CO-HONG BANKRUPTCIES

The 1760 reorganization concentrating trade in Canton and increasing the power of the Hoppo had not been in operation for more than a few years before mandarin squeeze on the Co-Hong merchants reached such proportions that a succession of them went bankrupt owing large sums of money to country traders. The Hong merchants' difficulties were considerable. Canton being far from the tea and silk provinces, orders had to be placed and cash advanced months ahead of delivery. The Hoppo's squeeze had to be paid on each sailing, and a great deal of lesser squeeze to minor mandarins. Seasonal presents had to go to the Governor and all officers of consequence; and on top of all this the Hong merchants were frequently fined, another indirect form of squeeze.

From the Europeans they did not receive much sympathy. Infuriated creditors among the country traders created disturbances at the bankrupt merchants' premises, and finally in 1771 the national companies joined in as a body by refusing to deal with the Co-Hong any longer. If the Hoppo chose to appoint the merchants who had a right to deal with foreigners, they explained, this was agreeable to them; but the selected merchants must be dealt with as individuals, not as a monopoly guild. For once the Hoppo, seeing that the Europeans were united and in earnest, capitulated, and the Co-Hong was abolished.

Mandarin squeeze continuing at the same rate, however, bankruptcies went on occurring with bewildering and exasperating frequency. By 1779 the debts owed by Cantonese merchants to foreigners ran into millions of dollars, affecting people as far away as Calcutta and Madras; and in that year Rear-Admiral Sir Edward Vernon sent a man-of-war from India to deliver a protest to the Chinese authorities.

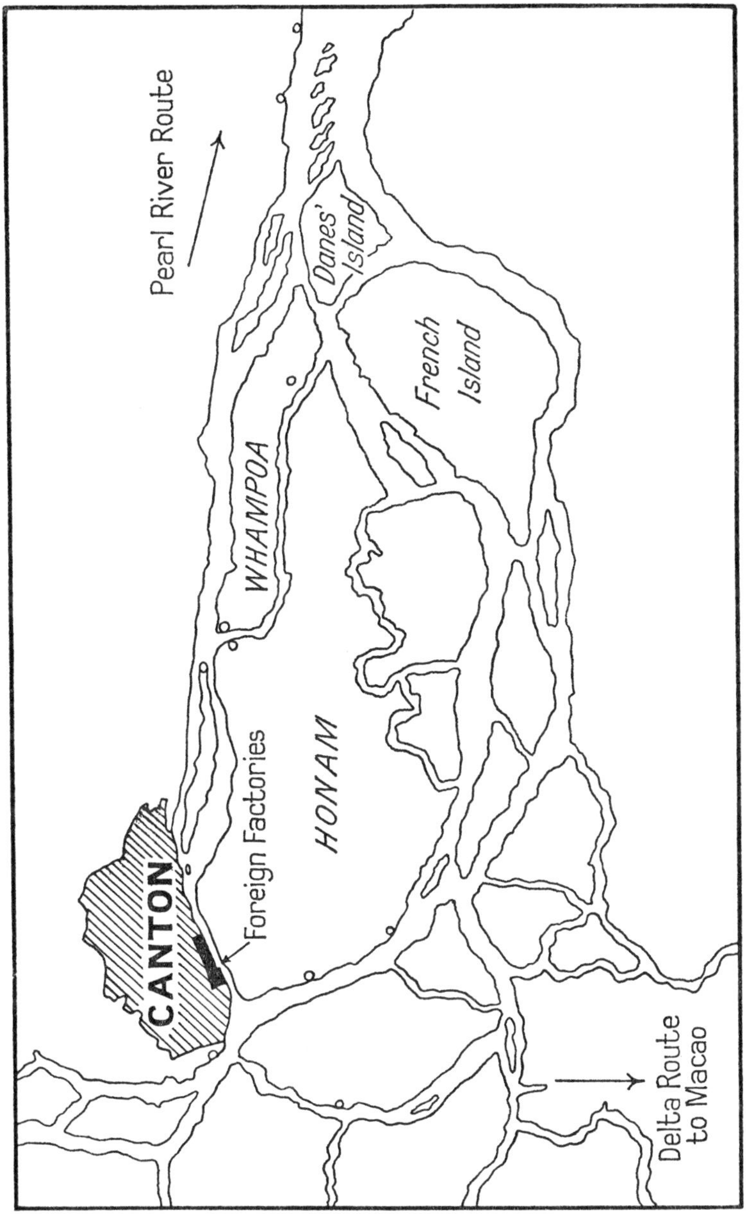

THE PORT OF CANTON

Pearl River Route

Danes' Island

French Island

WHAMPOA

HONAM

CANTON

Foreign Factories

Delta Route
to Macao

The Select were thrown into consternation. The last thing likely to improve the Company's position was the appearance of a British warship, and they did their utmost to dissuade her commander, Captain John Panton, from delivering the protest. But Panton obeyed his orders, and the note was handed in at the Petition Gate in Canton, the limit to which foreigners were allowed within the city. Surprising to relate, it received official attention, the Hoppo making an attempt to supervise transactions more closely to prevent the incurring of further debts. But characteristically two of the Hong merchants were banished to the outer provinces for having allowed the warship in.

In 1783 the Hoppo made a further modification in the trading system. The Co-Hong was revived, its membership limited to twelve, later increased to thirteen; and in this form the trade continued until the Opium War, giving Cantonese lore its name for the whole period—the epoch of the Thirteen Hongs.

IX: BRITISH DESIGNS ON MACAO

The overall size of the trade was all the time increasing. When Anson visited Canton in 1742 there were four Company ships in port; in 1780 there were twelve and twelve country ships. Up to this time smuggling tea into Britain and her American colonies had been a major source of profit for the other nations in the China trade, the Danes and Swedes smuggling to Britain, the French and Dutch to America. United States independence and Britain's 1785 Commutation Act, which reduced tea duty to a more reasonable 12 per cent of import value, caused an alteration in this pattern, knocking the bottom out of Danish and Swedish trade, these two national companies shortly folding up. The French and the Dutch adapted themselves, sending their usual four or five ships a year—these were now private voyages, their national companies having earlier been dissolved.

The really astounding feature of the years following the War of American Independence was the increase in British trade. By 1787 there were twenty-nine Company ships and thirty-three country ships at Whampoa. To appreciate the size of this it should be remembered that the East Indiaman of those days was the largest vessel to ride the seas.

In addition to their four houses on the Praia Grande, forming the great Company house at Macao, the British had by this time taken for the official residence of the President of the Select Committee the finest property in the place, a two-storey Portuguese house situated on high ground just within the old walls, with an unusually large and beautiful garden—whence the English name for the house, the Casa Garden—which embraced the tree-covered knoll of granite boulders known as the Rocks of Camões, where tradition holds that the great Portuguese epic poet wrote part of his masterpiece, *Os Lusiadas*, during a brief stay in 1557, the year of the settlement's foundation. Nothing symbolized more clearly than this unique acquisition the place the British had come to hold there. Macao had very nearly ceased to be Portuguese.

In fact, this was just the point. To a powerful nation expanding into empire Macao was a tempting proposition. The East India Company, though to the country traders they seemed to acquiesce in far too much, were actually not so insensible of British difficulties in China as might have appeared. Nor were they unwilling to take steps to see matters improved. Between Company and country the Company were very much the moving force, and continued to be so till well into the next century.

Of all the problems they were faced with none concerned them more urgently than that of Chinese justice. Naturally with scores of Europeans calling at Macao each year, and with the number of foreign sailors at Whampoa running into many hundreds, crimes were unavoidable, in addition to which there were the dozens of so-called crimes stemming from the Eight Regulations.

The degree to which Chinese laws were enforced depended on the character and whims—caprice was the word for it most favoured by the British—of the mandarins successively in charge at Canton. Some were easy-going, others aggressive, and foreign fortunes varied accordingly. Around 1779 an aggressive phase started, the mandarins widening the scope of their intervention in homicide cases to include crimes committed by one

European against another. One Dutch sailor having murdered another, the mandarins commanded the surrender of the culprit, and were only satisfied when he was hanged in their presence aboard his ship. A French sailor in 1780 murdered a Portuguese member of one of the Company's crews; the culprit took refuge in the French Consul's house, but finally had to be given up without trial, for strangulation.

The situation was no better in Macao, where the Portuguese obeyed Chinese orders without argument. One of the Company's servants, arrested in 1779 for creating a minor disturbance in the streets while drunk, was imprisoned by the Portuguese and only released after long negotiations. Another case was that of the Company's junior surgeon Abraham Leslie who, when one of the Cantonese merchants he was dealing with went bankrupt, occupied his premises with a posse of armed Indian seamen. The Chinese ordered his forcible removal from Canton and imprisonment in Macao, an order the Portuguese tamely carried out.

The Select Committee, commenting on all this to the Council in Calcutta, said they were placed 'in a worse Situation than are the Subjects of a Tyrranical Government—for we are liable to all the Severity and Injustice of Arbitrary Law, and yet do not enjoy its privilege or Protection'. Reporting various incidents, they described their position as 'disgraceful to us as Individuals & to the Company as our Employers, for in no part of the World are English subjects who are in trust, left so devoid of protection'.

The Calcutta Council, under its first Governor-General, Warren Hastings, had already formed their opinion of these difficulties. In their view what was needed was a formal agreement between Calcutta and Goa giving to British residents in Macao special rights similar to those granted to Britons in Portugal, or else more than that, the right to hold their own courts in cases involving Britons. In a memorandum to London they gave the first clear hint of what would be the best solution of all:

'Macao is so little known to the Court of Lisbon', ran the memorandum, 'and has been so neglected by the Government of Goa, that it is now the fit resort only of Vagabonds and

Outcasts. It has lost the valuable immunities formerly granted by the Chinese, & the Head Mandareen of a neighbouring Village exercises in it almost the Powers of Government.

'A place so little valued might perhaps be easily procured from the Court of Lisbon, and should it ever fall into the hands of an enterprising People, who knew how to extend all its advantages; we think it would rise to a State of Splendor, never yet equalled by any Port in the East.'

X: THE MISFIRED SALUTE OF THE *LADY HUGHES*

Thus things stood when in 1784 there occurred an incident more serious than any there had yet been. A country ship, the *Lady Hughes*, firing the customary salute on arrival at Whampoa, accidentally hit a small boat, seriously wounding three Chinese, two of whom later died of their injuries.

The Governor of Kwangtung wrote to W. H. Pigou, President of the Select Committee, ordering the surrender of the gunner who fired the shot. Pigou made the reply which more than any other exasperated the mandarins (but strictly from the Company's angle there was no other reply), reminding His Excellency that the East India Company had no control over country ships, and adding (which was perfectly true) that the gunner had disappeared.

The Governor answered that the gunner's disappearance was irrelevant. One Englishman must be surrendered, whether he was the gunner or not. Pigou declined comment, referring the Governor to the charterer of the *Lady Hughes*, who was—one might almost have known it—our old friend George Smith.

There was an uneasy pause for a few days, after which, when no one was surrendered to them, with the confusing rapidity of a single well-planned movement the mandarinate replied with action. Smith was seized by stratagem and flung into prison; the foreign factories were surrounded by Chinese troops; retreat to the sea was blocked; and every foreign house was cut off from supplies of food and water.

The serious turn of events, in which all Europeans were involved, rallied everyone in support of the British. A reasoned petition, signed by all nationalities, was addressed to the

79

Governor respectfully pointing out that the death of the two Chinese was an accident. By way of answer the Governor summoned all the foreigners except the British and tried to break their united front by explaining that he bore them no ill will, his displeasure being directed solely against the British. This endeavour did not succeed.

There was another pause, this time a more serious one, in that it became daily more evident that the Chinese did not intend to relent. Finally Pigou, from the solitude of his study, consulting no one, taking the full responsibility on himself, sent a letter to the master of the *Lady Hughes* ordering him to send up a man.

To the horror of all in the foreign factories, the master obeyed. The offending gunner still not having been found, the master selected the oldest and most decrepit sailor on board, whom he sent up with a pitiable letter pleading for mercy. He was handed over to the mandarins. Within an hour George Smith was released and everything went back to normal.

Several weeks passed by. Early in the new year the Hong merchants and two representatives of each foreign nation were ordered to appear before the Provincial Judge to hear the outcome of the case. The delay in dealing with the matter had been occasioned by the need to refer to the Emperor. His Celestial Majesty, the Judge informed the foreigners, had been graciously pleased to make an act of clemency. Although two Chinese had met their deaths, only one foreigner need be executed. Europeans were warned to be more obedient in future.

As the foreigners rose with angry protests from their seats, the Judge smiled pleasantly and withdrew. He alone knew that there was nothing more to be said. At the very moment he was speaking, in another part of the city the old sailor was being publicly strangled.

XI: HENRY DUNDAS ON THE BOARD OF CONTROL

The *Lady Hughes* incident sent sparks flying westward, to Calcutta and onward to London, as no former incident ever had. Pigou, who had shouldered the unenviable responsibility and

towards whom European hostility, even among his own colleagues, had at one stage been so intense that for several days
he had deemed it wise not to leave his rooms, was in a unique
position to word and sign the important despatch reporting the
incident. In this the Company's attention was drawn to the
criminal disgrace of Englishmen having to surrender innocent
men to be dealt with according to the degraded laws of China,
and for the first time the admission was made that if the present
deplorable state of affairs was not to continue indefinitely the
British Government must take action to redress merchants'
wrongs and put Anglo-Chinese commerce on a more equitable
basis. Extraterritorial jurisdiction, Pigou stated in so many
words, was probably the most practicable solution, and he
presented a worked-out scheme for this. The British needed a
depôt on the China coast in which they could be under their
own laws, unmolested by Chinese officialdom.

Thus the principle of extraterritoriality, destined to be forced
upon China in the nineteenth century, first really saw the light
of day. It was put forward by a highly reasonable and moderate
man, who due to the prevailing conditions in China had been
placed in an inhuman position, and to whom experience dictated that there was no other answer.

The despatch, signed by all three members of the Select
Committee and embodying the unanimous opinion of every
Briton on the China coast, was sent to the Council at Calcutta.
The Council addressed the Court of Directors of the East India
Company in London. The Court of Directors addressed the
Commissioners for the Affairs of India, popularly known as the
Board of Control, the body set up by Pitt's India Act of 1784
to supervise the East India Company's now enormous posses-
sions. There the circumstances of British traders in China
passed into the hands of one of the most influential cabinet
ministers of the day, the head of the Board of Control, Henry
Dundas, who, by consulting his colleagues on only unimportant matters and by relying on his friendship with the Prime
Minister, enjoyed a position similar to that later held by secretaries of state for India.

Dundas had no love for the Company. As a Scot he viewed
their affairs from a special angle. Though many Scots worked

in it, the Company was a London organization, supported by London funds, bringing profit to London. There had once, many years earlier, been a project for a Scottish East India Company; but since it had been shelved, Scots desiring to have commerce with the East had had to do so either as employees of the London Company or on their own account in the country trade. A number of leading country traders were Scots; their numbers were increasing. All that prevented them from engaging in oriental trade on a grand scale was the Company's monopoly.

The patent inability of the East India Company to achieve for British interests in China a status proper to the dignity of a great power provided Henry Dundas with an opening of advantage to Scottish and other private traders. As Dundas saw it, there would be no more of the Company's bungling attempts at diplomacy. They had not succeeded in getting beyond the Petition Gate at Canton; even a provincial Chinese governor would not open his doors to them. Matters would never be settled by haggling with subordinates. The proper way of proceeding was to go to the top. China, as was widely believed, was ruled by highly reasonable and civilized people; Voltaire and all the best *savants* of the *chinoiserie* had said so. True, what they said did not accord with merchants' experiences in Canton, but this was because Peking, being very far away from Canton, was probably unaware of what was happening. Let the matter be lifted out of the hands of the Company and put on a higher level. The King would send an embassy to the Emperor of China.

IV

LORD MACARTNEY'S EMBASSY

THE FIRST ATTEMPT to send an embassy came to nothing due to the death of the Ambassador, Colonel Charles Cathcart, while on his way to China in 1788. His instructions are, however, of interest in that they show the trend of British Government thinking, revealing also the care with which Dundas had examined the views expressed in Company documents and by private traders.

Cathcart was to have negotiated with the Chinese Government for the cession to the British Crown of a depôt for the marketing and storage of goods. A private letter from Dundas to the envoy suggested that a suitable place for this would be Macao. In the manner of acquiring Macao, the letter stated, there were uncertainties, and tact would be needed. (For of course the British Government knew no more than anyone else concerning the exact nature of Portugal's tenure of Macao. The Portuguese claimed to have sovereign rights there, yet they paid the Chinese an annual ground rent for the place.) It was suggested to Colonel Cathcart that the city would probably have to be ceded to Britain by Portugal, but only with the concurrence of China. If this proved unacceptable to the Chinese, a suitable alternative for a depôt would be Amoy or any other small port near the tea and silk provinces. In the depôt, if granted, the British were to be under their own laws, the Chinese under theirs.

Within a matter of months of the news of Cathcart's death at sea the French Revolution broke out, altering the preoccupations of every government in Europe, and it was four years before Henry Dundas had time to take up again the question of an embassy to China. When he did, in 1792, the Ambassador chosen was a more considerable figure—George, Viscount Macartney.

Ever since the age of twenty-seven when, being at the time one of the handsomest young men in London, he was sent as Envoy Extraordinary to the Court of Catherine the Great, Macartney had occupied a place of prominence in public life, as a Member of Parliament, as Chief Secretary for Ireland, as Governor of Grenada, and during 1781–6 as Governor of Madras. Although he had no direct knowledge of China, and although one of the criticisms levelled at him in India was that he had shown inadequacy in handling oriental princes, at the age of fifty-six Lord Macartney was a man of varied experience and undeniable social address. If it was possible for a Westerner to succeed in the Forbidden City, he had as fair a chance as anyone.

His instructions did not, as Cathcart's had, threaten Macao. They were drafted in the opinion that the acquisition of a depôt near the silk and tea provinces would be more suitable than a tripartite agreement with Portugal. The instructions loosely stated that the Ambassador should ask for rights at the depôt similar to those enjoyed by the Portuguese at Macao. The main purpose of the mission was to free trade at Canton from encumbrances and put it on a normal commercial basis, allowing the British to purchase Chinese goods at market prices from whatever merchants they chose.

Opium was mentioned in the instructions. 'If this subject should come into discussion', wrote Henry Dundas, 'it must be handled with the greatest circumspection.' If it should be insisted on as an item in a commercial treaty that British ships no longer carry opium to China, the Ambassador must accede to this. Greatly as it might harm the Indian revenue it must not stand in the way of a profitable treaty with China. And in the veiled language of diplomacy the Minister hinted that, even were the undertaking given, opium might still find its way to China, though by circuitous routes.

In the selection of an ambassador and the preparation of his instructions Dundas was sure of himself. He liked Macartney personally, and, as the instructions show, he thoroughly understood the commercial position. In the matter of presents for the Emperor and transport for the mission he was less certain.

Due to the many unknown factors involved, it was an exceptionally difficult embassy to provide for. Even the route to Peking was unknown. Information about China, most of it the work of Catholic priests and in French, was available to Protestant England only at second-hand, and much of what was known was decades out of date. It was known, for example, that suitable presents would be telescopes and guns. These were accordingly included in the gifts, on which a great sum was spent. The vogue for scientific gifts had, however, long ended. European priests and envoys had been bringing them to Peking ever since Ricci's day. The Imperial Palace was full of scientific marvels; there were roomfuls of telescopes and astrolabes—boring things which no one knew what to do with. The Son of Heaven was the most difficult person on earth to give a present to; he had all the things he wanted, and what he did not have he was not interested in.

This decline of interest in Western science being unknown in London, the British presents created the impression that here was another barbarian nation with its scientific contraptions, the same old thing again only not so good—for as Lord Macartney in due course saw for himself the British presents were inferior in quality to the exquisite European gifts already in the Imperial Palace, particularly those from France and Italy. Had Dundas known it, singsongs would have caused more pleasure and amusement, provided they were accompanied by presents of more substantial value. But how could anyone have believed this possible?

Even more cogent, how could anyone in the London of 1792 have believed it possible that since the Dutch mission of 1656 nothing in Peking had changed, that there was still no means of negotiating with the Son of Heaven, and that to prepare careful ambassadorial instructions was so much wasted effort? The Everlasting Lord was still receiving deputations of tribute-paying barbarians who touched their foreheads to the dust nine times as he appeared silent before them at the moment of dawn.

G   85

Lord Macartney's Embassy

Had Dundas thought of referring the point to Lisbon he might have obtained a clearer impression of what Lord Macartney would be confronted with, for since the Dutch mission the Portuguese had twice tried to improve relations with China by means of an embassy. The first of these was the most magnificent of all European missions, sent by João V in 1715 under Dom Alexandre Metello de Sousa e Meneses, whose cortège approached the Great Within scattering largesse in the streets of Peking, a custom the Chinese had never witnessed before and which roused great excitement. The second embassy, that of Francisco Xavier Assis Pacheco e Sampaio in 1752, after some difficulty in entering China, was received by the Emperor Ch'ien Lung who, one of the best royal calligraphists in Chinese history, even honoured the Ambassador by presenting him with a small casket of his own writings. Both embassies breakfasted in the Emperor's presence following the audience, and both achieved nothing, ending by being as baffled by the protocol of the Forbidden City as had been everyone before them. But as Chinese precedent dictated in the matter of foreign missions, both were received with the highest marks of benevolence.

In the case of Lord Macartney's embassy, to the usual marks of benevolence was added a distinct awareness that China was receiving the representative of the most powerful of barbarian tribes, and one who it was known in advance might refuse to perform the kowtow. There had been trouble before with Europeans over the kowtow. A Russian embassy, which was actually in Peking at the same time as the Dutch, had refused to perform it and been dismissed without an audience. The ceremonial of an audience in the Great Within demanded the kowtow. If Lord Macartney was to be received in Peking and refused to perform it, he would have to be dismissed as the Russians had been. But by stretching a long point it could just be said that there were certain precedents, albeit rather dubious ones, for a slight relaxation in ceremonial in the case of an embassy not actually given audience in the Great Within. The first Portuguese mission, for example, had in 1519 met the Emperor Chang Tê informally at Nanking while the latter was on a state tour. This appears to be the only possible explanation for the reception Lord Macartney was accorded. While determined that Macartney *would* perform the kowtow, the mandarins about the Emperor, who was by this time well over eighty, appear to have so contrived matters as to leave themselves a loophole which would in an emergency permit an audience to take place without the kowtow, thus avoiding giving offence to the British, out of whom, distantly through the Hoppo, they were making a very great deal of money. All apparently quite by chance, when Macartney reached Peking it was to find that the Emperor was not there, but at Jehol, where he had a hunting lodge on the edge of the steppes. Meanwhile, far away in Canton, from the moment news was received that a British embassy was on its way from England, treatment of British merchants instantly improved. To all, Chinese and Europeans, engaged in foreign trade, the embassy was an occasion of the greatest importance.

III: 'TREMBLINGLY OBEY'

H.M.S. *Lion*, bearing Lord Macartney and his suite, reached the islands off the mouth of the Pearl River in June 1793. The Ambassador himself did not land, but sent his Secretary of Embassy, Sir George Staunton, ashore to Macao to discuss matters with senior Company officials. Staunton, who had served Macartney in Madras, had been appointed Secretary at the Ambassador's request, and later published an account of the embassy. From his discussions at Macao emerged the proposition, later made in writing to the Emperor, that a suitable place for a British depôt would be one of the Chusan islands, off the Chekiang coast, and that the ports of Tientsin and Ningpo be opened to British vessels. After a few days the embassy sailed up the coast, landing at the mouth of the Peiho River, the nearest sea approach to Peking.

The boat bearing them up-river carried a banner describing the occupants as tribute-paying barbarians, but Lord Macartney, when this was explained to him, tactfully decided to ignore it. The question of the kowtow came up, and after repeated attempts to induce him to perform it he agreed to do so on condition that a mandarin of equal rank did the same to a portrait of King George III. This of course was quite out of the question, and in the end the officials fell back on what seems to have been their carefully prepared position of retreat. The kowtow was waived.

At the moment of dawn on 14th September 1793 the Son of Heaven, borne by sixteen bearers and attended in unique splendour, arrived to take his seat on a throne set within a magnificently caparisoned tent in one of the imperial parks at Jehol. There, arrayed in the robes of the Order of the Bath, Lord Macartney, on bended knee, placed in the hands of the Lord of Ten Thousand Years a jewel-studded gold box containing a letter in Latin from the King of England. Even in these informal surroundings an audience of the Son of Heaven was of a grandeur and magnificence such as every one of those present knew they would never live to see the equal. Even Lord Macartney, not given to exaggeration, wrote afterwards, 'Thus have I seen King Solomon in all his glory.'

This one remarkable departure from precedent excepted, the embassy proceeded (but the English did not know this) on the usual lines. The immemorial breakfast followed, and, like Assis Pacheco before him, as a mark of special condescension Lord Macartney was given a specimen of the Emperor's handwriting. Each of them in fact received a present, including Sir George Staunton's clever twelve-year-old son, who had been learning Chinese on the way up and whom the Emperor complimented on his knowledge. No opportunity was given for the embassy's business to be discussed.

After a few days, during which the Ambassador made every tactful endeavour possible to open negotiation, the Court returned to the Summer Palace in the Western Hills near Peking, and Lord Macartney and his suite were brought down to the capital. They did not see the Emperor again. On the three occasions when Ch'ien Lung spoke to Macartney he showed particular cordiality. But this was one of the Son of Heaven's disarming habits—beautiful manners, giving every embassy the impression it was doing better than its forerunners.

In due course—and by formal precedent it was the signal for their departure—the Emperor's letter to George III was received. The document, in a tone of exalted benevolence in which there was a calculated hint of admonition, commended the King's proper spirit in sending gifts and 'wishing to adopt Chinese civilization', and advised him of his duty to display in the future an even greater devotion. Accompanying the letter came munificent return presents. 'Reverently receive them', the letter concluded, 'and note the tenderness of our regard.' By Dragon standards it was singularly pleasant.

Lord Macartney's calm manner concealed a deep anxiety lest his costly mission be unproductive. How could he return to London with only this brief, inconsequential letter? As a last venture he presented to the Grand Secretary a short memorandum of the points he was authorized to raise.

Incredible to relate, the Emperor replied. Macartney received the letter just as he was leaving Peking to take the canal route southward. In tone the letter was very different from the first. Addressed to George III, it was majestic, thunderous, damning and final. Point by point it answered the memorandum without conceding an inch on any of the subjects raised. Lord Macartney was furthermore signalized as having shown himself anxious to introduce the English religion into China, an accusation added either in pique or on the prompting of the few Catholic priests still in Peking. It was difficult to imagine a more embarrassing document to have to carry back to an expectant King and Cabinet. From it, it would seem as if the Ambassador had bungled the entire mission, whereas in fact to have elicited a business letter from the Dragon was, like being presented to him without the kowtow, a unique achievement.

Once past the initial impression however, it could be seen that for all the grandeur of its language the Emperor's letter contained some strange things. How could they trade, asked Ch'ien Lung, at ports like Ningpo where there were no warehouses or interpreters? 'Nobody would understand your language, and no benefit could thence be derived.'

The same excuse was preferred for refusing to cede Chusan, and there was pathos in the warning that followed. Let the British not imagine that they could privily take possession of any such island. 'There is an accurate map of this Empire, and its limits are guarded with the strictest severity. Whether they be islands or inlets of the sea, every part of it has been surveyed, and is under a proper government.'

Doubtless the princelings of Cochin-China, the kings of Burma and Nepal, and the chieftains of Mongolia would have been impressed by the fact that China possessed a map. Such a remarkable document might even have magical virtues. It was unlikely that the Emperor's warning would make such an impression on their Lordships of the Admiralty.

After threatening the King that any attempt to disregard these restrictions would result in British ships being driven out by force, the letter concluded:

'Do not say that you have not been warned in time. Tremblingly obey and show no negligence.'

IV: THE MOMENT THAT NEVER CAME AGAIN

Hopeful even then of some result from his mission, when he reached Canton Lord Macartney tried to improve trade conditions by negotiating with the Hoppo and the Governor. But to no purpose. Coming down at last to Macao the Ambassador knew his mission had utterly failed. Although he concealed from the British there the true extent of the Emperor's contemptuous treatment of their King, the lack of visible outcome from the embassy told most of the story.

The Macartney embassy to China is one of those missed moments of history which have a transcendental quality about them. It is often regarded as the point beyond which there was no further hope for the Great Ch'ing, but this is surely an exaggeration. The British expected much of the embassy, but this was because they knew so little about the Great Within. Had they known more, they would not have entertained such hopes. It was still too soon to expect the Dragon to perceive the strength of the outside forces he sought to restrict and control, for these forces were far from apparent in China at that time. The Dragon needed to see more yet before he could judge.

What gives the Macartney episode its transcendental quality is a conjuncture of personalities tantalizing in the possibility they together held out to the future—Ch'ien Lung, connoisseur and patron of the arts, gifted and forceful ruler, in the mellow concluding years of one of the great reigns of Chinese history; Henry Dundas, who on the China situation was one of the best-informed men ever to hold Cabinet office in London; and Lord Macartney himself, a perfect ambassador. Such a conjuncture of personalities was never to come again. In China there was never to be another emperor of the calibre of Ch'ien Lung, the dynasty declining after him into a series of *rois fainéants*; while in London, as British power and responsibilities increased, the amount of time foreign ministers could devote to the complications of China became progressively less, till the time of Lord Palmerston when. . . . But let this story tell itself.

V

THE BRITISH THREAT TO
MACAO

THE FAILURE OF THE MACARTNEY EMBASSY—the failure to obtain a British depôt in China by a diplomatic approach to Peking—narrowed British possibilities to an arrangement with Portugal concerning Macao, transferring foreign rights there (whatever those rights were) from Portugal to Great Britain, if this could be done without a fracas with the mandarins—in other words, if there were some fully justifiable reason for such a transference.

In 1801 Portugal was invaded by French and Spanish forces. The Directors of the East India Company in London, fearing that this would be the prelude to French attacks on Portugal's overseas possessions, decided that Macao must be safeguarded by the despatch of British troops to reinforce its meagre Portuguese garrison. In March 1802 H.M.S. *Arrogant* arrived at Lintin convoying three Company ships each with a detachment of British troops on board whom it was intended to land at Macao.

The Select Committee took fright, informing the ships' commanders that they should on no account attempt to land troops without the consent of the Governor of Macao. To do so, they said, far from protecting British interests, was likely to wreck them. The naval and military officers commanding went ashore to meet the Governor, whom they found in the time-honoured position of being without orders from Goa.

These, he said, would have to be awaited. The officers stressed the closeness of the Spaniards in Manila, the Dutch and French in Batavia, but the Governor was resolute in prevarication.

Meanwhile in Calcutta an incorrect report had been received from Europe to the effect that France and Portugal had concluded a treaty of peace. Immediately sending two more ships to Macao, the Governor-General, the Marquess Wellesley, now authorized the troops to seize Macao by force, provided in the opinion of the Select Committee it could be done without upsetting relations with China. In a letter to the Governor of Macao Wellesley demanded that the settlement be placed immediately under British authority for the duration of the war. He went on:

'I have directed the Officer in Command of the British Armament previously to the employment of the force placed under his Command to propose to your Excellency terms for the peaceable surrender of the Settlement of Macao & its dependencies.

'Your Excellency's wisdom & discernment will suggest to you the inutility of opposing any resistance to the accomplishment of this measure, your Excellency's justice & humanity will not permit you to expose the lives & property of the inhabitants of Macao to the danger of an unavailing contest with the superior power of the British arms. . . . '

The letter was never delivered because the Select Committee would not allow it, but it explains what the Portuguese were up against. As Wellesley was doubtless aware, once the British were in control of Macao, with the overwhelming British commercial interests already installed there, it would cease to be Portuguese for ever.

None were more conscious of this than the Portuguese themselves, who came to know of the contents of Wellesley's letter. Behind the scenes the Portuguese Governor took the desperate measure of an appeal to Peking, asking that Macao be placed under the Emperor's protection. There was no quick reaction to this. The suspense lasted another two months, when a British despatch from Penang announced the cessation of hostilities in Europe (at almost the same moment the Peace of Amiens was signed), and without having landed any soldiers at Macao, Lord Wellesley's invasion force sailed back to India.

This fortunate outcome for Macao was not yet known in Peking when the Portuguese appeal for protection was presented by two Portuguese priests resident there, one of them employed on the Bureau of Mathematics. The Emperor Chia Ch'ing was at first impressed, but from Canton the Governor of Kwangtung, whose opinion of the British was not unfavourable, advised that the Portuguese were exaggerating the danger. This irritated the Emperor, who told the Portuguese fathers to keep out of politics, a rebuff which reverberated in Canton and Macao to Portuguese disadvantage, unforeseeably producing in due course the most extraordinary incident of the period—the British occupation of Macao.

II: ADMIRAL DRURY IN MACAO ROADS

The departure of Wellesley's force did not end the crisis. The terms of the Peace of Amiens had not even been carried out in India before Lord Wellesley received orders from London to hold everything, since resumption of war seemed imminent. In Macao the position thus remained unchanged. At any moment the British might again seek to 'defend' it from the French and their Spanish allies in Manila. When in October 1807 the forces of Napoleonic France under Marshal Junot invaded Portugal, the moment had come. The Governor-General of India was now Lord Minto, and the underlying tone of the proceedings was less herculean than it had been with Wellesley. A British force was despatched at once to Macao to safeguard British interests in China and protect the settlement of Britain's oldest ally. On 11th September 1808 Rear-Admiral William Drury stood off Macao with three hundred troops.

For the Portuguese, despite Minto's less threatening tone, it was a far graver crisis than that of 1802. Lord Minto had been in correspondence with the Portuguese Viceroy at Goa, who apparently approved of the British move. It was all very friendly and correct, the trouble being that these far-distant grandees did not appear to have understood the local predicament, which was that the presence of British troops would lead inevitably to *de facto* British rule, in the suite of which, once imposed, any attempt to prevent it in due course becoming *de jure* rule would be flying in the face of political and commercial reality. In unsuccessfully appealing to the Emperor for protection in 1802 the Governor and Senate of Macao had shot their bolt so far as that direction was concerned. Any further appeal from them could only result in the extinction of Portuguese authority by the Chinese. In addition, the Portuguese no longer had the Select Committee on their side. The diplomatic rebuff the Portuguese had received from Chia Ch'ing, coupled with a mandarin 'soft period' in Canton, during which relations between the British and the mandarins had been unusually good, had led the Select Committee to the conclusion that the Chinese would raise no more than formal complaints if British troops landed at Macao. This was the advice Admiral Drury was given on his arrival.

To add to the precariousness of the Portuguese position, the news from Portugal itself which the British brought with them was extremely grave. Junot's invasion had met with little resistance; the Prince Regent of Portugal and his family had fled to Brazil; a new government had been set up; and Portuguese were being recruited for service in Napoleon's armies. (Neither Drury nor the Governor of Macao knew that since then the arrogance of French behaviour in Portugal had led to a national uprising, and that British forces under Sir Arthur Wellesley were within weeks of coming to the rescue.)

The Governor of Macao at this critical moment was Bernardo Aleixo de Lemos Faria, who as usual was without orders from Goa. Drury had furthermore come without the all-important letter from the Portuguese Viceroy authorizing a British landing. With only a handful of third-rate soldiers in Macao, with the British force riding at anchor outside, with a powerful British resident community only waiting for Macao to become a British possession, with the French not far off and the Chinese inside and all around, the Governor could only rely on wit and luck.

He first reminded the Admiral of what was untrue, that Macao had concluded a treaty with China and was under Chinese protection. Only with Chinese consent, he said, could foreign troops enter. To Drury's assurance that he came in friendship to protect the city, Lemos Faria replied that he quite appreciated this, but that with such mistrustful people as the Chinese a British landing would do more injury than good to the Allies. Behind the scenes Lemos Faria then approached the Chinese prefectural authorities of Heungshan, from whom reply came that British troops were totally unnecessary for the defence of Macao, and that if the city was attacked, being part of the Chinese dominion it would be defended by a Chinese army. Threats were issued to the Portuguese if they allowed the British ashore.

Admiral Drury also resorted to threats. If the Portuguese would not agree to respect their national alliance with Great Britain, he informed them, he would be obliged to land his men at the point of the bayonet, and if the Chinese objected there might be bayonet points for them too.

Amid the reaction this produced in Macao, gesture nearly ran away with the situation. In an impassioned session the Senate swore the British would only march in over their dead bodies. Rusty old muskets were taken out and oiled, octogenarians volunteered, and the disposition of senators per fort was worked out. Caution only prevailed on the advice of Macao's Judge, Miguel de Arriaga, a person of great shrewdness in all that concerned Macao's relations with the Chinese. On his recommendation it was decided that the British request must be met on conditions, one of which was that only the Portuguese flag must be flown. Muskets were put away, and with all outward marks of politeness, rather as if there had never been any argument about it, the British troops were welcomed ashore.

III: THE BRITISH OCCUPATION OF MACAO

So the Napoleonic War, the first European war of sufficient dimensions ever to do so, reached out to China, and as befitted war in the world of opium, flagstaffs and singsongs there was a peculiar side to it. It was fought without gunpowder.

The British troops occupied the Forts of Guia and Bomparto; some were lodged in the East India Company's houses, some in the old Jesuit seminary next to the church of São Paulo, and some in tents along the waterfront. Those familiar with Macao will realize that by this time the city was almost bursting at the seams. The central fort—Monte—once the Governor's residence and traditionally the senior fort, was not sullied by foreign intruders. With a gesture all Macao understood, Lemos Faria temporarily moved his quarters from the Governor's Palace to the Monte where, the flag of Portugal flying bravely, he lived surrounded by an imposing array of mounted cannon, most of which—Macao was ordinarily a very peaceful place—were full of birds' nests.

From this eminence he looked uneasily down at a scene which rapidly deteriorated. The reaction of ordinary Chinese to the British soldiers and Indian sepoys was one of spontaneous hostility. Insults, jeers and taunts led to scuffles, broken heads and street fighting between bands of men of the different races. In drunken revels British soldiers broke into people's private houses and smashed up property, while sepoys committed other depredations including the desecration of Chinese tombs, which led to some of them losing their lives at Chinese hands. Canton and Whampoa could usually contain this kind of thing; Macao could not. It was too small. Within less than a week the temper of the Chinese had reached dangerous and vindictive levels.

But as he continued to look down on this unprecedented disorder Lemos Faria was no longer uneasy. Neither were the senators. They knew now that Arriaga's suggestion was wise. If the Chinese claimed Macao as theirs, let them show it. Let them get rid of the British. Macao had only to placate everyone on all sides—and wait.

With their customary grasp of affairs, the mandarins took no action directly affecting Macao. Instead, two weeks after the British installation all foreign trade at Canton was stopped. When this produced no result, a week later all servants were withdrawn from the factories and food supplies were discontinued. Retreat to the sea was left open, and a day or so later many of the British evacuated the factories and came down to Macao.

Shortly after this, on 22nd October, another shipload of troops arrived from India, landing at Macao amid renewed

97

objections from Lemos Faria and public threatenings from the Heungshan magistracy. Knowing what this last meant, the Chinese in Macao, sensitive to the least swing in the mandarin barometer, began to leave the city, carrying away their goods with them. Servants, hawkers, skilled craftsmen, even wet nurses and coolies, all were fleeing. Food prices rose alarmingly.

Admiral Drury remained obdurate. In a letter to the Governor of Kwangtung he explained the object of his mission. The Governor, who did not recognize the existence of foreign navies or their officers, did not reply. So far as he was concerned the spokesman of the British was John Roberts, President of the Select Committee, to whom he sent a verbal indication that the moment the Admiral sailed away trade would be resumed.

Chinese resistance of this kind, so bland and effortless, usually succeeded in arousing its opponents to fury. Long mandarin experience showed that such fury was invariably impotent. The tactics followed were thus repeated each time occasion demanded with baffling self-confidence.

The gallant Admiral's temper reacted in the classic manner. The candles on the Company's splendid dinner table flickered in the breath of fighting talk. The time had come for Britain to show the Chinese where they really stood. Canton would be bombarded from the river. Due to the density of its buildings, once fire was let loose in it the whole city would probably be burnt to the ground. It was the kind of lesson the Chinese needed to be taught. There was no other way to end the ridiculous conditions under which foreign trade was conducted. Drury and Roberts led the talk, which was so unrestrained that those present who did not concur—and there were several—had to hold their peace.

In preparation for this aggressive design Admiral Drury on 21st November gave all Britons still remaining in Canton forty-eight hours to be out, and ordered all British ships to leave Whampoa and come down to the mouth of the river. With misgivings the British at Canton obeyed and left. Roberts stayed behind at Whampoa on board a ship, from which he issued directions to all shipping requiring them to obey the Admiral's instruction and fall down-river.

None of the commanders, even of the Company ships, would move. Politely they pointed out, in a jointly signed letter to Roberts, that the steps being taken seemed to them likely to lead to a serious war, to their great loss (this was the point), and that if a peaceful approach consistent with the British character could be made to the Chinese, they considered this should be done.

One of the principal reasons that made the Company commanders venture to sign this letter was that they knew that Roberts was not supported by the rest of the Committee. It was the rule that Select Committee pronouncements on important matters must issue over the signature of all three members. The commanders were disinclined to risk their necks—and their profits—for the sake of one supercargo fancying himself as a general.

Lemos Faria, who had meanwhile been meeting Chinese threats to send troops into Macao by informing the mandarins that the discipline of the British forces had improved (which was true) and that there was now no need, was at this point formally notified through the Casa Branca that a Chinese army was being raised to invest the city. In desperation he informed the British that they must leave at once. At almost the same moment, after the refusal of the British captains to obey Drury's orders, the commander of the Bengal troops, Major Weguelin, advised the Admiral of the hopelessness of maintaining his stand. Between the Portuguese, the Chinese, the British civilians and his own military officers, Drury was enmeshed.

Weguelin, Arriaga and one of the supercargoes of the East India Company concluded an agreement for British withdrawal, formally notifying the Mandarin of the Casa Branca. After a few days the British evacuation started. When the last detachment was reported to have left, a Chinese general carried out an inspection of particular thoroughness, searching all forts for deserters or contingents secretly left behind. Satisfied at last, he signalled that the Emperor's orders were complied with. A week later normal trade was resumed.

The Governor of Kwangtung was dismissed for having allowed the landing to take place. A Portuguese priest who had acted as interpreter for the British was arrested by the mandarins, but later released on Arriaga's intervention. Thus ended the British occupation of Macao. In the words of H. B. Morse, historian of the East India Company trading to China:

'Admiral Drury in his encounter with Oriental passive resistance was defeated without the loss of a man on either side, and in the eyes of the Chinese he must have appeared to have saved all except honour. He had come to Macao with the most benevolent intentions: his object was to aid the Portuguese in defending Macao against the French—this aid was rejected both by the Portuguese, tenants of the port, and by the Chinese, lords of the soil.'

Looking at it from the viewpoint of today, it could be said that it was a pity that the Chinese should have had at so late a date yet another opportunity to demonstrate to the Emperor the perfection with which they handled foreign barbarians. This both sides owed to Admiral Drury, unknowingly a representative of that particular type of barbarian who, from the time of Weddell and before, the mandarins had shown themselves singularly adept at taming and driving away. Unfortunately their taming of Drury, at a date when their tactics were after many centuries at last quite definitely out of date, deepened their belief in the efficacy of age-old methods.

This was the last time Macao was ever to be quite so directly threatened by a British take-over, although for another twelve years the danger remained that at any moment it might become an item of British policy to try to acquire it. But when one thinks of the series of narrow escapes Macao had—the Warren Hastings recommendation, the instructions of the abortive Cathcart embassy, the Wellesley affair and the British occupation—it is almost as remarkable that the city survived from the British as it is that it has survived since 1557 from the Chinese.

For this Macao—and Portugal—has to thank a long succession of able men, of whom that cunning fox Miguel de Arriaga is one of the most famous in the city's annals. Their commercial and personal ties with the Chinese have been so extensive that in emergencies they have been capable of serving political ends. Time and again the Arriaga of the moment has steered the defenceless little city through the extraordinary hazards of its existence—while of course in Lisbon the governors got the credit. But when Macao people laugh at this latter element of the position, as they sometimes do, it has to be remembered that in one respect many a governor well deserved that credit. He knew how to recognize good advice when it was given him.

VI

HUMANITARIANS, NOT FORGETTING THE LADIES

DURING THE YEARS FROM 1800 ONWARDS a number of deeply important changes of a cultural and social nature started to make their impact on the thinking and ways of life of the China coast Europeans. Loosely speaking these developments may be linked together and jointly described as the arrival of English humanitarianism. In relation to the East they symptomatized the growing awareness in England that from trading had come power, and from power responsibility. It was no longer felt sufficient by educated and discerning men to come to the East solely to make money and be damned for the people from whom they made it. The idea had occurred—a revolutionary idea—that if one had anything in the way of special skill or talent to offer, one should not only get but give. In addition to making a great deal of money out of China one could perhaps contribute something for the general good, which included the good of the Chinese.

It has already been noted how the mandarins found it more difficult to understand a man of restraint like Anson than they did a Weddell or a Drury. The arrival of humanitarian England was to give power and permanency to this difficulty. Extraordinary as it may seem, the very factor which one would have expected to have contributed more than any other to an improvement of relations between Europe and China became in fact one of the most serious barriers to understanding.

Nothing is more traditionally perplexing to the Chinese than altruism. They admire it in theory, and also in practice where it has been patently proved to be altruism. But to prove such a case to a Chinese is exceedingly hard, the entire mental make-up of the people being to disbelieve it. The mandarins of those days, the most traditional of Chinese thinkers, distrusted appearances of altruism in their own people; still more did they distrust it in foreigners. From the arrival of humanitarianism there arose within the mandarinate a deepening belief in foreign hypocrisy, a belief that humanitarian activities concealed base ulterior motives. This belief in the hypocrisy of the British, the foreign nation with which the Chinese were chiefly concerned, was one of the main factors leading informed Chinese opinion into the state of bafflement and exasperation with foreigners which is characteristic of it in the nineteenth century. There had already been the irritating distinction within the British ranks between Company and country traders. This was now to be succeeded by a still more perplexing contradiction. With one hand the Europeans were selling opium, while with the other giving money to found clinics for the Chinese poor. To the mandarins it just did not make sense—and, as will be seen in due course, it is not too easy today for even us to make sense of it either.

The earliest representative figure in this new phase of China coast life was young George Staunton, who at the age of twelve had been Lord Macartney's page on his embassy to China and had in an astonishingly short space of time learnt enough spoken Chinese to be complimented by the Emperor and, even more remarkable, learnt enough written Chinese to draft simple letters for the Ambassador. Around 1800 this young man, now aged twenty, returned to China to become the East India Company's Chinese interpreter.

The mandarins had consistently refused to provide foreigners with facilities for learning Chinese. Severe penalties existed for any Chinese found teaching a foreigner. With great trouble the supercargoes had managed to discover a Chinese in Macao willing to teach them, but he would not dare come to the Company residences. The supercargoes had to seek him out in his small dwelling in 'an obscure and distant part of the town'. With Staunton's arrival all this, and much more, began to change.

Hitherto Europe's knowledge of China had come from two sources: the accounts of travellers who could not read Chinese and the writings of Catholic priests in China, the only Europeans who spoke Chinese, but whose mental approach was the dedicated and concentrated one of the missionary rather than the broader, dispassionate one of the scholar. The evidence concerning China as presented by these two sources conflicted strongly. Between Europe's breathless admiration for China, inspired originally by the French Jesuits in Peking, and the despising scorn of Anson's chronicler, describing how things were at Canton, lay an incomprehensible gap which George Staunton, in his studies and spare-time translations of Chinese books, began to narrow. At long last China's history and concepts, her religions and arts, her traditions and suscepti-bilities, and her weird cosmology found their way gradually into the English language in a presentation that was both well informed and unbiased. Staunton in fact set a tradition, being the first in a line of Chinese scholars in East India Company service whose books and articles are the foundation of our modern knowledge of China.

Another pioneer of this period was the Company's surgeon Alexander Pearson, who was foremost among those who con-sidered that European medical science must somehow be brought to the service of the Chinese. In 1805 Pearson vaccinated a number of Chinese against smallpox and wrote a pamphlet on vaccination for Chinese readers, which Staunton translated into Chinese and had printed at the Company's Canton press. It was the first event in a long and distinguished tradition of European medical assistance in China, producing as one of its more remarkable outcomes the fact that the founder of the Chinese Republic was a British medical graduate.

II: AN INVASION OF LADIES AT MACAO

In some ways the cultural and social changes afoot were no more than the extension of ordinary English life to the China coast, where till now European life had been decidedly abnor-mal. Concerning this aspect of things, by far and away the most important development was the arrival of the ladies.

Not forgetting the Ladies

No foreign women were allowed to come to China, which the East India Company, anxious to avoid misunderstandings with the Chinese, had always taken to include Macao. In Calcutta the Company was adamant that no berth in a China-bound ship must be given to a woman. At the same time there was a strict rule that no Company servant might marry a local woman, with the result that long after Englishwomen started taking residence in India, where the social life of a city like Calcutta was quite as gay as that of Bath or Tunbridge Wells, on the China coast European society was still womanless.

The various earlier references to ecclesiastical disapproval of foreigners at Macao will already have told much of the rest of this tale. While the Company forbade its servants to marry local women, nothing was said about mistresses, and in Macao practically all Company men had liaisons with local women, Portuguese, Chinese or Eurasian. Nor was the Company's regulation against marriage the operative factor. The distinction between European and Eurasian which had grown up had brought about a far more important unwritten code that no European, Company or country, might marry a Macao girl, the penalty for doing so being ostracism from European society and dismissal from partnerships or employment.

The stain of deep tragedy darkens these Macao liaisons, which were often of a lasting nature, terminated only by final departure from the coast. Even merchants without permits to pass the summer in China maintained mistresses in Macao. During absences remittances were sent to the women through one of the consulates, Prussia handling a good many of these. In correspondence the ladies were referred to as pensioners, a term innocent enough to meet the situation of an inquisitive wife in England or India nosing through account books to relieve the boredom of long years of separation.

The Briton who took care of himself socially, if he had children by his pensioner, prudently ensured that they were bastards, though while he was around they were provided for. When the time came to go home for good it was often another story, unless, as could sometimes be arranged, the woman and her children were looked after by the man's firm or bequeathed to a new arrival.

The first Englishwomen to wheedle their way through Company obstacles reached Macao in the last decade of the eighteenth century, and little by little—as in the mandarin view was always the way with women—the ladies established themselves as a permanent feature of Macao society. Around 1805 Company servants started bringing their wives and children with them on first arrival. The disapproving Select Committee considered sending the ladies back to England, but by one means or another they stayed on until it suited them to leave with their husbands. It was difficult for the Company to insist. One of its servants might leave England a bachelor, marry an English girl in Calcutta, and afterwards be posted to Canton. It was greatly preferable to accommodate his wife at Macao, where he could be with her each off-season, than leave her in the tedious and unhealthy heat of Calcutta during long periods of absence. Provided the rule was obeyed that none of the ladies came to Canton, it was in the end concluded that there was not much harm done.

The ladies, with their flounces and bonnets, were a source of rude astonishment to the Cantonese, used only to Macao women who had not such airs and graces. The word the Macao Cantonese coined for the ladies was an obscene pun, by which alas! European and American women are still known in all parts of the world where Cantonese draw breath.

Nor was there much fear of the ladies going up to Canton. The times in which these venturesome spirits came to the Far East were so dangerous that even a walk to the Macao barrier gate was an expedition demanding a strong male escort. Piracy, ever the scourge of the China coast, had become widespread since the beginning of Chia Ch'ing's reign, changes of rulership being the classic moment for the anarchic forces in Chinese society to break loose. The piracies in the Pearl River were so frequent and widespread that the delta route to Canton could no longer be used, and it was no longer safe to take walks on Lappa or other parts of the countryside near Macao. In 1807 pirates actually landed in Macao itself and only narrowly missed taking Guia Fort. Ships of several nations were attacked, among them British and Portuguese vessels in which every non-Chinese aboard was murdered. This general situation in the waters prevailed uncontrolled until the Opium War.

Then another pioneer arrived, the greatest of them all, and for all his peculiarities—irritating, narrow-minded, scornful and completely humourless—the man who by his endurance, his achievement and his moral bravery stands out inescapably as the most considerable European in China in the early nineteenth century.

He was English, but when the East India Company in London received his application for a passage to the East they coldly rejected it, their rule being never to carry such people, who ended up by being a political nuisance damaging to trade. He thus took ship to New York, where he boarded the American ship *Trident*; and on 30th August 1807 he stepped ashore at Macao as it were disguised as an American—if such a thing were possible, for he looked very English. He was a pink-faced young man of twenty-five, plump and soft, nervous, obstinate and unsmiling. As an even younger man he had hoped that God would select him for the most difficult of all work in connexion with His Word; and no one will deny that his prayer was answered. He was the first Protestant missionary in China.

Born at Morpeth, Northumberland, in 1782, Robert Morrison became obsessed at the age of fifteen by a deep sense of sin. Gravely concerned about his soul, fearful of eternal damnation, he turned to biblical study, meditation and prayer. Finding in this the answer to his mental anxieties he underwent training for the Presbyterian ministry, and applied to the London Missionary Society to work abroad. By the chance elimination of another candidate he was selected to start a mission to China, the land which an earlier intuition had suggested to him as his destiny.

Even before his selection he studied Chinese writings in the British Museum, and with the Mission's approval took lessons in the language with a Chinese in London. Although they had not studied the extensive Catholic continental literature on

China, the Society had some idea of the difficulties a mission would have to face. Their objects were limited and practical. Conversion was not to be Robert Morrison's aim. His soul's dearest wish was to convert 'poor perishing heathens', as he called them, but this, if vouchsafed him, would be a joy incidental to his main purpose, which was to compile a Chinese dictionary and translate the New Testament into Chinese.

The Society was careful not to restrict him; they gave him full discretion. But these were their hopes. Their attitude too is finely demonstrated in their instructions. There is in them nothing of the secrecy and political intrigue with which the history of the Catholic missions is intertwined. A new spirit was radiating from Europe. Morrison would undertake this literary work 'which may be of extensive use to the world,' the letter ran. A worldly-wise Catholic Provincial might have called it a mark of inexperience. But Protestants as missionaries were inexperienced. Morrison believed that the entire world could one day become Christian—at least, he did when he left England. A measure of Morrison's achievement, however, is that the work of the Protestant mission in the end obliged the Catholic Church to broaden the base of its own relations and teaching in the East.

It is hard to think of anyone who ever left the shores of England who was more shocked than Morrison by what he found beyond. Practically everything shocked him, including the shamelessly scant amount of clothing worn by the natives of tropical regions, only excusable due to their ignorance of religion. But what shocked him most of all were his own countrymen on the China coast, whom he regarded as completely depraved.

Among his letters of introduction was one for Sir George Staunton, who had by this time succeeded to his father's baronetcy. They met briefly at Macao. Though interested to meet another sinologue, Staunton was somewhat embarrassed by Morrison's call. The London Mission had stolen a march on the Company, which gave no encouragement whatever to missions in its sphere of influence. Staunton advised Morrison that it was hard to know which was the more dangerous for him, Macao or Canton. At Macao the Catholic priests were liable to make trouble, while at Canton as soon as it was discovered that a non-trader had arrived to learn the language the consequences might be equally serious. All told he might be less conspicuous in Canton, and Staunton concluded by asking him if he would be kind enough to continue being an American.

So Morrison sailed in the *Trident* up to Whampoa, and passed thence by sampan into Canton, amid the caterwauling boat people on the river, shouting, jostling, laughing and insulting one another. As he looked at them he said to himself, with the exactitude of observation which is a feature of his diary, 'O what can ever be done with these ignorant, yet shrewd and imposing people?'

In Canton the American Consul kindly offered him a room in his own house. On reflexion Morrison thought this would be disturbing, with too many callers coming. Instead he took over the basement of the Old French Factory, occupied by an American firm. His besetting sense of sin revolted against having servants to look after him. 'It would be impossible for me to dwell amidst the princely grandeur of the English who reside here', he wrote to the Mission. But after a few days he found that even basement life needed four servants: a cook, a house-boy, a coolie and a compradore to order provisions. Worse, when Sir George Staunton managed to send him a teacher the man turned out to be a Catholic. Worse still, the only Chinese with whom he could converse at all seriously were Catholics, and they, as he soon saw, only kept up with him so as to come now and then for a gift of money. His teacher, with whom he flattered himself as being on terms of real friendship, plainly intimated that unless he received better pay he would give no more lessons.

The servants were his first quarry. Pathetically, desperately he tried under the guise of explaining words such as law, promise, Sabbath, to interest them in Christianity. 'O that the blessing of God may follow these feeble endeavours!' he confided in his diary. 'Descend, thou Spirit of God! Open their hearts to receive the truth!'

But Canton was not the place for that. 'Truths which are the joy of my heart, excite with them a smile', he noted with accuracy. One man later on actually sat down in his room, read seventy-five pages of the New Testament in Chinese, and at the end simply said in pidgin it was 'all very good talk' and went away.

He was soon face to face with the fact that in Confucius and other classical writers the Chinese had a wide amount of moral teaching of their own, while being for the most part uninterested in metaphysics or miracles. 'They are unwilling to allow that any thing is new to them', he wrote. 'They are constrained to acknowledge that the words of our Lord are right words; but then they have something that is similar, they say, and equally good.'

In utter loneliness and despondency he devoted himself fanatically to his dictionary. One or two Chinese assisted him, reading Chinese books and helping him translate words, at the same time learning English themselves. On 24th April 1808 his diary reads:

'Learning with my two assistants the word "hope", we made two sentences to exemplify it—"I hope you are well", and "the hope of a future life". The former, when rendered into English, they learned with all eagerness, but discovered an aversion to the latter. I asked them how it came to pass that the affairs of the present life were esteemed so important, whilst those of a future and eternal state were neglected. Without returning an answer, and merely to gratify me, it was with a sneer that they desired me to teach them the English of the sentence in question.'

The Jesuits had been through it before.

Morrison, however, made it worse for himself. He was a shocked though silent observer of what he considered the immorality and self-indulgence of his own countrymen, an avowed enemy of the 'Romish' priests at Macao, a scornfully pitying critic of the Chinese Christians raised in Romish superstitions, the irreconcilable apostle sent by God to break simple Chinese respect for the deities of earth, kitchen, money and hell. He approved of no one.

John Roberts, President of the Select Committee, soon expressed an interest in the dictionary work. Sir George Staunton, as one sinologue to another, became a quietly influential ally.

Not forgetting the Ladies

When under the strain of his own immensely disapproving solitude Morrison began to break down in health, Alexander Pearson, the senior surgeon, attended him. At last, after several months, Morrison reached a profound decision: for his continued security in China the path of his duty was to be friendly with the English, whether he approved of them or not.

His health declined so considerably that when the hot weather started he had to go down to Macao, where Roberts procured him a house. There he worked on with his Chinese assistants. For fear of being seized upon by Romish hirelings he hardly ever left his house. Macao did not interest or delight him. It was full of sinful churches, one of which during his stay was providentially consumed by fire. When a little later the upper floor of his own house collapsed 'in a dreadful crash' there was a moment when it seemed as if perhaps Providence was behind this too, but this quickly passed. Providence was in the fact that no one was injured.

After three months in the better climate of Macao he returned to Canton. He was slowly fitting into the arabesque. Although moaning over the idolatry of their illustrations, he found great interest in Catholic books in Chinese; he was in fact obliged to study them in order to learn the Christian vocabulary. Money was transmitted to him from London through Cox's singsong and opium firm, then known as Beale and Magniac. After a few months Morrison was even advising people abroad to use Beale and Magniac's services when coming to China. They were such a convenient, efficient firm.

That was what the absent lovers thought too, remitting to their pensioners.

IV: MORRISON IN COMPANY SERVICE—HIS TRANSLATION OF THE
BIBLE INTO CHINESE

Before long Morrison again had to take shelter in Macao, when Admiral Drury was preparing to bombard Canton. It was the nadir of Morrison's mission. Anti-British feeling in Macao had never been stronger, while the Chinese were so thoroughly aroused by Drury that Morrison despaired of remaining in China. The alternative was to withdraw to Penang or Malacca, in both of which there were overseas Chinese communities among whom it would be possible for him to continue his work. But he did not want to go. Never was his diary more filled with moans and pleas for the Lord's help.

During these weeks of anxiety he was comforted by the companionship of some new-found friends, Dr. Morton, one of the Company's surgeons, his wife and their two children, Mary and William, still in their 'teens. More than this: there is a significant entry in the diary for 8th January 1809.

'Miss Morton too professes her faith in Jesus, and wishes to be devoted to him; to submit to him in all his institutions, and be resigned to his pleasure.'

The following month she married Robert Morrison.

At this moment Divine Providence, so often and piteously besought, intervened with unmistakable clarity to prevent the departure to Penang. On the very day of his marriage Morrison was offered by the East India Company a post as Chinese interpreter with a salary of £500 a year. Yesterday an impecunious, persecuted missionary, dependent for his livelihood on funds from the London Mission, today he was well-off, married, financially independent of the Mission, and with responsibilities great in terms of the prestige of the British nation and of the trade conducted by the Company, whose cargoes at Canton in a normal year were worth £1,000,000. The moral problems posed by the contradictions of humility and grandeur demanded by his two separate occupations, the missionary and the Company interpreter, stayed with him for the rest of his life, of which they are to a great extent the inner theme. In the end Dr. Robert Morrison, honoured by universities, received by the King on a visit to London in 1825, welcomed by the leading orientalists of Europe, and the mere mention of whose name in the House of Commons produced cheers, was still just recognizable as a missionary, though imperceptibly there had crept into his behaviour and correspondence the fussy tone of a civil servant concerned about precedents, increments and pension. It is hard to see how it could have been otherwise.

On his appointment as interpreter the Company officers, even including Staunton, made it plain that his engagement was due solely to his knowledge of Chinese. In 1806 the Court of Directors in London had ordered that church services be held each Sunday with compulsory attendance, an order the Select Committee ignored. Morrison's presence made no difference. If he wished to carry on his religious work, he was informed, that was his own affair; he need not expect the slightest encouragement from the Company, whom it would have suited better had he not been a missionary.

Blessed only with each other's company—the Mortons left soon after their daughter's marriage—Robert and Mary Morrison passed an aloof and lonely life in Macao. Mary spoke Portuguese, but was friendly with only one family. She read the Bible daily, and books on ecclesiastical history. The narrowness of Robert's outlook, his disapproval of Catholicism, made it hard for them to have friends. Mary, whose health was not good, longed for home.

While strictly maintaining their attitude to Morrison as a missionary, the Company, however, took a praiseworthy interest in his Chinese dictionary and grammar. The latter was sent to Lord Minto, who made funds available for the costly business of printing it at the Protestant missionary press at Serampore. The printing of the Chinese Bible—for Morrison extended his aims to include the Old Testament—was undertaken section by section by a Chinese printing firm in Macao.

When St. Luke's Gospel came out—the first section to be completed—Morrison published at the same time a Chinese tract and catechism. Christianity being now a banned religion in China and the distribution of complete biblical texts being contrary to Catholic practice in Macao, he was flying in the face of two authorities. The Portuguese, under a friendly Governor, Lucas José Alvarenga, who had even visited Morrison at his house, at first took no notice; but when in 1813 Morrison's long-awaited assistant, William Milne, arrived from London, Catholic pressure was uncompromising and Alvarenga informed Morrison that his new colleague must leave. Morrison entreated him, even going down on bended knee (surely the most astonishing action in his career), to alter his decision; but the Governor was intransigent. So was the East India Company which, true to its word, offered no assistance. 'I did not think that the society of English in this place would have treated me so unkindly', Morrison wrote. 'I never expected much; and the low expectations which I did form, have been disappointed.'

Still, by his own attitude to them he deserved no better.

The internal situation of China had by this time so deteriorated that the two missionaries concluded that to extend their work into the country was out of the question. The Yellow River was overflowing; famine was reported widespread; and in the disturbances occurring in several provinces it was being claimed that the leaders of rebellion were Christians, inspired by Catholic priests in Macao. Milne thus left—in due course to found the Anglo-Chinese College at Malacca and become one of the fathers of modern Malayan education—and Morrison continued his lonely endeavours unaided.

V: CHINESE OBJECTION TO ENGLISH INTERPRETERS

Morrison's assistance to the Company was quickly recognized as invaluable, and when the Court of Directors complained about the appointment of a missionary the Select Committee took no notice. Morrison's knowledge of Chinese surpassed Staunton's, and he was soon giving lessons to other Company servants.

The advent of Staunton and Morrison significantly altered the character of British relations with the mandarins. Hitherto, letters to the Hoppo or the Governor were submitted in English to the Hong merchants at their council chamber, known as the Consoo Hall. The merchants had the letters translated into Chinese by the linguists, who were Macao Chinese or Eurasians of the Norette type speaking pigdin English. No fine point of expression could be correctly translated by these men, whose knowledge of literary Chinese—which was what was needed when dealing with the mandarins—was in any case negligible. Furthermore, to avoid unpleasantness the Hong merchants always saw to it that the tone of every letter was suitably altered, so that instead of being, for instance, a firm demand for rights, it became a humble petition from self-abasing foreigners to the supremely civilized government of the Son of Heaven, represented by his superlatively gifted Governor. Conversations between foreigners and mandarins, on the rare occasions when they met, were even more misleading. Due to the mandarin tendency to arrest and flog the linguists whenever there was trouble, to be a linguist was a dangerous occupation and quite a number of the linguists were thus members of the criminal class—the only ones who considered the risks worth the profit— whose normal mode of speech was the lingo of the Canton underworld. When one considers that these were the sole means of official communication between the two races—unless a Catholic priest could be found willing to run the risk of assisting—it becomes slightly less surprising that educated Chinese should have underrated Europeans.

From the time of Staunton and Morrison the mandarins had the opportunity of seeing the British in a clearer light, and it was an experience they did not relish. Letters no longer went over to the Consoo Hall in English. By Morrison's insistence on seeing final drafts of all letters before the Hong merchants submitted them, Hong distortions were limited to the addition of honorifics and abasements. Letters were still headed 'Humble Petition' because this was the only kind of missive the mandarins would accept, but the exact substance of what the British wanted to say got through.

In conversation it was even plainer. For the first time, with English interpreters present, the mandarins heard outspoken criticism instead of watered-down pleas. It was an unpleasant experience all round. It broke the Chinese convention which makes it obligatory for all comment of a displeasing nature to be communicated indirectly. Staunton and Morrison knew this, but on the British side it was considered there was no other way. Morrison furthermore spoke the language as the mandarins themselves spoke it, with many marks of erudition, with the same vivid use of allusion and sarcasm that makes educated Chinese conversation pungent and stimulating. Not content with studying what he referred to as the vulgar Cantonese dialect, he took pains to speak with the proper Peking pronunciation and terms.

As transmitters of unwelcome information Staunton and Morrison inevitably classed themselves with the traditional recipients of bebostings. They became the immediate target of mandarin resentment, named in numerous threatening pronouncements as being barbarians of particular villainousness. Morrison was frequently in danger. Whenever there was an anti-Christian scare he had to hide all his books and send his assistants away to their districts. When not sent away, the assistants sometimes ran away on their own.

In mandarin reaction to Staunton and Morrison, which was violent, one senses an indication of future disaster. The mandarinate was at last placed in the position of having the means to understand in detail—and report to Peking—foreign viewpoints and quite a good deal concerning the background which had produced such views. Quite a number of them *must* have realized they were no longer dealing with barbarian tribes but with civilized and powerful nations who could be dealt with on terms of equality. Actually we know that some of them did realize this. There is that revealing moment when Sung, one of the friendly mandarins accompanying Lord Macartney on his return journey from Peking, and who of course remembered George Staunton as a boy, was in 1810 appointed Governor of Kwangtung and received Staunton privately in Canton. Alone with his guest he behaved with unaffected friendliness; in the presence of other Chinese all the traditional mandarin *hauteur* returned. More and more does that quality of deceiving Peking, first unmistakably noticed at the time of Anson's visit, become apparent; and more and more does the onus of the oncoming conflict consequently fall upon the mandarinate.

Admittedly a civil service is by its very nature an organism of conservation, to which nothing is more repellent than new ideas because of the anxiety they cause, the danger that at some point in their upward submission someone will be dismissed or relegated to a minor ministry for unreliability gauged according to strictly followed tradition. Admittedly too, remembering that the cosmology was concerned, the admission that the British were not tribal barbarians was a mixture of heresy and treason. But remembering against this the immense squeeze on opium and on foreign trade in general, it is impossible to avoid the fact that a main motive for mandarin deception was avarice.

VII

THE RIFT IS ABSOLUTE

THE 'SOFT PERIOD' in British relations with the mandarins, which had endured more or less since the Macartney embassy, came to an abrupt end at the termination of Sung's governorship in 1813, when under senior officials with different ideas things were once more plunged into difficulties. Proceedings in connexion with the murder of a Chinese some years before were resurrected; long and infuriating arguments went on about minor offences the British were alleged to have committed; there were objections to Company letters being submitted in Chinese, objections to Morrison, to his teaching Chinese to others on the staff, to a suspected Christian Chinese in Company employment. There was even a project to kidnap Sir George Staunton to prevent his ever leaving China with all the 'dangerous knowledge' he possessed.

In the same year the varied and powerful interests in London which since Henry Dundas' day and before had been intent on breaking the power of the East India Company achieved their first notable success. In 1813 the Company's monopoly of trade with India was abolished. Although the Company retained its monopoly in China, subject to revision after twenty years, and in theory still licensed all British traders coming to China, the termination of the Indian monopoly undermined the Company's position further East. The number of country traders coming to China rose markedly in consequence, many of them unlicensed, with the Company able to exercise little or no restraint on their activities. As Robert Morrison's experiences show, it was already easy enough to slip into Canton and stay there. In Macao conditions were still easier, added to which in its weakened state the Company found it more difficult than before to refuse licences. In Macao there were marriages, births and deaths, the religious services on such occasions being read usually by the President of the Select Committee. From 1820 there were resident Company chaplains, and in 1821, on the occasion of the death of Mary Morrison, a much-needed Protestant cemetery was established, today one of the most serene and tranquil beauty spots of the Far East.

At the bottom of the troubles with Canton lay the problem of singsongs, an item in the trade which had grown from a pleasant and amusing child into an adolescent monster due to mandarin demand for decorative and unusual clocks and watches. If the year's quota of these was considered insufficient, troubles were instantly created. The majority of all the disputes between 1810 and 1820 arose from the mandarinate picking upon technical infringements of the countless ignored or only partly observed laws in order to induce the Hong merchants to give them more toys.

The Hong merchants' position in the matter was ludicrous. As each consignment of singsongs reached Canton they were obliged to buy up the lot. As the foreign consignors knew the Hongs were obliged to buy, the clocks were sold at ridiculously high prices. Vainly the Hong merchants begged the Company to prevent the import of singsongs. If they could truthfully tell the Hoppo there were none to be had, this would finish the matter. As long as singsongs came into port there would be nothing but trouble, due to the nightmarish avarice of the mandarins to possess them.

A special fund had been established some years earlier, called the Consoo Fund, in which a reserve of capital was put aside, raised by a percentage duty on trade, to assist the Hongs in overcoming their otherwise incurable tendency to go bankrupt. Purchasing singsongs became such a strain on the merchants' resources, running into hundreds of thousands of dollars a year, that they were eventually debited to the Consoo Fund, being thus elevated to a form of taxation.

The Rift is Absolute

Within a few days of receipt of the news of Waterloo came a despatch announcing that another British embassy to Peking was about to leave London. No one appears to have asked for it or specifically to have expected it, and the moment was chosen in complete disregard of the worsening state of affairs in China. Two years earlier an attempt had been made on the life of the Emperor at Jehol; there were floods and drought. Before these clear portents of Heaven's displeasure the Emperor had publicly declared his own lack of virtue, accused his subordinates of corruption, and put to death several of the Court eunuchs. Ever sensitive of the condition and character of the authority over them, the Chinese were restless and uncertain. The fall of the dynasty was rumoured.

In London there was surprising negligence in the preparations for the embassy. No up-to-date advice was requested from Canton before the Ambassador's letter of instructions was drawn up, while the usual mistake was made of imagining that an embassy to China afforded an opportunity to discuss business with the Emperor or his close advisers.

The Ambassador, Lord Amherst, reached the China coast in July 1816. It was intended that Sir George Staunton and Robert Morrison should accompany the mission, but as both were in danger of being arrested by the Chinese if they tried to join Amherst openly they quietly embarked at Macao in one of the Company's cruisers, in which, crossing the Pearl River, they made their way among the islands on the far side to a secretly arranged rendezvous in the sheltered strait between the islands of Lamma and Hongkong. This incidentally is the first known British reference to Hongkong. There after three days the Ambassador's ship met them. They transhipped and sailed north together to the Peiho.

There was promptly trouble over the kowtow. Chinese officials sent to meet the embassy had orders only to allow the British to reach Peking if the Ambassador undertook to perform the kowtow. Amherst's instructions on the subject were not explicit and he himself was undecided about it, nor was his indecision dispersed by the two principal Company representatives with him, Staunton and Henry Ellis, urging him in opposite directions. Ellis was in favour of the Ambassador making the kowtow, it being a meaningless ceremony, while Staunton, with his recollections of Lord Macartney and his own fear that it would be interpreted by the Chinese to the detriment of the Company's status at Canton, was resolute in advising against it.

In the event, Amherst having led the Chinese to believe that he would kowtow, the embassy was allowed to reach the capital. He did not finally decide against the prostration until the imperial order to proceed was received and an hour fixed for audience.

In keeping with the slovenly state of affairs at Chia Ch'ing's court the date fixed did not allow enough time for the journey. Concealing this fact from Amherst, the Chinese officials in charge obliged the embassy to travel all night in an effort to reach the Summer Palace in time. The Ambassadors' carriage, unsuitable for stone-block Chinese roads, could only go at a walking pace, with the result that they reached the palace at the very moment when the Dragon was preparing to mount the throne to receive them. Sleepless, dirty, unshaven and jolted to bits by the journey, Lord Amherst was instantly summoned to the imperial presence. His complaints that the Prince Regent's letter and presents were in the baggage following them, and that he needed time at least to shave and change his clothes, were ignored.

Telling the Emperor that Amherst would surely perform all the ceremonies, and Amherst that the Emperor would not insist on the kowtow, the Great Chamberlain, who bore the responsibility for having allowed Amherst to reach Peking, tried to lead the exhausted Ambassador straight into the throne room in the hope of tricking him into making the kowtow while his will was weakened by sleeplessness. But Amherst refused to budge from the ante-chamber.

Commanded by the Emperor to explain the embassy's non-appearance, the Chamberlain informed Chia Ch'ing that the Ambassador had a stomach-ache so serious that he could not move. When Chia Ch'ing ordered the deputies to appear, the terrified official explained that they too had stomach-aches.

This was too much, even for Chia Ch'ing. Concluding that the barbarians were trying to insult him, he ordered them to leave the capital forthwith. As leave they did, by the inland canal route to Canton.

When the Emperor found out the truth, that his officers had bungled the affair, not adhering strictly to their orders, he published a statement to this effect, sent some presents to Lord Amherst, and degraded the officers responsible. But he did not recall the embassy.

They reached Canton in January 1817, and at a formal ceremony the Governor of the Two Kwangs[1] presented Amherst a letter from Chia Ch'ing to the Prince Regent. Although in addressing his civil service the Emperor laid the blame on them, to the Prince Regent he made no such concession. In the letter he accused the Ambassador of unprecedented rudeness, and told the Prince Regent it would not be necessary for him to send any more embassies.

Perhaps with great patience and tact, together with steady determination not to do the kowtow and a preconceived plan of campaign on how to avoid it, the embassy might not have been the expensive fiasco it was. Certainly in Staunton and Morrison the Ambassador could not have had better advisers. Yet surely the real truth is that even if the embassy had 'succeeded', it could not have achieved anything. The project was mistimed, and in that it required deviation from precedent if it was to effect any improvement in trading conditions, it was addressed to the wrong kind of emperor. It is relevant to remember that Europeans achieved most with the Great Ch'ing during the reign of its most outstanding emperor, K'ang Hsi. Where precedent is concerned it is surely universal that the smaller the mental stature of the man the less likely will he be to permit innovations.

At any rate Lord Amherst's conduct of the retreat was superbly correct. To the end he never omitted an iota in the affectation he was bound to support of injured majesty. The Governor of Kwangtung, obliged by the British to concede

[1] Governors usually, but not always, ruled two provinces, in this case Kwangtung and Kwangsi, the Eastern and Western Kwangs; thus the Governor of the Two Kwangs.

equality between the Ambassador and himself at the presentation of the Emperor's letter, sipped his tea afterwards with obvious embarrassment beside the stern peer in robes and coronet.

As had also been the case with Lord Macartney, Amherst's reputation was undamaged by his failure in Peking. After an eventful return journey which included a shipwreck and a meeting with Napoleon on St. Helena, Amherst in due course became Governor-General of India at the time of the first Anglo–Burmese war.

With on one side Chia Ch'ing's unwillingness to receive any further diplomatic approaches, and on the other side the serious weakening of the East India Company's restraining influence on the Canton situation, trade with China was for the next nineteen years allowed to take care of itself, which it quite soon proceeded to do in an alarming fashion. The failure of the Amherst embassy and we enter the final straight— the epoch of the opium clippers, leading onward to the conflict which already seemed to many traders to be inescapable, the only answer in a doorless impasse of gathering absurdity.

VIII

THE FIRST OPIUM CRISES

OPIUM HAD BEEN CONTRABAND in China since Yung Chêng's edict of 1729. The drug had been reaching China steadily since around 1685 in quantities which tended to rise, the edict having no effect on the trade because its regulations were not enforced. Cotton and opium, it will be recalled, were indispensable to the tea trade. As the volume of the tea trade rose, so did imports of cotton and opium, though towards the end of the eighteenth century with opium now observably gaining ground. The establishment of Canton's consular corps gave such a spurt to opium that even Peking took notice. To increase the efficacy of the laws the Emperor Chia Ch'ing in 1799 issued an additional edict forbidding the sale of opium from one merchant to another or to a consumer.

The Canton authorities went through all the outwardly correct motions of forbidding the sale of opium, which continued to arrive unmolested in large quantities through Whampoa and Macao. It would have been difficult to find any trader who was not in some way connected with it. Company servants, country traders, Britons, Americans, Portuguese, other Europeans, Armenians, Parsis and Indians, everyone dealt in it, directly or through an agent. The edict of 1799, in other words, was treated in the same manner as its predecessor. By unspoken mutual agreement it was ignored. One Hoppo after another condemned the trade in public while privately sharing in its very considerable profits.

From various references it will have been apparent that the Americans were by this time substantially engaged in the China trade. For convenience's sake I have not made much mention of them till this moment with a view to seeing in a more continuous light the curiously indecisive and often confusing part they played in the story of the opium trade while being at the same time so deeply involved in it.

Tea-drinking, as the eighteenth-century Spanish, French and Dutch smugglers knew, was quite as popular in the American colonies as it was in Britain. Not for nothing was the War of American Independence preceded by the Boston Tea Party. Once freed from Britain's overwhelming tea duties—these were in some cases as high as 127 per cent of import value—Americans wasted no time in getting into the China tea trade themselves. As early as August 1784—in terms of speed this voyage was a truly remarkable achievement—the first American ship, the *Empress of China*, reached Macao. Aboard her was Major Samuel Shaw, a supercargo bearing a commission from George Washington as United States Consul to China and India, surely in geographical dimensions the grandest consul who ever was. Expected to subsist as a business man, he incidentally received no salary.

His landing at Macao was a unique moment, when for once, along the Praia Grande and in all their usual walks, the British were not to be seen, though it may be presumed that many of them, suitably concealed by the curtains, were in fact glued to the windows of the great Company house, from which a front-line view was to be had as the French Consul, Monsieur Vieillard, stepped down the beach to welcome the Americans prior to entertaining them at his house in the company of prominent Portuguese. Copies of treaties between the United States and friendly powers were presented, after which five days later the Americans proceeded to Canton—promptly to be plunged into the drama of the *Lady Hughes* incident, a nice introduction to the problems of the tea trade.

In this crisis Sam Shaw played his part with the French in rallying all in support of the British—for the other Europeans had till then been thoroughly enjoying the discomfiture caused to the British by the American presence. He left for India soon after, but on this and his subsequent visit Sam Shaw established himself as a popular man all round.

The Americans, who quickly rose to a place second only to the British in the China trade, found themselves confronted by the same problem as the East India Company: there was no means of buying tea in sufficient quantities from the Chinese without importing cotton and opium. Needless to say, the Americans were not attracted to the avenues of commerce developed and commanded by the British. Instead within a short time they were importing to China their own United States cotton, and using Turkish opium exported from Smyrna as an alternative to the Company's opium from Bengal.

By 1807 foreign shipping in the Pearl River was almost entirely British and American. In Canton the Americans had taken over the factory of the defunct Swedish Company, the factory retaining its Cantonese name, the Suy Hong, for many years—one of the small perplexities of life on the China coast. There were some exciting moments between 1812 and 1814, when Britain was at war with the United States; but in 1815 things quickly settled down to another great period of trade expansion. By 1820 British and American shipping accounted regularly each year for between seventy and ninety vessels. Between 2,000 and 3,000 British and American sailors were at Whampoa each season, where there was an annual death rate of not less than 100. The fights and drunken orgies in Hog Lane and other lurid spots around the foreign factories at Canton were on a frightful scale. The Select Committee had for years frankly admitted that the behaviour of seamen ashore was disgraceful. In Robert Morrison's view seamen were not the only culpable ones. There were also the private merchants, adventurers and other riff-raff, 'unjust, covetous, avaricious, lying, drunken, debauched', as he called them.

Underlying this great scene of commerce there were, as explained, two rival brands of opium: Smyrna opium brought by the Americans and the British-imported Bengal product, known to the Select Committee's acute embarrassment as Company Opium. To these must be added a third brand, from Malwa, a part of Central India not yet absorbed into the East

India Company's dominion, and of which the Portuguese had hitherto been one of the importers.

In 1813 the East India Company, finding that the rising popularity of Malwa opium was threatening Company Opium, laid restrictions on the export of the Malwa brand through Bombay, thus throwing a growing and lucrative commerce into the hands of the Portuguese through their Indian settlements of Goa and Damão. For Macao, at the receiving end, this was a great opportunity for breaking in on the trade going on all around them but in which the Portuguese themselves had only a small share. More than this, the Macao Portuguese saw in Malwa opium a last chance of restoring their lost commercial prestige. Animosity toward the British, which reached its height during the Drury episode, was now joined by what Macao interpreted as a life or death struggle for economic survival.

Here once again, as on so many former occasions, the Portuguese wrecked their own chances by the legal limitations they imposed. The British country traders, now omnipresent, were naturally quick to cash in on the new Malwa opium routes through Goa and Damão. According to Portuguese law, exports from these places could only be consigned to a Portuguese destination and shifted in Portuguese holds. The British country traders thus chartered Portuguese vessels and brought their opium in at Macao.

Macao at that time was considered safer than Whampoa for the handling of opium but, as the country traders found, it had commercial disadvantages. The Portuguese customs, making the most of their good fortune, charged high dues on opium passing through Macao, whereas at Whampoa, where the trade was entirely illegal, there were no dues at all. Furthermore, it was much more profitable to deal with the Chinese direct at Whampoa than, as Macao law demanded, indirectly through solely Portuguese agents.

How the country traders dealt with this problem of Portuguese restrictions brought about an important change in the geographical layout of the opium trade—the development of Lintin Island as an opium depôt.

It was a risk to try bypassing Macao by sailing in a chartered Portuguese ship up to Whampoa. Symptomatic of how little things had changed in China, the Chinese restriction against Portuguese ships using the main channel of the Pearl River, which we observed in Weddell's day, still obtained; and if the Portuguese discovered that one of their chartered ships, evading Portuguese dues, had gone up to Whampoa, they were liable to report the fact to the Chinese as a means of protecting their own customs. On arrival from India therefore the country traders took their vessels only as far as Lintin, just comfortably within the shelter of the river, where they off-loaded their opium, sending it up to Whampoa by river boat, after which they crossed to Macao, arriving there blandly with their holds either empty or containing a few general goods of minor interest to the customs. At Whampoa the opium was meanwhile stored, prior to delivery to buyers, in mastless hulks moored in the stream, heavily armed and guarded—a floating opium headquarters.

Macao was so alarmed by these developments that in 1819 the Senate actually proposed to the Select Committee methods of dividing the profits of the Malwa opium trade. Needless to say, the Honourable Company made no reply on such a dreadful subject, but the following year they altered their arrangements in India and began competing with the country traders in the purchase of Malwa opium with a view to monopolizing it. This only drove the country traders more determinedly to the less restricted Damão route. With the aid of Sir Roger de Faria, a prominent Portuguese citizen of Bombay, they succeeded in bribing Portuguese officials in Goa and Damão to issue passes exempting opium carriers from going to Macao, thus completing their encircling stranglehold on the struggling, angry city.

II: MEN AND SILVER LEAVING CHINA

Whatever may be thought today of the activities of the country traders, the members of firms such as Beale and Magniac's were far from being the riff-raff Robert Morrison described. In the conditions of the times their business was a highly respectable affair. Thomas Beale, who in 1797 succeeded his brother Daniel as Prussian Consul, is one of the best-known figures of the period in Macao, greatly respected for his integrity. Practically everyone had dealings with Beale in one way or another. It was

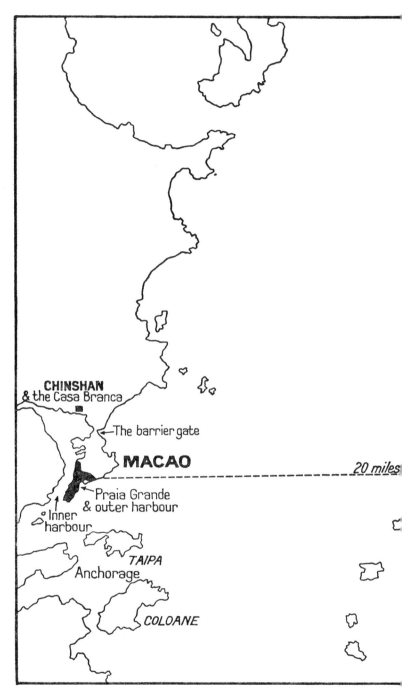

CHINSHAN
& the Casa Branca

The barrier gate

MACAO

Praia Grande
& outer harbour

Inner
harbour

TAIPA
Anchorage

COLOANE

20 miles

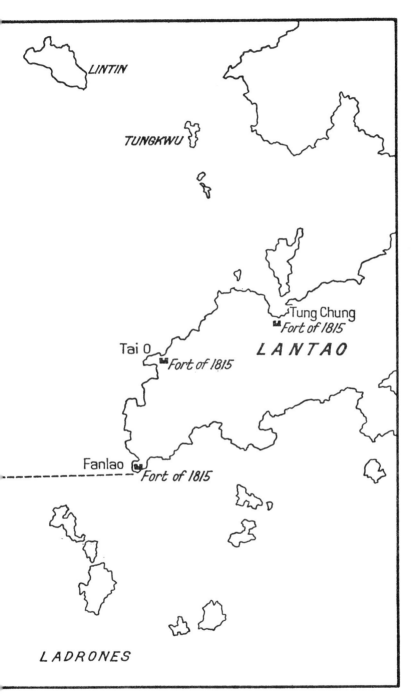

LINTIN

TUNGKWU

Tung Chung
Fort of 1815

Tai O
Fort of 1815

LANTAO

Fanlao
Fort of 1815

LADRONES

RL RIVER

convenient to have such a reliable person to handle private opium deals, act as banker between seasons, and dole out remittances to pensioners. William C. Hunter, the American trader and interpreter, described Beale in his later years as 'one of the old school in its fullest signification: stately in person, somewhat formal, with distinguished manners. . . . He occupied one of the finest of the old Portuguese houses, enclosed within high walls, on a narrow street known as Beale's Lane.' His garden was one of the sights of the city, and he kept an aviary of rare birds.

His firm, the most representative and significant of all the country firms, was in proper terms a house of agency, most of whose clients were from Calcutta, London, Bombay and other cities connected in one way or another with the China trade. The commodities they and the other more stable country firms handled were Indian cotton, sandalwood, tin and pepper as imports, with Chinese tea and silk as the staple exports. This was their licit trade. What of the illicit?

At the time of the Napoleonic War opium amounted to about one-eighth of the country imports. Its sale at the Calcutta auctions supplied one-seventh of the Bengal revenue. But in Canton, both in value and bulk, it stood far below Indian cotton, and also below English woollens, for which by dint of perseverance the East India Company had at last found an economic market.

Thus, though still valuable as an earner of silver, opium was no longer indispensable to the East India Company, nor need it have been to the Americans. Had its prohibition been seriously enforced by the Chinese at this moment, the Bengal revenue would have suffered; but the Company's tea exports, though they might have been reduced, would no longer have been curtailed to the extent they would have been in earlier times. In fact, with woollens, cotton and opium all doing well, the balance of trade was tipped the other way—and at this point let us remember Peking. Silver was flowing out of China.

The problem of silver in a commerce as large as that which the Pearl River trade had become was the simple one of sheer bulk versus limited space. All the foreign factories at Canton and a number of business houses at Macao had basements, known in pidgin as godowns, constructed of massive granite with huge iron doors, for the storing of silver. As British trade in cotton, woollens *and* opium improved, the mere physical problem of finding space for a constantly enlarging amount of silver absolutely necessitated the export of some of it to Calcutta and elsewhere, away from the cramped godown conditions of the foreign factories in Canton, where it was by simple geography impossible, or so it seemed, to ask for more land. Macao was not considered a safe place for storing such enormous amounts of silver due to Portugal's peculiar conditions of tenure and Macao's known capacity for safeguarding its own interests by reporting irregularities to the Chinese.

History has concentrated attention on the country traders' import of opium. More important in the context of then-prevalent Chinese economic theory is their export of silver. It was the knowledge that, using the same well-greased routes as served the import of opium, Company and country alike were ensuring the removal of silver in every ship leaving China that for the first time in all the years of foreign trade aroused mandarin concern.

Concurrently, by one of those spontaneous movements of which the history of China shows so many examples, a wave of Chinese emigration was in progress. Macao—and thus Portugal—was to bear the brunt of world criticism throughout the rest of the nineteenth century for facilitating Chinese slavery, just as the British bore the brunt of criticism for 'forcing' opium on China. The fact was that in the Chinese emigration rush on Macao, then and in the various other rushes that followed, the demand for space in foreign ships was so overwhelming as to be all but irresistible. Chinese were pouring in by the hundred— later in the century by the thousand. There was nowhere to house them; they refused to return to their districts; the Portuguese were left with them in their midst, their pleas to them to return home, their descriptions of the horrors that awaited them in the ships, being met by every conceivable subterfuge to obtain a berth in one. It was a kind of invasion.

Widely described later in the century as slave-trading, it was not exactly so, though the methods used (by all nationalities) to ship Chinese abroad were highly questionable. Chinese in effect pawned their own lives to pay for a 'free' passage in appalling conditions of overcrowded and suffocating holds, in which large numbers died, to one of the countries of migration favoured, where they were made over to such plantation owners and other employers who were willing to pay 'the cost of their passage', and for whom they subsequently toiled without pay until they had worked off this sum. By making opium available to them at plantation shops many employers ensured that they never did pay off what they owed, thus labouring for the rest of their lives for nothing. Yet—and who would have believed it at the time?—such is the resilience of the Chinese that it is from men such as these that descend many of the present-day Chinese of South-east Asia, with their graduates of Oxford and Cambridge and their members of the Inns of Court.

It reflects well on the East India Company that amid the strong demand for ship-space for human beings they never once resorted to this system. When Chinese migrants travelled in Company ships it was usually at the request of a British government in one of the new colonial settlements. Passages were paid in advance by the government requiring them, and the emigrants usually received an advance of wages before embarking. Java and Malaya were among the most popular countries of migration, but the movement was very wide, involving places as far distant as Trinidad and St. Helena, everywhere in fact where Chinese labourers were in demand as being more steady and reliable than the existing inhabitants. Napoleon's banishment to St. Helena obliged that island's Governor, Sir Hudson Lowe, to write urgently to Canton asking the Select Committee to send him 150 *more* Chinese in the first available ship.

The cardinal prohibition of Chinese cosmological economy was being broken. Men and silver were leaving China. Time was ripening as never before for a crisis.

III: A CHINESE ATTEMPT TO SUPPRESS THE OPIUM TRADE—THE AMERICAN SOFT LINE WITH THE CHINESE

In 1815 the Governor of Kwangtung unexpectedly arrested several Chinese opium dealers and ordered searches of all ships entering Whampoa and Macao. The bottom fell out of the

6. *Above* *Dr. Morrison translating*
the Bible into Chinese, from the
painting by George Chinnery.

7. *Right* *Chinnery's portrait of*
Howqua, the senior Hong
merchant, reputed one of
the richest men in the
world.

8. Self-portrait of the Irish artist George Chinnery,
who lived at Macao from 1825 till his death in
1852, and painted all the celebrities of the period.
The Indian landscape on the easel, and the framed
picture of the Praia Grande, Macao, on the wall
symbolize the two phases of Chinnery's career as an
artist in the Orient.

opium market and the trade came to a complete standstill. Everyone was involved, including the Americans and the Portuguese with their Smyrna and Malwa varieties. The East India Company, which in its usual way had issued credit bills in advance of opium sales, found itself down by over a million dollars, the ensuing litigation against creditors continuing for fifteen years.

It was the first serious measure taken by the Chinese to prohibit the opium trade, and it demonstrated the havoc into which it could be thrown whenever the Chinese chose to enforce their own laws. The immediate reasons for this first opium scare are not known, but that it was originally intended to bring about a suppression of the trade is suggested by the military measures taken, which included the building and manning of three new forts on Lantao Island at the mouth of the Pearl River covering the approaches to Lintin.[1]

In the outcome these forts were never used to any significant purpose, nor were the other restrictive measures sustained. It all proved to be a skirmish where a campaign was needed. Within weeks things were back to normal, and thus they more or less stayed until 1821, a year which a series of fortuities rendered one of the more exciting in the history of the foreign trade.

The season of 1821 began with a homicide case on classic lines, this time involving the Americans. An American sailor of Sicilian origin, arguing over shiprail with a Cantonese boatwoman selling fruit, became so irritated by her obstinate haggling and refusal to row away when he called the deal off that he threw an olive jar at her. The jar hit her on the head, she fell backwards into the sea and was drowned. The Chinese demanded the surrender of the sailor; the Americans refused. Their Hong security and their linguists were imprisoned. The Americans still not yielding, all foreign trade was stopped.

Unsure of themselves, without the backing of any great national organization like the East India Company, the Americans were disconcerted by this stiff reaction. Being seasonal traders, with

---

[1] The forts at Tung Chung and Fanlao still survive. Of the third, at Po Chu Tam, no trace remains, the site having been absorbed into the township of Tai O.

K

only one or two individual merchants residing in China, they had far less idea than the British concerning the background of the trade. The name *Lady Hughes* meant nothing to them. Dutifully they surrendered their man. He was questioned in secret by the Chinese and strangled, a conclusion the Americans accepted without any form of protest either by the American Consul or by individuals.

The entire British community, as may well be imagined, were shocked and indignant, describing the Americans as apathetic and inhumane, and fearing that this weak action would cause Chinese presumption to increase in the future. The truth was that in this particular instance the Americans found themselves in a situation so strange to them that, not knowing what reaction to make, they made none. But as the years passed and the Americans, in their own immediate trading interests, continued to follow a soft line with the Chinese in times of crisis, their attitude assumed more serious proportions. For fifty years and more the British and other Europeans had been striving to resist what they considered the inhumane procedures of Chinese justice and the unreasonable restrictions imposed on trade and residence; and now here, as the mandarinate saw it, was another barbarian tribe, second only in power to the British, who were altogether more docile and obedient. It strengthened the Chinese belief that the British were an unreasonable people whose views were not held by other foreigners. If one tribe could be docile, so could the British. It led to the reasoning that by the continuance of the ancient method of threatening, any situation could be brought under control. Had the Americans, as they were often invited to do, joined with the British in resisting Chinese pretensions, it is even likely that armed conflict with China might have been avoided altogether. For the British were at long last on the way to bringing about certain changes on the Chinese side.

This first became noticeable in the negotiations following another homicide case which took place the same year. A party of British sailors from H.M.S. *Topaz*, ashore on Lintin to fetch water and wash their clothes in a hill stream, were attacked by villagers. As the sailors were unarmed and were seen from the ship to be in some danger *Topaz* opened fire on the village, killing two Chinese and wounding four. The arguments following this affray lasted in all for five years, Robert Morrison playing an important part as interpreter. The Company maintained its policy of refusing to surrender anyone, and in the end the Governor of Kwangtung accepted the British statement that disciplinary action had been taken against those involved, according to British law. This was one of the incidents from which the British view developed that by determined persuasion backed by the presence of unused force the Chinese could be made susceptible to the need for changes. But if such an attitude was to produce results it was essential that all foreigners should stand together in the matter, which they unfortunately did not.

IV: JAMES MATHESON AND THE OPIUM SCARE OF 1821

Trade had not been resumed more than a few days after the American homicide case before the Pearl River was plunged into a second opium crisis. This time the reason was not that a governor wished to stamp out the trade. The cause of the crisis was accidental.

A few weeks previously a petty Chinese official had been arrested and charged at Heungshan with assaulting a Chinese in Macao. The charge was apparently of a serious nature, and faced with the likelihood that the magistrate would impose a severe sentence the accused man had sought to defend himself, with a view to rousing higher authority to come to his rescue and prevent further inquiry, by citing in court a number of senior mandarins who he claimed had committed various illegal actions. To the discomfiture of the entire hierarchy of mandarin corruption, the arrested man turned out to be the intermediary through whom the Heungshan authorities received their opium squeeze. The formality of the assertions made and the amount of gossip they caused obliged the Governor of Kwangtung and Kwangsi to make an investigation.

There was an immediate and intense application of the anti-opium regulations. Howqua, the senior Hong merchant, advised urgently that all opium ships leave the river, by which he meant in particular the floating opium emporium at Whampoa. After an extensive search of all foreign shipping, three private

British ships and one American, all accused of smuggling opium, were ordered to leave without an export cargo and never to return to China. Further to this, orders were issued that in future each ship arriving in the river must be inspected by two of the Hong merchants, the security concerned and one of the four senior merchants. If they were satisfied that there was no opium aboard they must sign a bond to that effect, to be deposited with the Hoppo.

The East India Company refused to countenance this. Bonds, as they saw at once, would become a source of squeeze worse than all those already available to the mandarins, and would probably ruin the senior Hong merchants, the only ones who were solvent and respectable. While this point was being either argued or squeezed to a conclusion, the four accused vessels and the opium emporium, consisting of the mastless hulks used as floating warehouses and various other craft, moved obediently down-river.

With limited obedience, however. Reaching the shelter of Lintin, the emporium and fleet came to anchor, waiting to see what the mandarins would do next. The principal figure in the affair, consignee of two of the accused vessels, was a twenty-five-year-old Scot named James Matheson, a country trader of a new and different type, at the mere description of whom we sense impending trouble. For James Matheson belonged to that class the mandarins found specially perplexing—he was a gentleman, an Anson but in opium.

A baronet's son, after leaving Edinburgh University he joined a Scottish firm in Calcutta, and as a travelling super-cargo made his first trip to Canton about the age of twenty-one. There he became so intrigued by the China trade and its possibilities that he left Calcutta and in 1819 set himself up in a partnership business in Canton. The following year his partner defaulted, but as, following current practice, Matheson was able to claim that each partner within the firm ran his own affairs separately, he managed to avoid being involved. At the time of the opium excitements of 1821 James Matheson was junior partner in a Spanish firm, Yrissari and Company, and, following the best country traditions, he was in addition the Danish Consul.

136

Handsome and gifted with a lively mind, Matheson was one of those rare men capable of putting their hand to almost anything and doing it well; and he delighted in adventure. In other places and circumstances one can imagine him being an outstanding naval officer or explorer; as fate was to have it, life led him to China and to the trade offering the most scope for adventurousness—opium. Destined by nature to be in the thick of things, whatever they might be, James Matheson did not take long to find himself in the thick of things Chinese. Indeed in the opium scare of 1821 the first of the two most formidable Europeans in the history of the Opium War makes his bow.

In the local scene Matheson occupied an unusual position from the start, being the first country trader to meet on terms of social equality the East India Company supercargoes, hitherto exalted above the country rank and file, whose activities the Company regarded in most essentials as Shoe Lane, London, transferred to Hog Lane, Canton. James Matheson further enjoyed special favour from the Company since he dealt in Company Opium, not the rival brand from Malwa; and when he retreated from Whampoa with the opium emporium, the Company, even at the height of the crisis, ensured that he received his export cargo of tea safely, delivered to him further down river against Chinese orders.

The decision to halt at Lintin proved justified. As might have been expected from the way the crisis started, the Kwangtung government did not sustain its repressive measures, which were motivated by nothing more than the mandarin need to save face. Peking was memorialized and tension relaxed, the mandarin position after this being that the opium ships had been driven away (to England?) but that occasionally they tried to come back to the outer fringes of civilization (Lintin) where they were dealt with by surprise naval sorties. On paper, in other words, proper measures were being taken. Not on paper, the channels of bribery were quietly reopened.

Lastly, marking the close of a year of unusual agitation and uncertainty, a huge fire broke out in Canton, raging for two days and three nights and destroying two-thirds of the city. Due to the refusal of the authorities to demolish unaffected buildings in the route of the fire the foreign factories were reached, all but three being completely burnt out. The Governor of Kwangtung ascribed the fire to a judgement of Heaven. Privately, and referring of course to a different Heaven, Robert Morrison agreed.

While the general effect of the 1821 measures against opium was negligible, merely removing the centre of activity from Whampoa to Lintin, which being further from Canton proved to be a much safer place for it, their effect on Macao was decisive in respect of the future. At the height of the scare Chinese vigilance in Macao was so strict that even house-to-house movements of small quantities of the drug were liable to be spotted and reported. All opium had to be innocently packaged to look like some other commodity. Macao in fact was seen to be a far more dangerous opium mart than Whampoa, although prior to 1821 the contrary had always been supposed.

British merchants, taking heed from this, now proceeded to withdraw all their direct opium business from Macao, storing the drug at Lintin and transacting the negotiations connected with it either there or at Canton. Macao tried by every means to induce them to return, but the country traders were unanimous on the subject. As a resting place Macao was delightful; as a residence for firms unlikely to have trouble with the Chinese it was adequate; but for the opium trade it was useless, offering neither concealment nor protection.

Strangled out of its Malwa opium trade, Macao by 1826 was little more than a spectator at events which under the guidance of new men such as James Matheson, and with the coming of faster ships, were expanding out of the historic canvas of the Pearl River into a frame of larger dimensions. Somewhere underlying British aims, if during such a policyless period there can be said to have been any, was the need to obtain a depôt of their own in China. Where such a depôt should be situated no one listening to the trend of conversation could have said. One conclusion alone was clear. It must not be Macao.

IX

HUMANITARIANS AT SEA
IN OPIUM

WITH THE SELECT COMMITTEE still grappling with the problem of clearing Canton of all Britons at the end of each season, the 1820s saw a revival in the glories of the consular corps. James Matheson represented Denmark; Dent and Company, second only to the Magniacs as an opium house, was the Sardinian Consulate; Ilbery, Fearon and Company represented Hanover; Robert Berry, a private merchant, was Vice-Consul for Sweden. A Scottish country trader, James Innes, did not trouble himself with such niceties. Repeating the tactics of old George Smith a generation before, he simply declined to move and defied the Select to do anything about it.

In effect, despite all the care taken by the Chinese to restrict and control foreign intercourse, the situation at Canton had come to look as though it was beyond the power of anyone to control. In addition to European traders there were now over two hundred Parsis who stayed on the coast during the off-season. The Company made no pretence about following their movements; it could not even find out where they all lived, some of them having succeeded in finding lodgings illegally in the city of Canton, away from the approved foreign residential area.

The Americans too had become a permanent feature of the landscape, their largest firm, Russell and Company, differing little in character and traditions from the larger rising British institutions. Beginning as a commercial agency in Canton and Manila, Russell's was in its earlier years outshone by the firm of Perkins and Company under the guidance of America's first China coast multi-millionaire John Perkins Cushing, who from 1803 until the mid-1820s did a tremendous, steady business. Cushing, a single-minded person with few friends and no interests apart from business, stayed for over twenty years on the China coast, 'living like a counting-house monk'.[1] Not even the Anglo-American hostilities of 1812–14 budged him. On one occasion his financial transactions were so cleverly contrived and on such a vast scale that he upset the East India Company's silver supply, making it necessary for more opium to be sent urgently from Calcutta to finance tea purchases. He was the close associate and protégé of Howqua, the leading Hong merchant, whom in asceticism and shrewdness Cushing somewhat resembled.

In the 'twenties, on the point of retirement, Cushing made over some of his interests to Russell's, and in 1827 returned home to Boston, Massachusetts, whence he sent his cousin to take over the firm. When the cousin was shipwrecked and drowned on the way to China, Cushing merged his firm with Russell's, which thus became for the Americans something of what the East India Company was for the British, an organization so large and influential that abroad it enjoyed almost the status of an embassy.

Throughout the same years Magniac and Company assumed a similar position in respect of the British private traders. The Magniacs had started, like Cox and the Beales, as a London singsong agency. In 1797 Daniel Beale had returned to London to join the Magniacs. Thomas Beale, who remained in China, got caught in the first opium scare of 1815 owing the East India Company $800,000 and went bankrupt, the most sensational bankruptcy of the period. Due to the prevalent system of separate accounts in partnerships, however, the firm survived, first as Shank and Magniac, later as Magniac and Company. A revealing point, incidentally, concerning the moral standards of the times is that even after the Company had written off Thomas

[1] Helen Augur: *Tall Ships to Cathay.*

Beale's debts, the company which had once been Beale's never gave him a cent of financial assistance. Beale lived for the rest of his days in Macao a ruined man, dodging creditors and keeping up a dignified appearance on borrowed money and small agency business, till his suicide in 1841.

In 1825 Charles and Hollingworth Magniac, wishing to retire to England, were looking round for a reliable partner to carry on the firm's activities with Daniel Magniac who was to remain in China. The man they invited was a Scot, a former East India Company surgeon named William Jardine, who was then working in Canton as an agent for a Parsi firm of Bombay dealing in Malwa opium. While in the Company's service Jardine had done well in private commerce, and since his arrival in China in the same year as Matheson he had shown extraordinary talent for the opium business. Jardine's acceptance of the Magniacs' offer brought into what was once Cox's little singsong firm the most forceful and determined personality on the coast. His Chinese nickname was the Iron-Headed Rat, which was not, as might at first appear, meant to be derogatory, Cantonese being like Cockney in inverting its compliments. The name referred to an occasion when, to the astonishment of the Chinese, Jardine walked on unconcerned after an iron bar had fallen on his head in the city of Canton. Like Matheson, he was a well-educated man with fairly wide interests, a supporter of early attempts to introduce European medical science in China, and who came to have a remarkable grasp of the political situation as it affected Britons in China. That he was a formidable, indrawn person, more feared than liked, is best exemplified in the fact that in his office there was by tradition only one chair—his own. When being received by Mr. Jardine one stood.

Two years later James Matheson, having scooped one of the largest opium profits ever made in a single voyage by peddling the drug at ports far up the China coast, also joined the firm. The Prussian flag, lowered at Charles Magniac's departure, was replaced by the colours of Denmark, Jardine as the senior partner becoming Consul in succession to Matheson. The firm's good repute was then tarnished by Daniel Magniac's insistence on marrying his pensioner, rendering his elimination essential if Magniac's was to survive in the tight conditions of morality prevailing on this point. The last of the Magniacs was dismissed with a meagre pension, leaving Jardine and Matheson in control, with Hollingworth Magniac as sleeping partner in England. In 1832 the firm was reconstituted as Jardine, Matheson and Company, the name under which it rose to be the commercial colossus of the China coast, from one end of which to the other it became known without irony as the Princely Hong.

The conjunction of these two remarkable men as partners in the house of Magniac acted as a catalyst to the entire China situation. As if an irresistible force had taken over, everything from this moment began to speed up. A sense that there was no turning back seeped into the till then strangely changeless atmosphere, and in the extraordinary way in which one thing led to another, both in England and in China, soon practically nothing was the same.

Matheson's peddling voyage up the coast clearly revealed that enormous as the opium trade already was, the demand for the drug in China far exceeded the supply. The opium trade had hardly started. Matheson's example was quickly followed by others, notable among them James Innes. If Magniac's was to hold its own in what was in effect a new avenue of trade an entirely new technique of trading was required, a tip-and-run technique involving speed.

The Americans, since entering the China trade, had developed a new type of vessel, the Yankee clipper, smaller and much faster than the Company's slow and cumbrous East Indiamen and to the speed and performance of which the Americans owed much of their success. Taking a leaf out of the American book, Jardine and Matheson started to build a fleet of ships of similar though still more modern design, the opium clippers, the fastest ocean-going ships in the East. Dealing in such a sensitive commodity as opium, fast delivery from Calcutta and Bombay was indispensable. By being able to answer demand quickly as and where it occurred along the coast, Jardine and Matheson sent up the volume of the opium trade in a disturbing manner, being time and again able to effect speedy deliveries in safe areas before the Chinese authorities woke up to what was happening and imposed restrictions.

Concurrently, within and around the house of Magniac, anti-Company opinion among the British concentrated and found voice. Though neither of them came to China with the least idea of assuming the leadership of a political struggle, Jardine and Matheson by their sheer qualities of leadership, by the place which their outstanding commercial success and their personal ability gained for them among their countrymen, came inevitably to be the main spokesmen in demanding the freeing of trade and the attainment of proper rights for British traders in China. From the vague talk of earlier years grew a policy, one of the canons of which was that private merchants must no longer be under the restraints imposed on them by the Company, whose China monopoly, due to expire in 1833, must not be renewed by Parliament. On the other main question, of obtaining better treatment at the hands of the Chinese, there was less certainty, though a general view began to evolve of some kind of forward policy supported by force.

William Jardine and James Matheson thus found themselves the prime movers in a dual movement of such extraordinary contradiction and illogicality that their own real motives in it, if these were at bottom anything other than the most completely convinced self-interest, will perhaps never be completely understood. While superintending the deterioration of British trade into highly organized sea-pedlary, they led the formal demand of British merchants for what they considered to be their just rights in China. To look for logic here one looks in vain, but to understand the mental climate in which such actions could take place without being dubbed the most blatant hypocrisy (for that this was what it was did not seem to occur to anybody) one perhaps obtains a clue in the fact that a favourite topic of conversation in the Canton and Macao of those days was to cast scorn on the Americans for selling Smyrna when Company Opium was available and so much less deleterious to smokers. Traders prided themselves, in other words, on dealing only in opium of the best quality. And to this clue of doubtful worth it must be added that the British by and large were so absolutely fed up with the hypocrisy of the Chinese, with their everlasting double façade of restrictions and bribes, that their own hypocrisy in the matter seemed so negligible as hardly to merit attention.

Humanitarians at Sea in Opium

The Americans tended to find Canton less annoying than the British did. William C. Hunter, one of the most popular of all the Americans, endowed with a never-failing sense of humour, and who from 1829 worked as a Chinese interpreter with Russell's, of which he eventually became a partner, wrote in his reminiscences of those days that people assumed life in Canton to be 'a heap of restrictions, a long conflict with the authorities, of trials, of threats, of personal danger, and of a general uncertainty as to what the morrow might bring forth'. Admittedly, he continued, the foreigners were told to listen and obey, to tremble, and not by obstinacy and irregularity to court the wrath of the Imperial Will. They were reminded that they sojourned in the land on sufferance, through the benevolence of the Celestial Dynasty. They were threatened and re-threatened with the direst penalties if they continued to sell foreign mud (opium) to the people, ruining their health and plunging them in inanity, while precious metals oozed out of the country. Forbearance, they were told, could no longer be exercised.

The drug traffic, however, carried on as usual.

The receiving ships at Lintin were ordered to cease loitering at that anchorage, but forthwith come into port or return to their respective countries. The heart of the Ruler of All within the Four Seas was full of compassion, yet now no more delay could be granted. Cruisers would be sent to open upon them irresistible broadsides.

But despite these terrors the ships never budged.

Except on fixed days, three times a month, foreigners were forbidden to wander about, and never without a licensed interpreter. But foreigners walked when they pleased, remained as long as they pleased, and never took interpreters.

Foreign devils were ordered to sail away to their own countries at the end of the season, or at least go to Macao. But they only did so when it suited them.

Each factory was allowed eight Chinese servants and a compradore, but actually all employed as many servants as they chose.

Smuggling between the factories and the ships at Whampoa was prohibited under serious penalties. But those whose duty it was to guard against it—customs boatmen and the watch-force men opposite the factories—were the medium by which, on payment of a fee, foreigners were relieved of all embarrassment in the matter.

Foreigners were ordered by the Regulations not to present petitions at the city gate, lest His Celestial Majesty's sacred glance be turned from them. But they took their petitions just the same, while the guard *protected* them from the crowd. The mandarins would soon make their appearance, take them mildly to task for their wayward disregard of the Will of the Son of Heaven, and accept the petition. A little pleasant conversation would ensue; the officers would offer tea and accept cheroots, then retire, ordering the *guard* to be bambooed for letting the foreigners in. Meanwhile the foreigners returned unharmed, much exhilarated by the pleasant walk.

And so, Hunter concluded, by the foreigners acting in direct opposition to everything they were ordered to do, business went on smoothly and harmoniously.

III: THE HEYDAY OF THE BRITISH AT MACAO—GEORGE CHINNERY

The American attitude that the British in general tended to exaggerate the difficulties was shared by many Chinese, in particular by Howqua, who preferred the Americans to the British, though he dealt with both. Howqua—his Cantonese surname was Ng—was the most successful of the Thirteen Hongs, reputed one of the richest men in the world and well known for his acumen and sagacity. As he and other critics saw it, the British were insufferable sticklers on matters of dignity and principle. The smallest incident would send them into huffy silence, or produce protests, demands for satisfaction, and a general attitude of injured righteousness which Chinese found disconcerting, in that it intruded an element of principle into what in their eyes were matters concerned solely with value, risk and expediency.

It is the important fact that on this particular point American and Chinese attitudes, specially in commerce, resembled each other with surprising closeness—and still do, for such things do not change—that rendered hypothetical any concerted Anglo-American action towards the Chinese. As seen in the inner sanctum of Russell and Company, the Americans were doing well because they understood the Chinese better than the British did—by which was meant Chinese like Howqua. And there was another point. The Americans had had no experience similar to that of the British in India, where for example in Calcutta a Company bachelor's household might consist of forty or fifty servants, including—besides cooks and house servants—punka-wallas, sweepers, grooms, gatekeepers and carriagemen. It was coming as they did from this kind of background in India which made it steadily less likely that the British would tolerate indefinitely the Canton conditions which Americans were readier to accept with a laugh and make themselves comfortable in.

Compensatingly, of course, the profits of private trade and the salaries of Company men were considerable. In a good year the President of the Select Committee could expect to make £10,000 (multiply by fifteen for today's money), while a writer of seven years' service jogged along on £1,000 a year. These incomes were relatively moderate to those of some of the country traders. Many Britons of this period kept wardrobes so large they were able to send their laundry to Calcutta and wait four months or so for it to come back.

In Canton, where they spent about eight months each year, they were expected to live in a state of monastic celibacy. The fact that they did not entirely do so is suggested by the occasional accusations made by the mandarins that the less respectable Hong merchants were smuggling flower-boat girls into the factories, and boys posing as domestic servants. Earlier we observed the East India Company referring to Howqua and the four senior Hongs as the only ones that were solvent and respectable. The fact was that among the Thirteen were a number who made up for their lack of success in business by pandering to foreign requirements in Canton's unusual circumstances of daily life.

The atmosphere of the foreign factories, with their drinking parties and long-drawn-out after-dinner sessions of stories and port, was like that of a row of officers' messes. Amusements included amateur theatricals with men taking the women's parts and music played by the bands of the Company ships, with character dances and other buffoonery afterwards. From Willie Hunter's descriptions it can be seen that the traders adapted themselves to the peculiar frustrations of life and contrived to make time pass as cheerfully as possible.

During the summer the celibates relaxed at Macao, where all the principal characters in the story, even those most insistent on going down from Canton only when it suited them, maintained houses. Entertaining at Macao was on a smaller scale than in Calcutta, but twenty servants in a bachelor's house at Macao was not considered ostentatious. Though there were a few carriages, the generality of Englishmen rode out on horseback.

Much of our visual knowledge of Macao at this time—the heyday of the British there—is derived from the sketches and portraits of the London-born Irish artist George Chinnery, who arrived in 1825 and remained till his death in 1852, painting while there all the works for which he is today famous, 'Dr. Morrison Translating the Bible into Chinese', the charming portrait of Harriet Low, the portrait of Howqua in the Tate Gallery and the self-portrait in the National Portrait Gallery.

Chinnery was the ugliest fellow imaginable, with shaggy eyebrows, a high forehead with hair all over the place, a rock of a jaw and a lower lip so big that when he closed his mouth it almost hid the upper one. But, as it did not take people long to perceive, the ugliness radiated good humour. He had spent the preceding twenty-three years in India, and on arrival in Macao announced without reserve that he had come to escape from his wife, 'the ugliest woman he ever saw in the whole course of his life'. 'Her beauty', as he put it, 'even surpasses my own.'

It did not of course take long for Macao to discover that Chinnery was also escaping from his debts, which in Calcutta ran to the astonishing figure of £40,000. But he was such an entertaining fellow, an inexhaustible raconteur with all the latest Bengali jargon at his command, that people said little about the creditors and concentrated on the wife.

After he had been about three years in Macao there was a rumour that Mary Ann was on her way from Calcutta. Chinnery took no risks. Packing his bags as soon as the rumour became serious, he left for Canton.

Regulation No. 2, debarring devil women from entering that city, had been improved in literary appearance since we last encountered it. It now read, 'Neither women, guns, spears, nor arms of any kind can be brought to the factories.' It certainly showed a wonderful prescience about Mrs. Chinnery.

'What a kind providence is this Chinese Government', said Chinnery to the nineteen-year-old Willie Hunter, 'that it forbids the softer sex from coming and bothering us here. What an admirable arrangement, is it not?'

It proved to be a false alarm, however, and Chinnery returned to Macao. But there were several more similar alarms, during which the artist retreated to Canton, to the great amusement of the European and American community among whom Mrs. Chinnery became a byword.

By 1827—another sign of the coming of a more varied and normal life—the community had their own newspaper, the *Canton Register*, printed on a small hand-press lent by James Matheson and his brother, and operated in a godown at one of the foreign factories, the editor—he was American—being also the compositor. The *Canton Register* added a new touch of make-believe in the best tradition. While opium traders were being threatened with dire penalties, each issue of the newspaper carried with impunity the latest opium quotations.

IV: AMERICAN DOCTORS AND MISSIONARIES—OPIUM WITH
HYMNS ON SUNDAYS

And all the time the humanitarian advance was proceeding. The earliest attempts to introduce Western medicine to China had been spasmodic, due mainly to the constant changes of personnel among Company surgeons and the small number of surgeons available and willing to undertake such work. After Alexander Pearson's attempt to introduce vaccination nothing substantial was done till 1820, when Robert Morrison and the Company surgeon John Livingstone, one of Morrison's few personal friends, opened a clinic at Macao for the Chinese. An interesting feature of this was that with Morrison's assistance the

. Above James Matheson, joint founder of Jardine, Matheson and Co., 'the Princely Hong'. Portrait by Chinnery.

10. Right   Portrait of Harriet Low, by Chinnery, 1821. Harriet and her aunt were the first American ladies in China.

11. The Protestant Cemetery, Macao, with a view of the 'Casa Garden', once the residence of the East India Company's senior supercargo.

beginnings of a proper study of Chinese herbalism were made and a herbalist was engaged to work with Livingstone at the clinic.

This work came to an end when Livingstone left the coast, the next medical institution of its kind being a free ophthalmic clinic started by another Company surgeon, Thomas Colledge, at Macao in 1827. Jardine, keenly interested, helped to overcome the initial difficulty of persuading Chinese to submit to treatment by paying the first man operated on. Needless to say, this procedure had to be rapidly abandoned. The clinic anyway proved a success without it.

Then in 1834 the medical side took a great step forward with the arrival from the United States of Dr. Peter Parker to open the first Western hospital in China. Subsequently known as the Canton Hospital, it operated in a house made available freely for the purpose by Howqua, and after a short time gained the confidence of large numbers of the poor of Canton. Parker, a man of outstanding ability as a doctor and as an observer of political events, later held the post of American Consul in Canton, and was for many years an on-the-spot adviser to the United States authorities on their policy in China. In his hospital the first Chinese surgeons and doctors in Western medicine were trained. The earliest of these, known in English as Kwan Ato, was a nephew of one of Chinnery's pupils, the Chinese artist Lamqua. Thus inconspicuously, and regardless of the mandarins, another inroad was made, surely the most important of all—the inroad of knowledge.

On the missionary side of things Robert Morrison, after labouring alone for so many years, was joined in 1829 by the first two American missionaries, Elijah Bridgman and David Abeel, the former of whom, working in close collaboration with Morrison, started a new printing press in Canton publishing religious tracts in Chinese, and in 1832 founded an English periodical, *The Chinese Repository*, a valuable new medium for the spread of knowledge concerning Chinese history and customs, also running informed comment on the commercial and political situation. In the same year Bridgman in addition started teaching English to Chinese students in Canton.

In 1830 one of the most extraordinary figures of the period arrived, the indefatigable Prussian, Charles Gützlaff of the

L   149

Netherlands Missionary Society, who developed an amazing command of the Chinese language, and with his vehement manner of speech and curiously Chinese appearance could always count on an audience in the mission field. Going up the coast even as far as Korea, Gützlaff's main aim was to distribute Chinese Christian publications (the earliest ones were published by Milne in Malacca) as widely as possible, letting them thereafter do their own work. He has come to be remembered, however, as the person in whom the contradictions of humanitarianism and the opium traffic reached their most astonishing embroilment. In 1832 Jardine invited Gützlaff to take the post of interpreter in one of his ships.

It was one of those small masterstrokes by means of which Messrs. Jardine, Matheson and Company always managed to keep ahead of everyone else, and has that touch of intellectual daring which is so characteristic of the two great opium princes. Jardine's letter was cautious, worded with delicacy and care. Without precisely mentioning opium he made it plain that Gützlaff, if he accepted, would be expected to interpret illicit opium deals. For some days the missionary hesitated, going through intense self-questioning. His own work demanded that he travel far up the coast to as many places as possible; Jardine's ships travelled further than any and to more places, besides which they were safe, fast and comfortable. Gützlaff accepted, and was thereafter seen in many an unexpected spot on the China coast, preaching vigorously to wondering Chinese crowds, handing round pamphlets, and then hastening back to assure some merchant that the opium supplied by Jardine Matheson's was guaranteed the very highest quality.

No better person could have been chosen by Jardine to assist in sending up sales of opium, and no man made a greater impact on more hundreds of Chinese people in the interests of Christianity. To Gützlaff it was the latter that mattered. How does one assess this unique figure? The fact is that on the European side no one ever has, except by a gasp of astonishment tailing off into what must surely have been Jardine's own reaction—a perceptible twinkle in the eye.

Next to join the missionaries, in October 1833, was a twenty-one-year-old American, Samuel Wells Williams, a person of unusual grace and balance of mind, who in the course of time became the United States' leading sinologue and first great authority on the Chinese people and their culture. In the crucial years that followed, this group of missionary sinologues— Gützlaff, Elijah Bridgman and Wells Williams—performed, apart from their religious work, tasks of the greatest political importance as interpreters in the difficult negotiations that gradually drew China out of her lofty seclusion.

The missionaries were disapproving onlookers of the enlarged opium trade, but whatever influence they tried to exert over the traders was ineffectual. One of the missionaries' peculiar difficulties was that with which we ourselves are still faced when discussing them: that a number of the opium pedlars could, if opium were discounted, be called in Christian terms good men. James Innes, for example, read a chapter of the Bible every day, even when aboard ship running the drug up the coast; Jardine contributed to medical treatment for the Chinese poor; Matheson, apart from interests in printing and music—he owned Canton's only piano—left with the Governor of Macao a substantial sum to be used on charities chosen by the government; and all the leading opium men, after the death of Robert Morrison, subscribed to found a Morrison Education Society as his memorial, providing Chinese youths with free education in English and Chinese.

The rate of Chinese conversion to Christianity remained extremely low during these early years of the Protestant missions. In 1832 there were ten Chinese Protestants in China, one or two of them being from Malacca. Wells Williams later recorded that in his own mission he could not recall a single Chinese conversion prior to 1850. But in other ways the impact made by the Protestants was plain for all to see. Protestant services were now conducted in a room in the Canton factories and in the chapel within the walls of the Protestant Cemetery at Macao. The congregations were made up of British and American traders and (at Macao only) their wives, officers of the Royal Navy, merchant captains and seamen. Occasionally the Bethel flag would be hoisted and lustily sung hymns would resound from the decks of the ships at Whampoa.

In 1832 Robert Morrison, then in his fiftieth year and conscious of death's approach, could with justice sum up the Protestant achievement and his own part in it. 'There is now in Canton', he wrote, 'a state of society, in respect of Chinese, totally different from what I found it in 1807. Chinese scholars, Missionary students, English presses, and Chinese Scriptures, with public worship of God, have all grown up since that period. I have served my generation, and must—the Lord knows when—fall asleep.'

X

PALMERSTON'S NEW RÉGIME

I: THE SELECT COMMITTEE'S ATTEMPT TO IMPROVE TRADE
CONDITIONS—FEMININE INVASIONS OF CANTON

JARDINE, MATHESON AND THEIR FRIENDS on the China coast
might well inveigh against the East India Company and determine on a forward policy towards the Chinese; a forward policy
would require British government assistance, and in London
the prevalent attitude in regard to China was totally unfavourable to anything of this kind. Cabinet Ministers and many
responsible members of the British public were seriously concerned by the continued growth of the British dominion in
India, as with seeming effortlessness one Indian ruler after
another came within the shade of the Company umbrella. The
practical problems raised—how this vast empire of alien races
was to be looked after—were by many people regarded as of
disturbing magnitude, the consequence of such an outlook
being that in dealing with China the most important consideration was to do nothing that might involve Britain in any more
commitments of the Indian type.

It was recognized in London that there was a certain demand
for the abolition of the Company's China monopoly, principally
on the grounds that while British trade was limited, Americans
were free to plunge in as energetically as they wished. But if
the monopoly were abolished and a new trading system started
with China, the innovation must not commit British power.
The approach to the Chinese must be firm and dignified, but
not threatening or antagonistic. In keeping with this moderate

outlook the Court of Directors of the East India Company, then in the last decade of their China monopoly and already uncertain of the future, advised Chicheley Plowden, the President of the Select Committee at Macao and Canton, to do nothing likely to upset trade.

The ten years after Waterloo had brought home to the British overseas their new and unchallenged position in Asia, accentuating the absurdity of their helplessness on the China coast; but so far as Britain itself was concerned, the situation in 1829, when Jardine and Matheson completed their fourth year in the house of Magniac, was in effect that the British Government, in possession of the full facts, declined to take any notice.

Within the Company personnel at Canton was a small group who, well aware of the trend of talk at Magniac's and disturbed by the potential threat it posed to Company leadership of the British in China, resolved to ignore the Court of Directors' orders and initiate an attempt to improve matters. As some of the more cynical country traders saw it, the group had a desire to shine in Canton and Macao society as leaders of a forward policy. Leader of the group was a senior supercargo and member of the Committee, William Baynes, who with others on the Committee outvoted Plowden, and in 1829 attempted to force the Chinese to yield better conditions under threat of a British trade embargo of Canton. Under Baynes' orders British shipping was ordered to leave Whampoa and join the opium vessels at Lintin, after which the Committee made its demands: more Hong merchants to be appointed, taxes and duties to be lowered, restrictions to be relaxed on the renting of offices and warehouses, and a number of other unspectacular but practical requests.

The Governor of Kwangtung dealt with the matter politely but without yielding. After months of discussion and correspondence, in which the Company achieved nothing but a delay in its own shipments, Baynes and his party considered they had made one or two satisfactory points and the embargo was lifted in expectation of improvements. But as Plowden, Morrison and others with more wisdom than Baynes realized from the outset, the inevitable capitulation of the Company without gaining anything of importance made the British lose face, thereby reinforcing the Chinese belief that foreign complaints could with impunity be ignored.

The rebel group did not consider they had lost face. In the next season, Plowden having returned to Europe, Baynes, now President, flouted the regulation concerning engines of destruction by taking his wife to Canton. With them went Mrs. Robinson, wife of another supercargo, and Mrs. Fearon, wife of the Hanoverian Consul. They were not the first English-women in Canton; a few years earlier a lady had been conveyed there by accident and returned to Macao. But Mrs. Baynes and her friends were the first to go there in deliberate defiance of the Second Regulation.

In fact, when the Chinese classed women as dangerous they were being cleverer than they knew, for without doubt the presence of Englishwomen in Macao was one of the factors operating to send up the political temperature. Men by them-selves were not particularly bothered by the Chinese restrictions except at times of crisis, such as when there was a homicide. A good deal of the rest of the time they either cursed or laughed and put up with the restrictions, or else ignored them.

Women saw in a different light the rules about Chinese servants, sedan chairs and restriction of movement to within Macao. Instead of funny, they found the rules irritating and inhuman. Nor could they understand why the men were so supine. Of what importance or power was the government of a people of such low standards and primitive mentality as the Chinese they saw around them in Macao? It was time, in the ladies' opinion, that a ridiculously tyrannical government was put in its place.

Nor was it only Englishwomen who envied Mrs. Baynes her trip to Canton. 1829 saw the first two American ladies in China, Abigail, wife of William Low, one of the partners in Russell and Company, and her engaging and vivacious niece, Harriet Low. Prepared to find the Company atmosphere in Macao dull and the Company people pompous and condescending, Harriet soon had her attitude changed for her. English ladies, full of curiosity but prepared for the worst, found on calling that their cautious reserve was returned by the Salem ladies, whose social stock rose rapidly in consequence; while as for the Company gentlemen, Harriet was surrounded by their attentions and thoroughly enjoyed herself—in the most correct manner, be it understood, as befitted a strict Unitarian. The dreadful thing was that she and Aunt Abigail found they really rather liked the English. The Reverend George Vachell, Company chaplain, was very attentive; so too the Company surgeon, Dr. Thomas Colledge; and of course she sat for her portrait by Chinnery and heard the latest tremors from Calcutta about Mary Ann.

William Low came down from Canton to join them as soon as he could. Harriet wanted to know all about the city and whether there was the slightest chance of her going there. When, after all the assurances she received about it being impossible, Mrs. Baynes actually went up, Harriet determined not to be outdone.

Mrs. Baynes' visit was brief, a trade stoppage having been hinted at unless she went back to Macao. But in the autumn of 1830, with the excuse that Baynes was an invalid and that she had to be with him to nurse him, up she went again with a friend.

The Governor of the Two Kwangs was in the midst of trouble with the British, who were refusing to give up three Parsis involved in a homicide case. The additional disobedience of Mrs. Baynes' arrival caused a gubernatorial outburst. As Morrison put it, 'Out came a thundering edict to expel the "foreign woman", and disallow sedan chairs. *Barbarian* merchants must not presume to overstep their rank, but walk on foot.'

As this had no effect, the Governor next intimated through the Hong merchants that if Mrs. Baynes did not leave after a few days, soldiers would be sent to force her away. Baynes replied by bringing up two eighteen-pounders and a hundred Company soldiers, making a fine display on guard at the factory in their red coats, with muskets, swords and pistols. The eighteen-pounders were mounted at the factory gate, facing nothing in particular but looking like business. A few days of suspense followed.

The Governor, troubled by an insurrection in Kwangsi province, then decided that in the disposition of his troops the rebels were more important than the lady. His tone becoming less dictatorial, the Company soldiers and eighteen-pounders were sent down to Whampoa. But the lady stayed.

At this moment Harriet and Abigail Low came up from Macao. Though unaccompanied by military display (the Americans alas! had no troops to protect the charming Harriet) the Lows' visit was of the two escapades the greater social occasion. The American gentlemen were at sixes and sevens. With the arrival of ladies at Canton all their freedom came to an end. Shortly after the Low ladies' coming young Hunter noticed some of his older confrères 'in immense coats, which had been stored away in camphor trunks for ten or fifteen years, and with huge cravats on, and with what once were gloves, on their way to make visits'.

Fortunately they were not required to undergo such severe strain for long. Threatened with a stoppage of Russell trade, the Low ladies returned to Macao after eighteen days in Canton, being seen off on the river-front by the entire American community, which afterwards tore off its cravats with immense relief. One sour old fellow said he hoped they would never be bothered with ladies in Canton again.

II: MANCHESTER'S INTEREST IN THE CHINA TRADE

William Baynes was dismissed from the Committee the following year and his sympathizers were removed from the ladder of promotion, their places being taken by comparative juniors. But the Baynes comic opera of improving matters with the Chinese demonstrated sharply to the British private merchants how small were their chances of obtaining better conditions without the formal intervention of the British Government. At the end of 1830 they took the unusually forward step of petitioning Parliament for a permanent ambassador to be sent to Peking and for an island off the coast to be acquired as a trading depôt. Lintin was named as a possibility, another suggestion being Taiwan.

The private traders were not alone in resenting the negative attitude of the British Government toward the China situation. Chinese treatment of the Royal Navy, the ships of which were classed with the meanest opium smuggler, infuriated all

Englishmen, Company and private. Even Robert Morrison was disgusted by it, expressing his incomprehension that His Majesty's Ministers could be content to tolerate such affronts.

The petition to Parliament failed to produce any results, but in 1832 a new and effective medium of appeal to the British Government and people unexpectedly presented itself in England. The Manchester Chamber of Commerce, in the name of wider markets for its manufactured cotton goods, began to arouse public attention to the importance of abolishing the East India Company's monopoly. Interested persons, including Jardine's politically able agent in London, quickly took advantage of this more or less spontaneous action by encouraging other commercial organizations to voice similar opinions. As a result of one of the modern world's first examples of what would today be called a public relations campaign, within a few months the Board of Trade was receiving petitions from chambers of commerce all over the country demanding the right of free trade in China; and at last the Government moved. A parliamentary inquiry into Eastern trade was instituted, and as the time drew near for the India Bill to be debated at Westminster the trend of parliamentary and public opinion bore heavily towards the abolition of the monopoly.

Far away in China this trend was, with the usual time-lag, reflected at Canton and Macao, the last years of the Select Committee's existence being clouded by the increasing certainty that it was soon to be disbanded and its personnel returned to India. Trouble was no longer taken to oblige private traders to leave at the end of the season. Consular flags lost their former value. The foreign population at Macao increased more rapidly.

Nor was life as easy there as it had been. Still bearing resentment against the British for having thrown them out of the opium trade, reducing Macao to a mere seaside resort, the Portuguese adopted an attitude of non-cooperative pique. Rents increased, until for lower-paid employees they were prohibitive, and in 1831 the Portuguese authorities even tried to prevent any further increase in the number of foreign residents, a measure the British were obliged to circumvent by appealing to the Governor-General of India to communicate with the

Viceroy at Goa, who ordered the abrogation of the Macao residence order.

The degree of Chinese interference at Macao was during the same period (1830–3) particularly tiresome. Repairs to various old buildings were forbidden; certain commodities were declared illegal imports; the sedan chair order was enforced; and Chinese were ordered to quit their employment in European homes. In keeping with former times none of the restrictions were enforced for more than a few days, but they were irritating, particularly as Europeans now understood that by the Chinese authorities pinpricks such as these were what was considered necessary—and sufficient—to keep foreigners humbled and controlled.

III: THE END OF THE COMPANY'S CHINA MONOPOLY

Early in 1834 news was received that the great event so long awaited and so universally demanded had taken place. In the Commons debates the free traders had won the day. The East India Company's monopoly had been abolished.

It was realized in London that a central authority was needed in China to replace the Select Committee, to ensure law and order among British subjects and obedience to Chinese rules, and to be the channel of communication between British merchants and the Chinese authorities. To perform these functions a committee of three was to be formed, of which the senior member was to be known as His Majesty's Chief Superintendent of British Trade in China. Jardine feared that Sir George Staunton (now a Member of Parliament) or one of the other former Company supercargoes would be appointed to this post. Staunton's criticism of the Government's measures, however, ruled him out, and the final choice fell upon Lord Napier, a former naval officer and an authority on the rearing of sheep.

It was also realized in London that some reorganization of trade was required. What form this should take—the establishment of a British Chamber of Commerce in Canton, an approach to the Chinese Government for the abolition of the Co-Hong—was left as a matter for discussion between Lord Napier and the British community.

This was innocuous enough. Lord Napier's instructions, however, went further. The Government's main intention in appointing the Chief Superintendent was to have on the China coast a representative of sufficiently high status to be able to deal on terms of equality with Chinese officials. The old procedure used by the Committee of communicating only by petition through the Hong merchants was to cease. The annual migrations to and from Macao were another relic of the past that must be discontinued. Canton would in future be the sole headquarters of British trade. In effecting these changes Lord Napier was to treat the Chinese authorities with consideration and politeness, was not to use force or threats, and was to show respect for Chinese established customs.

As will be observed at once, these instructions, in the context of Canton and its Petition Gate, were nonsense, impossible of fulfilment. To Lord Palmerston, the Foreign Secretary, they seemed to be moderate, fair and sensible, and Sir George Staunton's warning criticism of them was dismissed. People like Staunton were still thinking in terms of the old Company days. A completely new system had begun. This would have to be explained to the Chinese. There seemed to Lord Palmerston to be no reason to suppose that this would cause trouble. In fact, from this moment one begins to despair of the British Government almost as much as one despaired of the mandarins. With the experience of the Macartney and Amherst embassies to go on, with a mass of information to be had from the East India Company and from the publications of Staunton and Morrison, and with Staunton himself at hand in England to advise, there was no longer at this date the excuse there had been in earlier times for ignorance of the difficulties of dealing with China. Lord Palmerston, whatever his achievements in other fields, emerges through the documents surrounding the Opium War in a peculiarly uninspiring light. Throughout he never understood, or refused to believe, even the initial point of encounter, which was that no communication with the mandarinate of China was possible unless worded in the form of a petition. It certainly seemed, and was, highly incongruous for a British government of the nineteenth century so to have to proceed, but there it was, and it could surely have been used as a temporary expedient to effect introductions. You do not use the telephone to communicate with ministers of a country that has not yet been connected with that instrument. Anyway, Palmerston had made up his mind to do something of the kind, and Lord Napier, little knowing that he was heading for humiliation and death, sailed for China.

IV: LORD NAPIER IN CANTON—THE DEATH OF ROBERT MORRISON

Jardine realized in advance that Napier's instructions were likely to be unsatisfactory, but he was not particularly concerned. As the senior and most prosperous British resident in China, the last of the Company's supercargoes being younger men with less experience then he, Jardine was in a position to take Lord Napier under his wing, as it were, a position he intended to take advantage of.

The Chief Superintendent of British Trade in China, with his wife and two daughters, arrived at Macao in July 1834. To signify his break with the old régime he did not move into the Casa Garden, but occupied a large house on the Ridge placed at his disposal by Jardine and Matheson. To signify that the break was not as complete as this might suggest, he announced the appointment of two former Company supercargoes as Second and Third Superintendents, John Francis Davis, one of the more promising sinologues of the day, later to be distinguished as a writer on China and a Governor of Hongkong, and Sir George Robinson, of the same vintage. Captain Charles Elliot, R.N., whose rise to being the key figure in the Opium War and the foundation of Hongkong begins here, was appointed Master Attendant. Other members of the Royal Commission were J. H. Astell, a former Company servant, as Secretary; Alexander R. Johnston, later to be Hongkong's first Colonial Secretary, as Private Secretary to Lord Napier; and Dr. Robert Morrison as Chinese Interpreter, with a good salary and—at this moment he really does almost cease to be a missionary—orders to wear a vice-consul's uniform as soon as one could be obtained.

The offer of the house on the Ridge was the first pawn moved in Jardine's game to ensure that the Chief Superintendent began on the right foot, that is to say, as the protagonist of the policy advocated by Jardine and Matheson. This policy was in essence simple. Long experience of dealing with the Chinese showed that their officials would only grant more favourable conditions under threat of violence. This did not mean that war with China was unavoidable; war should at all costs be avoided. But a demonstration of force, and even the use of it in some minor engagement such as the seizure of a coastal island—Lintin, for example—was essential before proceeding to talk about a new basis for trade.

Not all the merchants supported this view. Some were for a less aggressive approach. Others opposed it simply because it was supported by Jardine, who with his stern manner and uncompromising methods had a number of prominent British enemies. Opposition to it centred around Lancelot Dent, senior member of the house of Dent, the largest British firm after Jardine Matheson's.

It is unlikely that any of the senior merchants with a knowledge of the gist of Napier's instructions imagined that a new régime was really about to be inaugurated. But after the years of waiting for the Committee's demise great things were expected of 1834, and when at the end of July Lord Napier, without asking for a pass from the Governor of Kwangtung and Kwangsi, sailed up to Canton to open negotiations, nobody talked much about the difficulties. The prevailing mood was of relief that at last something was happening.

Morrison translated Napier's opening letter to the Governor, announcing his arrival, and Morrison's son, twenty-year-old John Robert Morrison, a brilliant sinologue like his father, went with Astell to deliver it at the Petition Gate. As it was headed 'Letter' and not 'Petition', and as it was evidently from the mysterious barbarian official who had recently entered Canton without authority, it was not accepted; and as Lord Napier refused to yield by delivering it via the Hong merchants, there was deadlock from the start.

Robert Morrison's anxiety at the experience before him—for it was evident that if Napier really was to converse with Chinese officials the official interpreter would be required a great deal—and the intense strain of translating, to Howqua and others whom Lord Napier met, opinions, statements and questioning certain to produce only consternation and dispute, caused the missionary's health to fail rapidly. The headaches from which he had suffered since childhood had for some time been growing worse, preventing him from sleeping. For a day or so more he managed to attend Lord Napier's interviews, going to and fro by sedan chair, thickly curtained lest the authorities see a foreigner was inside it. After this the chair coolies refused to take the risk (to themselves) of carrying him any more. For the last three days of the month he was confined to his house, where Colledge strove to save him and even Jardine was asked in for his professional advice. On 1st August he died. He was fifty-one.

Lord Napier and the entire foreign community, including the Indians and Parsis, accompanied Morrison's remains as they were borne from his house to the quay, whence they were shipped down to Macao for burial in the Protestant Cemetery. There was greatness about Robert Morrison, and everyone was aware of it; yet even in the terrible moments of his first year in Canton there is something in his character and outlook that provokes more admiration than sympathy. Even Samuel Wells Williams, the most gracious of the missionaries, and who like all of them regarded Morrison with esteem and affection as the great representative of their common cause, remarked that Robert Morrison 'was not by nature calculated to win and interest the skeptical or the fastidious, for he had no sprightliness or pleasantry, no versatility or wide acquaintance with letters, and was respected rather than loved by those who cared little for the things nearest his heart'.

V: THE WORSTING AND DEATH OF LORD NAPIER

At Canton the Napier fizzle, as it was called by Hunter and his waggish friends, continued for another two months. The Governor ordered Napier to leave; but as the order was sent through the Hong merchants, from whom Napier refused to receive it, he was for a time unaware of it. By mid-August Napier had clearly come to the conclusion that in the peculiar circumstances Jardine's views and his own personal reactions as a former naval officer were the only landmarks to follow if he was to steer clear of the utter confusion between his London instructions and the Canton situation. He was by this time seeing more of Jardine than he was of Davis, the Second Superintendent, while within other walls Dent and his group were beginning to criticize and even decry the Commission. As Jardine's association with Napier became more widely realized, the British community split into two camps, for and against His Majesty's Commission; and as it did so the Governor of Kwangtung, informed of what was happening, was reassured: he had only to sit firm and wait. By way of a little prod he ordered a partial stoppage of trade.

A few days after this Napier found a way out of the impasse created by his and the Governor's refusal to open each other's letters. Convinced that Chinese common folk were the unwilling servants of their Manchu overlords and that disaffection could easily be fomented to advantage, Napier caused a proclamation to be written in Chinese in which he accused the Governor of ignorance and obstinacy, and laid upon him the responsibility for bringing ruin to all the thousands of Cantonese put out of work by the partial trade stoppage. This proclamation Napier had posted up in such streets of Canton as his men could reach.

It was certainly effective in conveying his views to the Governor, but it was a game two could play at. In reply came a proclamation describing Napier, whose name in Chinese was rendered by the characters signifying Laboriously Vile, as a lawless foreign slave and a barbarian dog. This was followed on 2nd September by a total stoppage of trade, the announcement of which, to make sure Napier read it, was posted at the Company's front door by a platoon of soldiers. And of course, as will have been realized, Napier's incitement of the common folk produced no effect whatever.

Subtlety, diplomacy, patience, good manners and luck were the ingredients Napier needed. Unfortunately the poor man seemed at this moment to possess none of them. Even his manners forsook him when, in ridiculous imitation of the Governor's style of letter-writing, he closed one of his letters by telling the Governor to 'tremble, tremble intensely!' Anson was the type of man who might have mastered the situation. Napier, faced with placid Chinese methods of self-defence, quickly made the classic reaction of exasperation. This made him physically ill, and with the outcome of a tropical fever he became mentally upset. Ignoring his royal instructions, he resolved to counter the trade stoppage by resorting to aggression.

Since Admiral Drury's visit no outright challenge to Chinese power had been made, and Jardine, Matheson, Innes and their group were keenly interested to observe what effect such a challenge might have. For years a section of the British traders had been saying that a few broadsides on the city of Canton would quickly resolve most troubles.

In spite of enjoying Napier's confidence, Jardine could not risk openly advising such a step, for there was every reason to suppose that the use of force would fail, and even at this late date no one was quite sure what superior forces China might have in reserve. In the event, Jardine and his friends had but to nod their heads in agreement when His Lordship touched the subject, and let His Majesty's representative carry out on his sole initiative the experiment which might point the course of the future. It was a situation of remarkable convenience for the forward group. On 5th September Lord Napier ordered the frigates *Imogene* and *Andromache* to enter the Bocca Tigris and come up-river as far as Whampoa.

This they did. The forts put up a braver show than usual, but despite the calm weather (and consequent slow progress of the ships) they made few hits and killed no one. Throughout the engagement Captain Elliot, following in his cutter, *Louisa*, sat on deck and watched, imperturbable beneath an umbrella.

The Governor at once organized defensive measures. To prevent the ships reaching Canton from Whampoa a number of junks filled with stones were sunk across the river, and a fleet patrolled the area. After the ships passed the Second Bar steps were taken, if need should arise, to block the river there too, preventing egress to the sea.

The need did not arise. Lord Napier saw at once that his aggressive tactics had failed; the ships with which he had intended to terrify Canton were immobilized. His fever rising with his frustration he retired to bed, with Dr. Colledge in attendance.

Satisfied with themselves and with the situation in general, the Chinese authorities complacently informed the Hong merchants that as soon as the ships left the river and Lord Napier returned to Macao trade would be resumed. It was to be the same classic story in essentials: Laboriously Vile, a dangerous barbarian sent to China as a Confidential Eye, had uttered threatenings and brought warships, but all had been driven away by the superior power of the Celestial Kingdom. Furthermore this time, due to the unusual amount of publicity given as a result of Napier and the Governor addressing each other by printed proclamation, the whole city of Canton saw for themselves that what their Governor said was true.

For his part, Napier realized he must leave with as much dignity as was possible after this dismal defeat. It would have been purposeless to have sought to open negotiation on another, a humbler footing, in that by resorting to force he had played into the Governor's hand and totally lost face. Nor was there any appeal he could make to his own countrymen, for having unwisely allied himself with Jardine too closely, to the exclusion of the more moderate party under Lancelot Dent, he no longer commanded the obedience of the British community. Nor, finally, could he have left John Francis Davis behind to negotiate as his deputy, because the alliance with Jardine, between whom and Dent existed a mutual relationship of unmitigated contempt, had so incensed the moderate party that it had irreparably damaged the reputation of the Royal Commission itself in the eyes of the British, a fact of which the Governor of Kwangtung was fully aware. Few downfalls have been more complete than Lord Napier's.

Colledge advised that it was in any case imperative for Napier to be brought to Macao as soon as possible, which might, it could be supposed, have provided him with a *porte de sortie*. But here the Governor from the unseen mystery of his yamen imposed on Laboriously Vile a set of additional, distinctively Chinese humiliations. Napier was virtually besieged in Canton, after all, from which he could not withdraw except on terms—the Governor's terms. These were negotiated between the Hong merchants (the first humiliation) on one side and Colledge and Jardine on the other, and were approved by the Governor. Under them Napier ordered the retreat of the warships, and in a humble petition (the next humiliation) begged the officers of His Celestial Majesty for the issue of a standard red permit giving leave to depart (signifying that he had paid all debts incurred during his stay and inferring that he was a common trader). The permit was issued, but only (for the importance of which door you enter and leave by is important in China) on condition he left Canton by the inferior route, the delta channels used by the Portuguese, and (the final insult) under armed Chinese escort.

Napier agreed to everything and departed. The journey through the delta was made by houseboat and took a needlessly long time, a slow pace being set by the escort. At Heungshan they were delayed for two days, Canton having failed to send orders to allow them to pass the customs post. Heungshan was a busy place. Cymbals beat as dignitaries passed this way and that on the river; firecrackers exploded in celebration of weddings and other festive occasions. Amid the endless disturbance of the journey Napier's fever increased, and when he reached Macao and his family he was in a critical condition. For just over two weeks he hung on to life, with unabated fever, and on 11th October he died.

One would have thought that with the Amherst embassy the British had reached the low-water mark in the indignities to which they laid themselves open by failing to make proper preparations for dealing with so strange a country as China. The Napier mission was an even worse fiasco than that of Amherst. Admittedly Lord Napier was an unsuitable choice to head a mission to China, an example of the fallible British tendency to select men for high appointment on grounds of breeding or other standards not necessarily relevant to affairs of state. But the impossible position he was placed in, rendering him a figure of tragedy with whom one has every sympathy, was caused entirely by his instructions and Lord Palmerston's refusal to heed the expert advice which was available to him.

VI: QUIESCENCE—RAPID EXPANSION OF THE OPIUM TRADE

The disagreements misguidedly stimulated by Napier among the British merchants left them at his death leaderless and unrestrained, at a time when the opium trade was entering a new phase and assuming enormous commercial proportions.

John Francis Davis succeeded Napier as Chief Superintendent, with Sir George Robinson as Second Superintendent and Captain Elliot promoted to be the Third. Though distinguished by his scholarly attainments, Davis had what would be described today as a civil servant's mentality. High principled, with the moderation and correctitude so highly valued by the Honourable Company, he lacked the qualities the merchants demanded at this particular moment, those of a man of action capable of rallying his countrymen together in a deteriorating situation. As a former supercargo he enjoyed scant respect among his own people—Jardine and his friends could not abide him—and as a comparative junior he was left at a crisis in Britain's relations with China without guidance from the British Government, Lord Napier's instructions having nowhere entered into the possibility of his mission being the total failure it was. Davis accordingly wrote urgently to London for further instructions, removed the Commission to Macao, and enjoined upon his countrymen a policy of absolute quiescence, which should not, he added, imply acquiescence.

Given the opium taipans he was dealing with, this last was a culminating mark of fatuity. Jardine's new technique of fast-sailing opium clippers, making four journeys per year between India and China instead of the old East Indiaman's two, was producing effects. The amount of opium annually reaching China rose from 20,486 chests in the 1833–4 season to 30,202 chests in 1835–6, and by 1838 was well over 40,000 chests. In 1837 the number of floating warehouses at Lintin had risen from five to twenty-five. In other words the trade, already large, doubled in five years, until it amounted to three-fifths of all British imports to China. (The Americans also were trading heavily in opium; the chest figures given above include their shipments.)

The result of Davis' quiescence was that His Majesty's Chief Superintendent of Trade ceased to be of any importance, while in an atmosphere of irresponsibility illicit business was conducted on an unprecedented scale. The end of the monopoly brought to the Far East increased numbers of new British traders, many of whom the Company would formerly have considered too disreputable to obtain a licence, and no self-imposed commercial restraints succeeded those imposed by the Company.

Early in 1835, after three months living at Macao like an exiled monarch with the remnants of his court still making obeisance to him, John Francis Davis withdrew from the post of Chief Superintendent and went back to England. He was succeeded by Sir George Robinson, with Captain Elliot as Second Superintendent and Alexander Johnston as Third.

Sir George Robinson, in whom the lordliest and most tiresome characteristics of Company men found their apogee, quite rightly observed (but in the circumstances also quite pointlessly) that as long as British merchants hastened back to Canton the moment trade reopened, and only left when forced to by the Chinese, there was little chance of negotiating for better treatment. What he had in mind—and he mentioned it in a despatch to Lord Palmerston—was to prevail upon the entire British community in Canton and Macao to suspend all trade, board ship and leave, taking shelter in one of the pleasant anchorages of Lantao or Hongkong. If necessary one or two Chinese coastal forts—he appears to have had in mind those on Lantao—could be reduced, allowing the British to establish themselves ashore.

It will be seen that this proposal, involving virtually the seizure of a coastal island such as Lantao, did not differ substantially from Jardine's policy. But it did require force and leadership to carry it out; and while Sir George Robinson had enough force at his disposal to ensure British safety on an island at least temporarily, he was not in a position to lead in anything. The rift among the British merchants and the decline in the Chief Superintendent's prestige rendered it impracticable to impose any policy on anyone. Had Robinson been able to persuade even one group of the merchants to his idea it might have succeeded. But he could not. No one would listen to him. Clash of personality was in addition never more marked than at this juncture. Robinson regarded Jardine as an utter bounder and many of the others with contempt; Jardine and his friends considered Robinson a pompous ass. The rest shrugged their shoulders at His Majesty's representative and went on with their opium peddling. After holding on at Macao for the best part of the year, Sir George, irked by the close proximity of his free-trading countrymen, resolved that if they would not accept his advice and leave Canton and Macao, he would set a proper example and leave alone.

Which in November 1835 he did. Installing his entire office, including the archives, in the cutter *Louisa*, he sailed out to Lintin and anchored with the maximum of inappropriateness beside the opium clippers and floating warehouses.

Even from Whitehall it was obvious that Sir George's move could only serve to complete the sterilization of the King's Commission as a means of effecting any change. In June 1836 Palmerston wrote abolishing the post of Chief Superintendent, ordering Robinson to hand over the archives to Elliot, who thus became head of what remained of the Commission, with Johnston as the other member. This despatch was received and put into effect five months later. Thus things stood in December 1836.

VII: MATHESON IN ENGLAND

Meanwhile James Matheson had been active in what had become more significant as a scene of operations—England.

At the height of the Napier episode a British Chamber of Commerce had been formed in Canton, with Matheson as its first chairman. The Chamber did not represent all the British merchants, and from the composition of its members gave little promise of becoming the restraining influence which was really required, but it did start the campaign which was at last to produce results, awakening Britain to the need to improve the status of her countrymen in China. Late in 1834 the Chamber addressed a petition to the King-in-Council requesting that an ambassador be sent to China, supported by warships, to demand the opening of more ports and the abolition of the Co-Hong system.

By this time Jardine, Matheson and the other leading men in their group had realized very fully that nothing was likely to be achieved on the basis of action in China and communication with London by correspondence, as hitherto. The petition to the King would not arouse the Government to take any real interest unless informed and influential opinion in London could also be aroused to awareness of conditions in China. What was required was action on the basis of a two-pointed prong, one point set firmly in China, the other in England, where the Government clearly understood very little concerning China and where considerable effort would be needed to make them understand. With the aim of stirring things up in England James Matheson combined courtesy with mercantile interest by accompanying Lady Napier and her daughters on their unhappy homeward voyage.

Once in London, Matheson set to work, beginning his operations with the Government. Palmerston, whom he had counted on meeting, was out of office. Instead, Matheson was heard by the Duke of Wellington, Prime Minister of the short-lived government of November 1834 to April 1835. To the Iron Duke the problems of petty merchants in China were of no interest, and after an unsatisfactory interview, at which Matheson concluded there was nothing to be gained by pressing for attention in that quarter, he turned to the direction from which the China merchants had received help before—the chambers of commerce of Britain's great industrial cities.

Thus began a second and equally effective public relations campaign. Matheson toured the country addressing interested bodies. In 1836 he published a pamphlet in London entitled *The Present Position and Future Prospects of Trade in China*, and the three most important chambers of commerce in the land—those of Manchester, Liverpool and Glasgow—all addressed the Board of Trade on the matter.

This created the extraordinary dual situation without taking stock of which the actions of the British Government—and the sentiment of Britons at home—during the period of the Opium War appear totally incomprehensible. It may be called a duality between action in China and ideas at home. It may even be called a duality between theory and practice. In effect it was no more than an extension to England of a duality long existent among the British in China, and of which James Matheson made the British public aware in suitably censored amounts. At one and the same time, while private merchants in the Pearl River were bringing to China every ounce of opium they thought the Chinese could smoke, in London—with little reference to opium—strong arguments were being put forward in the name of justice and national honour to end the abuses Englishmen had suffered too long at the hands of the Chinese.

For bringing about this amazing contradiction much of the credit—or blame—must go to James Matheson, who knew how to pitch his appeal to British interests exactly in the manner to provoke a response. Throughout his campaign the question of opium was treated as being of secondary importance, the potential Chinese market for British manufactures being the main issue commercially. Nor in fact—a point to be remembered regarding Matheson's integrity—was he exactly hoodwinking the British public. As can be seen from an examination of the China trade, opium *was* of secondary importance. Due to various reasons, among which stand out the decline and fall of the East India Company as a restraining influence and the period of British governmental indifference to China in the nineteen years between the missions of Amherst and Napier, the opium trade had been allowed to grow into a huge bubble whose reflections have hypnotized many even among ourselves into believing that opium was the major issue of trade that led us to force China to open up commercially. This is not the case. Opium could certainly have been described as a major issue in the days when it was an essential financer of the tea trade; but those days had long ago passed. At any moment from 1815 onwards the expanding opium balloon could have been pricked and burst had the Chinese so chosen, the operative factor being Chinese—meaning mandarin—choice in the matter, as is proven by what now took place, in order to observe which we must pass through the Petition Gate at Canton into the great country beyond, entering the inner courts of the mandarinate and the seat of the Chinese Empire.

XI

THE CONFRONTATION

I: MEMORIALS TO THE SON OF HEAVEN

As JARDINE'S CLIPPERS sent imports of opium rocketing up, so within China did a phenomenon occur portending developments of great importance. The highest echelon of the Chinese civil service, those few at the top who were the supreme guardians of tradition and security, provincial governors and other officers of long and varied administrative experience, awoke to their responsibility for protecting the health and morals of the people. Not only did they awake but they took action in the form most dangerous to themselves should their words go unheeded or be considered worthless—in the form of memorials submitted through the Board of Censors for presentation to the Emperor. Every one of them knew that the Emperor was indirectly one of the greatest beneficiaries of the opium trade. To touch upon the subject was to touch the Emperor's purse, even to offend his celestial dignity. Yet one by one from all parts of China the memorials arrived, penned only by the highest—none less could so venture. Perhaps there was collusion—who could say? In the extreme summits of the mandarinate were many who must have known each other at a distance for the best part of their lives. Perhaps on the other hand it was spontaneous. In Peking it appeared so, and was all the more significant for that.

The tone of the memorials was sober and responsible. Shorn of decorative verbiage the documents read today, as does so much concerning the mandarinate at all times, with a compelling sense of modernity. Barbarian traders, the Emperor was humbly informed, would continue bringing opium to China until foolproof measures were taken to prevent the disgraceful habit of smoking it. The barbarians, it will be noted, were not particularly blamed. To refer much to foreigners in a memorial was indeed beneath the dignity of a great officer of the Chinese Empire. It was inferred, and believed, that nothing better could be expected of barbarians than to bring deleterious drugs if they thought they could earn silver thereby. Those singled out for blame were the smokers. At present, the memorialists submitted, the number of smokers was increasing acutely, and action by the Government was imperative. If there was delay, and the present increase in the popularity of opium smoking continued, it might soon be too late to control the traffic or prevent the morale of the people from being broken by it.

It was grave and disturbing reading, demonstrating to us today that when the Chinese talked about opium plunging the people into inanity those were not mere idle words. As the highest and most responsible officers of China saw it, the danger of such a terrible eventuality was imminent. Nor did they mince matters in ascribing the principal cause of trouble to Chinese craving for the drug—the inexplicable root factor without which most people throughout the world today would never have heard of opium.

Most of the memorialists mentioned the other serious problem related with the drug—the drain of silver. And from what they said it is evident that there was a general belief at Court (which at Canton has been observed as entirely correct) that the import of opium was the prime reason for the drain in the country's silver. (In fact the drain had now reached serious proportions and was causing a peculiar inflation of smaller coin, a tael of silver, normally 1,000 cash, fetching at this time 1,600 cash.) Not all the memorialists agreed that opium was responsible for this, or that the suppression of the trade would necessarily end the drain of silver. Argument in most of the memorials concentrated on whether the trade should be suppressed altogether or controlled by licence—and on the subject of control some of the writers showed a sensible regard for the need to prevent what they described as petty corruption—and whether it should be the smokers or the Chinese dealers (not the foreigners) who were to be the more severely punished.

Up to the middle of 1836 the current of opinion in Peking was that the wisest procedure would be to legalize the opium trade as a means of bringing it under a workable system of control, either by accepting opium on a basis of barter, or by restricting the price and the amount annually imported. While the memorials continued to come in, the Emperor Tao Kuang held his hand, undecided what to do.

II: CAPTAIN CHARLES ELLIOT AS SUPERINTENDENT OF TRADE

Whitehall did the same in respect of the petitions it was receiving demanding better treatment for British traders in China. Wellington's ministry was out, and the Whigs were back in power with Palmerston again Foreign Secretary. Undecided what to do, Palmerston held his hand in expectation of further developments on the China coast.

There the removal of Sir George Robinson as Chief Superintendent had brought to the conduct of British affairs a group of men who, had they been supported by an understanding Foreign Secretary in London, might well have drawn the Pearl River make-believe into the world of reality without the crude wrench of war.

'Few foreign officials who have come to China', wrote Wells Williams, 'have been superior in talent to Capt. Elliot, or better fitted than he to fulfil the important duties devolving upon him. He had also the advantage of having as interpreter and adviser John R. Morrison, Dr. Morrison's son, a man whom it was impossible to know without loving, and who, born in the country and familiar with Chinese from childhood, was in some respects better qualified than his father to act in these capacities. . . . Both he and Captain Elliot recognized very clearly the ideas which the Chinese have on the subject of their unchallengeable supremacy over all other nations. . . . Indeed, it is hardly to be wondered at if they felt themselves vastly superior to the handful of foreigners who dwelt in the Canton factories, intent only on trade, which . . . is the lowest of the four categories into which the Chinese divide human professions and pursuits.'

Without instructions to the contrary, Elliot resumed contact with the Canton authorities in complete conformity with Chinese rules. He humbly applied for permission to come to Canton, and waited at Macao until answer was received from Peking. When it came, in March 1837, it was found to be satisfactory. Though not conceding Elliot's status as the representative of the King of Great Britain it did acknowledge that his status differed somewhat from that of former Presidents of the Select Committee (in that he was not a trader), and that provided he obeyed the Regulations, addressed all correspondence through the Hong merchants, and did not loiter about in Canton after the season, he might be regarded as the barbarian headman. This in fact was a distinct advance according to the only practicable method, the step-by-step system.

Next, by the same system, Elliot reached the point where although letters from the Governor continued to be addressed to the Co-Hong for transmission to foreigners, Elliot's letters to the Governor were delivered sealed to the Co-Hong, with merely a covering note requesting transmission.

The Governor of Kwangtung, Têng Ting-chên, was, as mandarins of his rank usually were at all times in Chinese history, well informed from private and official sources of the trend of affairs in the Great Within. At present, for example, he was aware of the memorials being received by the Emperor on the subject of opium, and of the Emperor's indecision. As Têng saw it, whatever the final decision as regards legalizing opium or suppressing it altogether, it behoved him, should the decision arrive tomorrow, to be manifestly engaged in driving opium ships away. Just before Elliot assumed control Governor Têng, acting possibly on a rumour from Peking that the alternative of suppression was gaining ground, expelled twelve opium merchants from Canton—eight of them were British subjects—and ordered increased vigilance throughout the entire area, the movement of foreign ships being reported by all coastal forts and naval patrols. Elliot, from his assumption of office, had a series of complaints from the Governor about opium vessels loitering in different parts of the river and in Hongkong harbour, to all of which he replied that he had no jurisdiction to order the ships away. This was the kind of reply which in former days had infuriated Canton officialdom. Such were the good relations that Elliot was steadily building up that this time there was no such effect. In fact, being strongly opposed himself to the opium trade, Elliot would have liked greater control over shipping; but when he had earlier tried to exercise it he was warned by Palmerston to beware of exceeding his powers.

The corollary to Governor Têng's improved preventive methods was of course that improvements also had to be made in delivery arrangements for the opium on which Governor Têng and other high officers received their squeeze, for whatever outward appearances might suggest, underneath it was still very much business as usual. In 1836 an unwritten agreement was reached between the British at Lintin and the Chinese junk squadron on duty in the river, whereby for a monthly fee of 36,000 taels of silver the war junks convoyed the opium safely to Whampoa. The following year the war junks actually carried the opium themselves for greater safety, in return for a percentage amount of each cargo which they then presumably sold to dealers themselves.

As a convinced opponent of the opium trade Elliot was already in an unenviable personal position as the representative of Great Britain at such a time as this. His position was now to be made still worse, and his work undermined, from an unforeseen and unanswerable quarter. Lord Palmerston had received the first of Elliot's despatches written as head of the Commission, and been appalled to discover from them that the old methods of communicating by petition through the Co-Hong were still being used. His answering despatch reached Elliot in November 1837, its tone critical and authoritative.

'It might be very suitable', Palmerston wrote, 'for the servants of the East India Company, themselves an association of merchants, to communicate with the Authorities of China through the Merchants of the Hong, but the Superintendents are Officers of the King, and as such can properly communicate with none but Officers of the Chinese Government.' He added that Elliot must on no account head any further correspondence to the Chinese with the character meaning 'petition'.

Immersed as he was in the affairs of Europe, Palmerston had still learnt little of China. It was furthermore the age when orientals were being put increasingly in their places, the age when a masterful attitude of clean Christian decency was demanded of ambassadors in the face of oriental political intrigue. Unfortunately China, though oriental, did not present problems of that kind at all. It is perhaps too much to expect that Palmerston could have understood the importance of the character 'pin'. Unfortunately, too, the problem had that quality of so many initial problems: it had a deceptively small appearance. Yet surely, one thinks—Palmerston, the great Foreign Secretary. . . . He had the Napier fiasco to account for, and he had Napier's and Elliot's despatches; yet he proceeded to place Elliot in the same impossible position as Napier had been placed in. By this despatch of 1837 Palmerston deprived the British representative in China of the means of communication with the Chinese. Surely no envoy was ever given a more perplexing instruction.

With great deference Elliot informed the Governor—they were in more or less daily correspondence—that he would no longer be able to address his missives in the form of petitions. The Governor replied that no other form was acceptable. The situation in the Pearl River was deteriorating still further and rapidly. British and American armed boats were fighting their way through from Lintin to Whampoa carrying opium. If it went on much longer, Governor Têng was liable to be in trouble with Peking. When therefore the Governor insisted in the matter of petitions, Elliot made use of departure to Macao as a gesture to impress upon the Governor the fruitlessness of the position he was taking. He might very well have need of Elliot's restraining hand on the British.

The gesture, which may perhaps be regarded as one of Elliot's few errors of an otherwise formidably correct judgement of the Chinese, produced no response from Governor Têng, while by moving to Macao and staying there (it was difficult to see what else he could have done when the gesture failed) Elliot cut himself off still further from intercourse with Chinese authority.

The Confrontation

Macao remained Elliot's headquarters throughout the year 1838, which was dominated by rumours of gathering strength from Peking that the Emperor was proposing to suppress the opium trade, and by increased British and American determination to force their opium through to Whampoa past Governor Têng's defences. Macao meanwhile, packed as never before with Europeans, noticeably took on the tense and uncertain character of a neutral city important to two contestants in time of war.

To the Governor and Senate of Macao, the most experienced of all observers of the China scene, it was evident that matters between the British and the Chinese were heading for disaster, and that if Macao was not extremely careful, maintaining the strictest neutrality towards both sides, she would be involved and obliterated in that disaster. Many Portuguese now expressed emotions of relief that their city was no longer an opium centre. That it was not an opium centre gave a more genuine appearance to neutrality.

Occasionally the Portuguese Governor overstepped the mark in one direction or the other, producing remonstrances from whichever side felt itself aggrieved. After Napier's death the Governor declined to acknowledge the official status of the British Superintendents, obliging Palmerston to address Lisbon on the matter. After this, from mid-1837, relations between Elliot and the Portuguese Governor improved, though perhaps only on the surface. As often befalls with neutrals, the British were convinced that Macao was pro-Chinese, while the Chinese suspected the Portuguese of being hand in glove with the British. It was an uneasy and anxious period all round, in which from Elliot's point of view a main point of concern was the number of British women and children in Macao, who if the Portuguese should finally feel obliged to choose the Chinese side would be left completely undefended.

Then the general situation took on a more sinister light. In April 1838 Governor Têng, whose profits from the opium squeeze were an open secret, ordered the public execution in Macao of a Chinese convicted of disobeying the opium edicts, following this with a series of such executions held there and in Canton. Before such inhuman hypocrisy and injustice a wave of shock and disgust swept the foreign community, generating the feeling that *au fond* they were dealing with a barbarous and horrible government undeserving of further patience or respect. It was an intense and universal feeling, extending to the humblest European on the China coast. The West had just about had enough.

The mood was thus when in December of the same year a consignment of opium was seized in front of the house of James Innes in Canton. Innes was given ten days in which to leave the city, and his security merchant was paraded through the streets with a square wooden cangue round his neck and his crime written above his head, the Chinese equivalent of being put in the stocks. A day or so afterwards, under official Chinese orders, a cross was erected in front of the foreign factories and an attempt made to strangle a Chinese opium dealer. A group of foreigners, led by William Hunter, protested against the use of their recreation ground as a place of execution, but the Chinese officer in charge took no notice. A posse of British sailors, disembarking by chance at this moment and seeing what was about to take place, without the need for any orders set upon the officer and his men, overthrew the officer's table and teapot, smashed the cross, and drove the Chinese party helter-skelter out of the square, whereupon a mob of the lowest elements in the city, aroused by the incident and intent on exterminating every foreigner in the place, surrounded the factories, where howling disorder prevailed for several hours. Every window had been broken and battering rams were being placed against the doors when Hunter and another American, Gideon Nye, managed to escape over the rooftops from the besieged area and get Howqua, unaware of what was happening, to send for the police. These arrived soon after, dealing with the crowd with customary ruthlessness, slashing out at them widely with bamboo poles. Many left the square with broken arms and bleeding heads, and in the stampede to escape several were pushed by others into the river where, being unable to swim, they drowned, some of them within a few yards of boats whose occupants, as was ever the case in China, made no attempt to save them. Within a short time there was tranquillity again.

From Macao Elliot, alarmed by report of the riot, which was certainly the gravest there had ever been in Canton for the foreigners, came up at once to Canton without a pass. In company with a section of the British merchants he believed that a catastrophe was imminent. Calling a general meeting of his countrymen he urged them to cooperate with him in stopping the illegal movement of opium between Lintin and Whampoa. But many of those present had too much experience of China coast crises to be upset by this one. Elliot seemed to their supercilious eyes to be inexperienced and emotional, while his clear intention of damaging their opium profits strengthened the dislike and misgivings they had felt about him from the start. Only very few paid attention to his appeal.

Undeterred by their attitude, Elliot reopened correspondence with the Governor in an endeavour to veer off the crisis of whose approach he rightly remained convinced. But Palmerston's insistence about petitions had damaged the status Elliot had been gradually gaining by his own methods, and he now found himself obliged to correspond on a lower level, dealing solely with the Governor's subordinates, through the Co-Hong. He accepted this as a compromise necessitated by the urgency of the situation, but in doing so he aroused toward himself violent ill-feeling among the British mercantile community. From this moment forth nearly everything that Elliot did was wrong according to the opium merchants, for whom he became the target of their own frustrations, anxieties and discontent. Elliot was not at his best when dealing with the merchants. In word and action he had a tendency to be off-key with them, as he often was in his despatches to Palmerston. The opium merchants were, however, a group of whom one can still wonder that they excited the sympathy they did.

But here, though no one in Canton knew it at the time, the die was already cast when James Matheson, by his public relations campaign, dropped the pebble which rippled the waters in England. The event which was to make that ripple tremble into the reverberation of war was the crisis Elliot foresaw approaching and which struck a week or so after his arrival in Canton.

Late in January 1839 the Emperor's decision on the opium issue became known. Within a few hours the opium trade withered away. The greatest and most sudden drop in prices ever recorded took place. Even the Calcutta market stagnated. It happened without any action on the part of Governor Têng, though this officer continued issuing stern warnings and in February succeeded in having a Chinese opium dealer strangled in front of the factories. The standstill in the Pearl River actually took place without any action by anyone locally—merely as a result of a brush-stroke by His Celestial Majesty in Peking.

In order to observe what happened then we must be introduced to the most celebrated Chinese personage in the history of China's maritime relations with barbarians, to a name known today from one end of China to the other, renowned as a hero and extolled as one of China's greatest public servants, an ever-living example of incorruptibility and devotion to duty. I find it necessary to describe him thus at the outset because otherwise no occasion will occur to place him in his true Chinese perspective, where he stands prominent in the roll of honour. We, due to the circumstances in which we met him, have ever since found ourselves looking more at his shortcomings than at his virtues. Since for this reason he has often been underrated in the West, let us begin by being quite clear that we are now encountering one of the great names in the history of the Ch'ing dynasty, a person of whom Chinese today will hear no wrong. That done, let us be honest about him as we see him, which is not in all respects quite as the Chinese do.

IV: THE ARRIVAL OF LIN TSE-HSÜ AT CANTON

The most impressive memorial on the subject of opium to be laid before the Dragon Throne during 1838 was written by Lin Tse-hsü, a Fukienese official at the time Governor of Hupeh and Hunan. The memorial was longer than most, masterly and forceful, indeed even today one of the most remarkable documents ever written on the subject, displaying the most detailed knowledge of opium smoking, the trade, the smokers, their habits and the drug's effects. Lin Tse-hsü wrote with assurance because, as he explained, he had recently had to take stern measures against the vice in his provinces. He recommended the application of a similar policy in Kwangtung.

The memorial demonstrated such a grasp of the subject that the Emperor called Lin to Peking, and after many interviews decided that if opium was to be suppressed (which was Lin's considered advice) Lin Tse-hsü was the man to do it. Lin was elevated to a rank superior to Hoppo and Governor, superior in fact to any official Canton had ever seen. As Imperial High Commissioner, personal emissary of the Emperor, embodied with imperial power, he was to go to Canton and stamp out the opium trade utterly and for ever. Secondly, because of the old story that the imperial exchequer could not afford to be without revenue from foreign trade, he was to re-establish normal trade relations at Canton as they had existed prior to 1834, i.e. under the East India Company. Lin Tse-hsü confidently undertook to the Emperor that these two orders would be carried out. It was the mere knowledge of his approach that made the opium trade wither away.

In March 1839, watched by a concourse of thousands of people on the river—the only time within living memory that the human turbulence of the river was hushed into silence, the greatest Chinese mark of respect, all the river's hundreds of boats momentarily still—the Imperial High Commissioner arrived, seated alone beneath a canopy at the head of a fleet of mandarin boats ornamented in black and gold, with coloured flags streaming from them. Stern of mien, looking to neither right nor left, he passed amid the awesome quiet.

Lin Tse-hsü was portly, with long black moustaches and a smooth and even countenance. 'Of all the Chinamen I have ever seen', wrote Wells Williams, 'Lin was decidedly the finest-looking and the most intelligent. He was indeed a very superior man, and if he had only been better informed he might have brought the difficult business intrusted to him to a much more creditable issue than he did; but this his ignorance and the conceit that accompanies ignorance prevented. . . . He was naturally much elated at his rank, and the absolute power entrusted to him led him to commit acts of rashness which recoiled upon himself.'

It was to be the greatest occasion when the age-old Chinese belief that barbarians could be controlled by threats was put to the test—and the last. For this was what Wells Williams meant when he referred to Lin's ignorance. Like every educated Chinese of his day Lin knew nothing about foreign nations or their institutions. In assuming a threatening attitude, a course he appears to have decided on prior to arrival, he made no effort to weigh up the forces against him. He had no opinion of foreign intelligence or power. He did not even know where England was, apparently reckoning it to be some 2,500 miles from China. Like most Chinese of his rank he was aware that Britain was master of India, which one would have thought could have provided him a clue; but in China the size of India was unknown, and there was no reliable information about it dating later than the seventh century—a mere twelve hundred years out of date—while popular belief was that India was a land of monsters, deformities and wild animals—hardly an important conquest. Indeed the more one examines what Lin knew, the greater grows the tragedy of what he did not know, for he was in truth, as Wells Williams said, a very superior man. The tragedy, if one analyses it, is that he did not turn to a single European source of information before taking action. All his information about foreigners, the opium trade, the importance of the China trade to the foreign countries concerned, all the information in sum which could have formed the basis of a settlement between the Canton authorities and the traders, was gained from Chinese sources, most of them unreliable.

Charles Elliot missed the spectacle of Lin's arrival. Realizing that the British were in for serious trouble within a matter of days, he had gone down to Macao to take what precautions were possible for the safety of British men and women there. On his way down-river he noticed large fleets of war and fire junks assembled, evidently for a surprise assault on the Lintin anchorage, which was now clearly no longer safe. At Macao he advised all British shipping to leave Lintin and shelter for the time being in Hongkong harbour. He then asked the Governor of Macao, Adrião Accacio da Silveira Pinto, if all British subjects in Macao could be placed under Portuguese protection, a request which the Governor granted in the case of all except those engaged in the opium business. Ambiguous as this was, Elliot accepted it as a step in the direction he had in mind, which was that if the Chinese really turned on the pressure and the British were forced out of Canton, Macao was the only place they could sensibly turn to for accommodation and safety. Elliot had privately concluded, in other words, that the Portuguese must and could be induced out of their neutrality, coming down firmly on the British side.

V: THE SIEGE OF THE FACTORIES

In Canton, after a few days of private investigation, the Imperial High Commissioner issued an irrevocable order that all the opium stored at the factories and at Whampoa was to be surrendered forthwith for destruction. Foreign ships at Whampoa were cut off from those at Lintin and Hongkong by heavy Chinese naval forces, and troops surrounded the factories, from which a line of boats across the river made escape impossible.

Quite a number of the opium merchants still did not appreciate that this was no ordinary crisis, and when Lin made his demand the foreigners, acting on the advice of the Hong merchants, offered to surrender 1,037 chests of opium, as it were to propitiate the High Commissioner. But Lin Tse-hsü was a very different type of mandarin from those to whom Canton was accustomed. After rejecting the foreigners' offer outright, he sent word to Lancelot Dent, who was believed to have about 6,000 chests, inviting him for an interview within the city.

The foreign community of all nationalities combined in a resolve that Dent should on no account go. All Chinese servants were thereupon ordered to leave the factories, and all supplies, including water, were cut off. A few days of impasse ensued, during which Lin repeated his demand to see Dent.

At that moment occurred a picturesque scene which comes to us vividly through the surviving documents of the time. Leaderless, besieged and beginning to be anxious, the British unexpectedly found the Queen's representative in their midst. Elliot, having bravely made his way up from Macao past all Chinese obstacles, reached the besieged factories, before which

185

he symbolically hoisted the Union Jack. Even among that gang of respectable, God-fearing drug-pedlars not a few hearts were stirred. After this, with a gesture Dent did not entirely relish, Elliot placed him under his personal protection, obliging him to share his rooms.

Elliot's instructions from Palmerston were scarcely relevant to ordinary circumstances in the Pearl River, and contained nothing relevant to a crisis such as this. But someone had to take a lead, and among the British it could be none other than Elliot himself. He thus proceeded to deal with the situation on his sole initiative and responsibility. He first asked the Chinese for permits for the whole British community to leave. When this was refused and Lin remained unalterable in his demands, after three days Elliot ordered that all British-owned opium be delivered to him for surrender to the Chinese, the British Government to decide at a later date what compensation should be paid to the merchants.

They, hearing there was to be compensation, complied readily enough, though doubtful of the necessity. Their doubt increased when they discovered that Elliot intended surrendering every chest of opium they possessed. Despite Elliot's offer to Lin to do this, however, the situation in the factories remained extremely uncertain. In addition to ordering the total surrender of opium, Lin was demanding that every merchant sign a bond undertaking never to bring any more opium to China and acknowledging themselves punishable by death according to the laws of China should they ever be found to have broken their undertaking. When Elliot, in the name of the entire British community, refused to countenance this, it touched a responsive chord among his fellow-countrymen, whose memories of Chinese law as administered by Governor Têng were recent and vivid. Though the merchants did not really agree with Elliot's policy in surrendering so much opium—it was a question of degree; everyone realized that some opium must be surrendered—they were united with him to a great extent on the question of signing bonds.

With the siege of the factories in its fourth week the position had been reached that Elliot had offered Lin 20,283 chests of opium, but was still arguing to obtain a lifting of the siege without the traders having to sign bonds, the British position being weakened and the siege unduly prolonged by the fact that Americans and others were signing bonds as required. Concurrently Elliot had come to the conclusion that to continue using Canton as a commercial base, where the British were so completely at the mercy of the Chinese as the present situation showed them to be, was unfeasible. More than ever his ideas were veering to the alternative of Macao.

In a despatch to Governor Silveira Pinto, Elliot now offered on behalf of the British Government as much credit as the Macao government needed to put the settlement in a full state of defence. He suggested arming a number of vessels to act as coast-guards, and that in the event of siege by the Chinese there should be arrangements to provision the city direct from Manila. In such an eventuality, Elliot stated, British subjects could by his authority be at the Governor's disposal for the protection of Macao in the interests of the Portuguese Crown.

Silveira Pinto declined these suggestions, explaining that in the peculiar position of Macao he must maintain his neutrality as long as he could. But within a few days Lin Tse-hsü started turning on the pressure around Macao as well as at the foreign factories, making Silveira Pinto realize he might soon be glad of British help. Chinese at Macao's barrier gate increased their scrutiny of goods passing from Macao into the country, and there were clear indications of a build-up to one of the immemorial blockades which in the past had invariably brought Macao to heel. In haste Silveira Pinto ordered all godowns and warehouses in the city to be emptied of opium, the 3,000 chests thus declared being put aboard ship and despatched to Manila, where incidentally James Matheson too was arranging to transfer his opium headquarters.

In May, when the siege of the factories had lasted six weeks and while the removal of the vast quantity of opium quoted by Elliot was being effected, all foreigners unconnected with the opium trade were permitted to leave Canton. Americans, feeling they were less involved than the British, in general stayed on and did well for themselves in consequence. But the British, who had been pretty shaken by the siege, had had enough of Canton for the time being. As throughout the month of May the siege was gradually lifted they reassembled at Macao, where to their surprise they were cordially received by Governor Silveira Pinto. A suggestion made recently by Lin that he might find it necessary to occupy the forts of Macao had un-expectedly brought the Portuguese closer into sympathy with the British than they had been for more than fifty years. Elliot's views being what they were, it seemed as if, under some such arrangement as that which he had earlier proposed, Macao would become the next seat of British commerce in China.

Of all the British besieged in Canton, Elliot was the last to leave. In the end he won his point about bonds. No Briton signed one. But the point was only gained by a compromise whereby sixteen of those whom the Chinese considered the worst opium offenders gave written guarantees to leave China and never return. Trade was resumed. News of the surrender of the opium chests caused the price to rise slightly in Calcutta, enabling trade to be resumed there too. In other words . . .

'This affair has been well managed', wrote the Emperor Tao Kuang after reading Lin Tse-hsü's report.

XII

THE BRITISH WITH THEIR
BACKS TO THE SEA

I: LIN'S UNYIELDING POLICY

UP TILL NOW everything had gone well for Lin, and he shines
from whatever angle one looks in a very favourable light. His
magnanimity and consideration toward Elliot, once Lin knew
that the Englishman was in earnest about surrendering all
opium, show Lin Tse-hsü to have been an unusually pleasing
person, generous in his response to honour. Indeed the con-
frontation of Lin and Elliot is a fascinating spectacle. Here in
a setting of utter dishonesty, hypocrisy and double-dealing
stood, at the head of their respective nations, two men similar
in their transparent honesty, in their courtesy and forbearance,
and in their detestation of the opium trade. The difference
between their outlooks at this point is that Lin believed he had
prevailed upon the barbarians to reform their ways, that a
new and better era had been inaugurated, contemplating which
he was elated and very confident, while Elliot knew too well
that unless Lin did a great deal more and continuously the
entire episode would rank as nothing more than another
skirmish where a campaign was needed. It was Elliot's certainty
that there would be further trouble once the fresh opium already
on its way from Calcutta started arriving—that it was impossible to stop the British bringing it or the Chinese smoking it—
that made him so determined to shift the headquarters of trade
to Macao. Opium traders or whatever they were, never again

must the British be placed within the jaws of that vice at Canton.

In effect Lin Tse-hsü had so far performed only part of his duties. He had yet to undertake the second item of his instructions, to restore normal conditions of trade—which meant the old seasonal trade at Canton. It was now June. By September he had somehow to effect the return of the foreigners to Canton for a normal season. He was elated and confident. By threats and intimidation he had succeeded over the opium. He now proceeded to deal with the restoration of trade in the same manner.

But whereas on the earlier occasion the British were within Lin's grasp at Canton, they were now no longer so. They were down among those islands where barbarians were traditionally told not to loiter. The reason why after telling them not to loiter there the Chinese traditionally never did anything further was that they knew full well it was beyond their capacity to control this area. Not without good reason did the Portuguese give the islands at the mouth of the river their European name, the Ladrones (*ladrões*), the Robbers. One of the most lawless areas in China, only two administrations (the Mongols and the present government) have ever made any pretence at keeping the Ladrones free of pirates and robbers. What line of reasoning, one immediately asks oneself, could have made an intelligent man like Lin Tse-hsü believe that by threatening and intimidating the barbarians when they were down there he could induce them to return to Canton? Far more likely—and one is initially amazed that Lin did not appreciate this—was that the British would either seize an island and be damned with Canton, or would sail away to Manila.

Basic in Lin's reasoning was the belief that the lure of money among the barbarians was so great that nothing would ever persuade them to leave China, a belief supported by the fact that Americans were throughout this period doing without protest everything they were asked in their determination to carry on trading, signing whatever they were told to sign, acknowledging themselves subject to Chinese criminal law, and accepting every condition Lin chose to impose. Here at its clearest is exposed the curious part the Americans played, by their very lack of policy, in the events leading to war with China. It was the old story. If the Americans could be obedient, so could the British. Lin seriously believed that by making things thoroughly uncomfortable for the British down at the mouth of the river he could force them *in*, not out, to place themselves once more within the jaws of Canton.

II: LIN'S INTIMIDATION OF THE BRITISH—A MURDER AT
KOWLOON—THE BRITISH WITHDRAWAL FROM MACAO

The British were now concentrated at two places, on land at Macao and on shipboard in Hongkong harbour. Hongkong has gently grown into these pages much as it grew upon the British of those times, and before it grows any more it should be explained how this came about.

In the days when the trade lay between Macao and Whampoa, in the heyday of the tea trade, Europeans had little reason to go near Hongkong and its neighbouring islands, which were off their beaten track. As the papers of the Amherst mission show, by 1816 the British knew about Hongkong, which had already acquired its inexplicable name (in Cantonese Heung Kong, meaning Fragrant Harbour).[1] But it was not at that time realized that between Hongkong and the mainland lay one of the largest and most perfect natural harbours in the world. The development of Lintin as an opium depôt from about 1818 onwards brought the British nearer the region, but it was not until Baynes' embargo of 1829 that Hongkong really comes into the picture. At that time the withdrawal of British shipping from Whampoa necessitated a search for good anchorages within easy distance of Lintin, and it was in the course of this search that the advantages of Hongkong harbour were

---

[1] Chinese do not usually give names to islands as large as Hongkong, i.e. to islands which cannot at once be *seen* to be islands. Thus when in the Introduction to this book I refer to the islands of the region as 'nameless', this is not meant to imply neglect on the part of the Chinese authorities. Minor islands were usually identified by the name of the principal village on them. There was no village called Hongkong, and it can only be assumed that the appellation was a fishermen's name for a stretch of water adjacent to Hongkong Island, and where there was good fishing. The name applies to water, and not to land. The most likely place is on the south side of the island, between Aberdeen (Heungkong Tsai) and the protecting islet of Aplichau; but this has not been definitely established.

discovered. From 1829 not a year passed without some British ships anchoring in the great sheltered space of water between Hongkong and the mainland.

Ten years later it was still a remote and neglected area, Hongkong a gaunt granite sea-mountain with patches of scrub growing where it could amid the rock, down which the summer rain cascaded in lugubrious waterfalls. Facing the harbour were one or two small villages, but the mark they made in the grim landscape was so insignificant that only with the aid of a glass could it be seen that the island was not entirely uninhabited. Opposite on the mainland, where now stands the glittering, skyscrapered mass of Kowloon, was a peninsula of low, rocky hillocks among which trees grew in isolated clumps in the neighbourhood of secluded villages, near which there were small patches of cultivation. To the British the sole amenity the place offered was its anchorage. To have suggested in 1839 that Europeans might inhabit either Hongkong or the Kowloon peninsula would have been inconceivable.

Lin Tse-hsü now proceeded with his oddly conceived and unrealistic campaign of threatening the British at Macao and Hongkong as a means of driving them back to Canton. To render conditions precarious for them at both of their stations he organized impressive demonstrations of Chinese military and naval strength. In the near neighbourhood of the British ships at Hongkong he constructed forts, and installed large bodies of soldiers at the foot of Kowloon peninsula, which here juts out into the main waters of the harbour, almost bisecting it. Around Macao the military build-up was so extensive that it appeared to the Portuguese as if Lin was preparing to invest the place.

Well-informed concerning Elliot's good relations with Silveira Pinto, and appreciating that so long as these friendly relations subsisted it would be difficult to persuade the British to think otherwise than in terms of making Macao their next commercial centre, Lin now set about inducing a formal breach between the British and the Portuguese. The Chinese military preparations around Macao served Lin unexpectedly well in this context. Ordinary Macao Portuguese became so alarmed by them that there was a lessening of popular goodwill toward the British, who were seen to be a dangerous liability. Lin was also clever enough to realize he had made a mistake in mentioning the Portuguese forts. This he rectified by assuring Silveira Pinto privately that he did not after all intend occupying the forts. With considerable astuteness he also warned the Portuguese Governor that the British were like birds that seek to possess the nests of others, a warning which at the time bore an uncomfortable resemblance to the truth.

On the British side, since the Chinese were once again insisting on all traders signing bonds before their ships could enter Whampoa, Elliot ordered a total suspension of British trade. Again this was rendered inadequate as a means of obliging Lin to come to more equitable terms due to the large amount of American commerce being conducted in accordance with Lin's requirements; but Elliot considered this was the best he could do in the circumstances.

This situation prevailed, with a certain amount of British trade being done indirectly through Macao, for another six weeks. Then, on 7th July 1839, there occurred one of those classic incidents which had consistently been the landmarks of trouble in Chinese relations with the British. A drunken brawl took place on Kowloon peninsula between British and American sailors and some Chinese ashore. One of the Chinese was killed.

Elliot hastened across from Macao to try the case. At the inquiry it was found impossible to determine which of the sailors was responsible for the death, but several of them were deprived of their freedom on Elliot's orders and compensation was paid to the dead man's family.

Inevitably the incident came to the knowledge of Lin. Shortly after Elliot's return to Macao a Chinese notice was posted at Lin's orders on the Praia Grande accusing Elliot of hushing up by bribery the murder of a Chinese A day or so later came a formal demand for the surrender of the guilty sailor, or any other Englishman, to be dealt with under Chinese law. When no one was given up, the Casa Branca ordered the removal of all Chinese servants from British homes in Macao. For another week the British held on, the Portuguese assisting them in procuring food, while a series of pronouncements was issued threatening that the British would pay for it with their lives if the sailor was not surrendered. Silveira Pinto was requested by the Casa Branca to ensure that no Portuguese assisted the British, who should be left without food and water until they did as they were told. Compared with earlier occasions, on which an incident of this kind would have caused the barrier gate to be closed and the whole of Macao cut off from food supplies, it can be seen that Lin was still treating Silveira Pinto with kid gloves on in an endeavour to split the two nationalities; but as Elliot and Silveira Pinto both realized, this forbearance was unlikely to last more than a few days.

At a meeting of the British community Elliot advised that if they remained any longer in Macao the consequences to the Portuguese might be extremely grave. He announced his own departure, with his family, to join the ships at Hongkong, and urged everyone to take the same action. The day after his departure a small British schooner, in use as a passage boat between Macao and Hongkong, was set upon by Chinese who murdered the entire crew, all of them British, and left the single passenger with an ear cut off. It may have been a chance action by sea-marauders, but it had an electric effect on Macao, where it was followed by Governor Silveira Pinto's final warning to the remaining British that he could not be responsible for the consequences if they were still in the city eighteen hours later.

A final meeting was held at which it was decided that everyone would leave the following morning. As a night attack by the Chinese on individual British houses was feared, most of them spent the night awake. Next day, 26th August, they embarked, every one of them, even Chinnery (who was found trembling at the head of his own staircase, afraid even to come down), each of them taking a few possessions. The neutral, diplomatic, considerate, but profoundly anxious Governor saw them off, completing his display of friendliness to the British side by handing the ladies aboard.

Eight days later Lin Tse-hsü entered Macao to enjoy the triumph of the second of his victories. First he had suppressed the opium trade. Now he had succeeded in reducing the number of British stations at the river mouth from two to one. Next before him lay the crucial engagement of forcing the British out of Hongkong harbour and back to Canton. Needless to say, the perfectly neutral Portuguese Governor welcomed Lin as courteously as he had bidden farewell to the British. For Macao's survival there was no alternative.

Life in a ship in Hongkong harbour was not easy. Although water could be procured without difficulty from hillside streams on Hongkong Island, it was virtually impossible for Shaukiwan, Wongneichong and the other small villages facing the harbour to provide enough livestock and vegetables for the large concourse in the European ships. To land on the Kowloon side of the harbour (the mainland) would certainly lead to collisions with Chinese military forces, in addition to which Lin was causing notices to be posted up in all coastal villages inciting villagers to attack any Britons attempting to land.

Cramped, uncomfortable, not particularly aware of being threatened by the Chinese, fed up with Elliot's trade stoppage, and unable to see where all this shipboard discomfort was leading, the British reached a peak point in their dissatisfaction with Elliot's leadership. Delayed-action resentment at having been forced to surrender so much opium had swollen on gossip emanating from the Hong merchants to the effect that if Elliot had not been so hasty Lin would have been perfectly satisfied with a surrender of seven or eight thousand chests instead of the formidable twenty thousand actually turned in. It was this—having yielded too many chests—that the opium merchants never forgave Elliot. Their 'experienced' view that from the start he made a mountain out of a molehill so pervades the thought of the period that even today is is quite hard to perceive the truth, which was that Elliot judged the situation correctly and took the only possible course. He might indeed have held back a few thousand opium chests hidden away somewhere, but the risk of doing so with a man like Lin was tremendous, besides which Elliot's honesty would not have enabled him to countenance such a subterfuge. Reference is made on many occasions to the fact that even Howqua said

Elliot surrendered more opium than he need. Howqua was merely being polite to Britons who had already made up their minds on the matter. What Howqua said to the Americans is more to the point, when he warned them even before Lin reached Canton that the opium trade would be finished. There can be no doubt whatever that Elliot's appraisal of Lin Tse-hsü was a correct one.

As people saw it in the ships at Hongkong, however, Elliot had so far done nothing but lead them backwards. The retreat to Hongkong had achieved nothing, and in addition there were those smaller things which at such times figure so large. The weather was at its hottest and most uncomfortable, periods of broiling sunshine being interrupted by torrential tropical downpours. Many of the evacuees had left at Macao beautiful houses, splendidly furnished with valuable possessions, now left uncared for, at the mercy of anyone who cared to walk in and help themselves. In a mood derived from such considerations British unity was not to be counted on.

Elliot, aware of this and of the fact that he himself was the main target of dissatisfaction, opened negotiations almost at once for a return to Macao. His first letter to Silveira Pinto arrived when Lin's visit to the city was daily expected, and the reply was consequently on the usual tone of neutrality. Later in September three-sided negotiations began between Elliot, Silveira Pinto and the Mandarin of the Casa Branca (reporting to Lin). Meanwhile, fed up with ship life and with the general hopelessness of the situation, individuals began returning to Macao—to find incidentally that their Portuguese neighbours had taken care of their houses, from which nothing was stolen.

When the Mandarin of the Casa Branca reported to Lin that Elliot had opened negotiations, the Imperial High Commissioner deduced that his threatenings had been effective and his policy proved entirely correct. He had the British on their knees at last, begging to be allowed to return. In accordance with this misguided judgement, as the negotiations continued he increased his demands. He sent down orders that whatever the conclusion reached, every Englishman on arrival in China, whether trader or not, must sign a bond placing himself voluntarily within the jurisdiction of Chinese law. Elliot, who still held firmly to the view that the British must never again place themselves at the mercy of the Chinese even by installing themselves within the Bocca Tigris, maintained his absolute refusal to allow any Briton to sign a bond.

The arguments proceeded for a month, nearing deadlock, until in the latter part of October a British ship, the *Thomas Coutts*, arriving from India, ignored Elliot entirely, sailed to the Bocca Tigris, signed the second of the bonds demanded by Lin, and proceeded to Whampoa, where the Chinese treated her with every consideration.

It was just the situation Lin had been waiting for. Promptly breaking off discussions with Elliot, he issued notices declaring that unless within three days every Briton signed the required bonds the European ships in Hongkong harbour would be attacked and the houses of all those people who had returned to Macao would be surrounded.

Elliot had at his disposal two recently arrived British warships, H.M.S. *Volage* and H.M.S. *Hyacinth*. Captain Smith, commander of *Volage*, was an officer of enterprise and resolution. Though under orders from the Admiralty to avoid direct hostilities with the Chinese, he now suggested to Elliot that he answer demand by counterdemand. Accordingly on 2nd November 1839 Elliot and Smith sailed with the two warships to the Bocca Tigris to deliver to the Admiral in charge a letter addressed to High Commissioner Lin and Governor Têng demanding that within three days proclamations be published by the Chinese stating that the offensive notices concerning Britons landing ashore were withdrawn and that, in effect, British traders and their families might resume residence in Macao without fear of interference with their servants or supplies.

It happened that Lin and Têng were inspecting the Bocca defences. When therefore Admiral Kwan T'ien-pei, in charge of a fleet of twenty-nine powerful war junks, replied that Elliot's letter would be delivered promptly and that until a reply was received he would be obliged if the British ships would move slightly downstream away from the junks, the British anticipated an early reply and complied with the Admiral's request.

No answer was received that day. The ships passed the night without significant movement. In the morning, however, the Chinese fleet was seen to be forming to bear down upon the two British frigates. The British quickly weighed anchor and prepared to meet attack, seeing which Admiral Kwan, his ships now a good deal nearer them, ordered his fleet to anchor. The British did the same.

Captain Smith next requested John Morrison, who was with the expedition, to translate into Chinese a peremptory demand that the Chinese retreat to their former positions. In reply came a note from Kwan saying that if the British sailor responsible for the Kowloon murder were surrendered forthwith he would retire, but not otherwise, and returning unanswered Elliot's letter to Lin.

It was unsafe to allow the Chinese fleet to remain where it was until nightfall. Having fallen downstream the British frigates were in a wider part of the river, and the Chinese might easily slip past in the night and carry out their proclaimed intention of attacking the merchant ships at Hongkong, between which the frigates rode as the sole defence; while to retire—the pacific alternative—after the exchange of communications just recounted 'was not compatible with the honour of the flag', as Elliot expressed it to Palmerston. With Elliot's approval therefore, at about noon on 3rd November 1839, Captain Smith hoisted signals for an engagement; and the Chinese, having dealt with Europeans on their coasts for three hundred and twenty-seven years, at last found themselves at war with them.

XIII

ELLIOT'S MISUNDERSTOOD
COURSE

THE BRITISH FRIGATES, as Elliot afterwards described the event, 'then lying hove to, on the extreme right of the Chinese force, bore away in a line ahead and close order, having the wind on the starboard beam. In this way, and under sail, they ran down the Chinese line, pouring in a destructive fire. The lateral direction of the wind enabled the ships to perform the the same evolution from the opposite extreme of the line, running it up again with the larboard broadsides bearing. The Chinese answered with their accustomed spirit; but the terrible effect of our own fire was soon manifest. One war-junk blew up at about pistol shot distance from the *Volage*, a shot probably having passed through the magazine; three were sunk and several others were obviously water-logged.'

Admiral Kwan, in complete disregard of his own safety, personally directed the Chinese part in the battle from the bows of his flagship in the thick of the fire. 'In less than three-quarters of an hour, however, he and the remainder of the squadron were retiring in great distress to their former anchorage.'

Considering they had done enough, the British withdrew to Macao to take aboard any of their countrymen who might think it advisable in view of the new and more serious turn events had taken to quit the city once more.

This brought to an end the action known, after the part of the river in which it was fought, as the first Battle of Chuenpé. Its first immediate result came three days later, when news of it was reported to the Chinese military forces on Kowloon peninsula, who by way of answer opened a shore cannonade on the British merchant ships. The gunfire was not particularly effective, but it decided the Europeans to evacuate Hongkong harbour and move to an anchorage beside the small island of Tungkwu, situated between Lintin and the equally sharp mainland hill known as Castle Peak.

The general Chinese reaction to the battle was the same throughout—a hardening of attitude. When news of it reached Peking the Emperor issued a decree debarring the British for ever from trade with China, while in Canton, though there was cosmologically no such thing as a war with maritime barbarians (from the sea there were only pirates to fight), additional forces were raised and things put on a war footing.

When the Emperor's decree was published in Canton, on 6th December 1839, Elliot negotiated first with Lin and then with Silveira Pinto in an effort to obtain trading rights at Macao, but without result. The Battle of Chuenpé had made it even more important to the Portuguese Governor to demonstrate to the Chinese the coolness of his relations with the British. Not only did he refuse to allow British goods to be stored temporarily in Macao, but when a fresh batch of Chinese notices was issued actually inciting Chinese in Macao to murder all Britons, the Governor allowed them to be posted up.

War or no war, however—and to most foreigners it looked strangely unlike a war—trade was once more in full swing. British goods, including opium, were passing up-river from Tungkwu to Whampoa in American and other neutral ships, all of whose owners had signed the bonds demanded by Lin. The Americans were doing such a swift business out of this that several of their leading firms, including Russell's, established additional agents on shipboard amid the British at Tungkwu. At Macao the same indirect trade arrangements were in operation, benefiting those British merchants who had returned to the settlement.

On 4th February 1840, as soon as he became aware of the murderous notices being exhibited, Captain Smith sailed H.M.S. *Hyacinth* into Macao's inner harbour to effect another British evacuation, causing the highest alarm to the Governor and Senate, who refused Smith all facilities and ordered him to leave at once, which he was reluctantly obliged to do unless he would risk endangering the British community still further.

Meanwhile Lin Tse-hsü, become Governor of Kwangtung and Kwangsi in succession to Têng, hastened on his programme of armament, even purchasing foreign ships from the Americans (the summit point of the American soft line) and attempting to train his levies in Western methods of warfare. Volunteers were raised from the lowest elements of Chinese society, pirates, bandits and fishermen, and prices were placed on the heads of the principal Englishmen involved, the highest being Elliot, whose head was valued at $5,000. For the first time it appeared just possible that the British might soon be in sufficient danger to necessitate a temporary evacuation on a larger scale than hitherto.

II: JARDINE IN LONDON—A BRITISH EXPEDITIONARY FORCE AT CHUSAN AND TIENTSIN—THE APPOINTMENT OF KISHEN AS NEGOTIATOR

But this was not to be. Public opinion in England, where nothing was yet known of the Battle of Chuenpé or that a virtual state of war existed between Britain and China, had at last been roused. The siege of the Canton factories, reported in London in the latter part of 1839, served to deflect attention from the opium issue and concentrate it on the simpler and more dramatic theme of British lives in danger. Jardine, who on Matheson's return to China had left on retirement six weeks before Lin's descent upon Canton, found himself in London at a moment when his presence could not have been more appropriate, and took pains to exploit the siege of the factories to the best advantage. Significant of his political shrewdness, he who in China was an arch-opponent of Elliot, in England stressed the indignities suffered by the Queen's representative. In January 1840 the young Queen Victoria, in her speech from the Throne at Westminster, referred to events in China that affected the interests of her subjects and the dignity of the Crown; and in the following month Jardine was advising Palmerston on the measures needed to protect the British in China.

This time Palmerston listened to a man with experience of China and whose advice was unquestionably sound, doubly so in view of the fact that, though neither of them knew it, war had already broken out. Jardine was far more Palmerston's type of man than George Staunton or any of the other sino-logues would have been, men whose counsel the great Foreign Secretary would have found altogether too intellectual, am-biguous and complicated, almost sinister in its sinuosity as enunciated in the crisp air and cool temperature of Whitehall, far from the balmy climate and strange realities of the Pearl River.

In such circumstances it was not surprising that the Govern-ment's measures embodied precisely what had all along been advocated by Jardine and Matheson. An expeditionary force was prepared, with orders to use the maximum restraint before committing any action involving bloodshed, the force's main purpose being to provide a suitably impressive escort for the delivery to Peking of a despatch from Palmerston making certain demands. These included reparation for the insults offered to the Superintendent of Trade (Elliot) and his formal recognition as such, the opening of additional ports to foreign traders, an indemnity for the surrendered opium and other losses suffered by British merchants, and proper security in future for Britons residing in China for lawful purposes.

As compensation for the indignities offered to the Queen's representatives and subjects in China the British Government was prepared to accept the cession of one or more islands on the coast, and it would be desirable for some such islands to be taken by force prior to negotiation (one of Jardine's main points). 'If, however, the Chinese Government should express a wish that instead of making the cession of such islands, they should give by Treaty, Security and freedom of commerce to H.M.'s subjects resident in China, the British Government would not object to such an arrangement, and would in that case forego the permanent possession of any Island on the Chinese Coast.'

Two plenipotentiaries were appointed, Rear-Admiral George Elliot and his cousin, the Superintendent, Captain Charles Elliot. The forces were commanded, under their orders, by Commodore Sir James John Gordon Bremer, the force consisting of three battleships, fourteen frigates and sloops, four armed steamers of the East India Company, and about 4,000 British and Indian troops conveyed aboard twenty-seven troopships.

Late in June 1840, after the force had assembled in Hongkong harbour and the local situation of war had been assessed, Bremer declared a blockade of Canton, and accompanied by the two plenipotentiaries sailed northward, seized Tinghai on the island of Chusan, and at Tientsin presented Palmerston's despatch to the Governor of Chihli (modern Hopeh) for transmission to Peking.

In the south Lin Tse-hsü continued his former tactics. In August, whilst the British were waiting for the Emperor's reply and trying to consolidate their hold on Chusan, more notices appeared in Macao; a young British missionary was captured while having a swim; and it was reported that Lin, angered by the return of the British to Macao, was proposing sending an army to drive them out.

Captain Smith, feeling the situation demanded another of his demonstrations of force, sailed an armed steamer near the barrier gate, landed some British troops north of it, and after a short engagement, in which he completely routed the Chinese soldiery, destroyed the barrier buildings and barracks. Thousands of Macao Chinese watched the engagement, but without excitement; 'they quietly looked on, and when the action was over, returned home to tell what they had seen', wrote Wells Williams, adding that many of them were not displeased to see their braggadocio troops routed—'for to understand this feeling it should be mentioned that a body of soldiers is one of the greatest annoyances to a Chinese village that can infest it'.

At the end of August, after three weeks of waiting, Kishen, the Manchu Governor of Chihli, was authorized by the Emperor to negotiate with the British in the Peiho. Charles Elliot was the spokesman, and after heated argument and much plain speaking with Kishen it was agreed that if discussions (to be held, at Chinese insistence, in the south—always with the aim of keeping unpleasant things as far away as possible) for a resumption of trade at Canton and Macao were put in hand forthwith, British forces would be withdrawn from all parts of the coast except Chusan, which they would continue to hold as a pledge of China's serious intentions.

After another three weeks the Emperor ratified this agreement. What it conceded was slight, but it was already too much for Tao Kuang. Lin Tse-hsü was dismissed and formally disgraced. In his place the Emperor put what surely must rank as one of the most impossible combinations of men ever formed in any civil service. Kishen was transferred from Chihli to Kwangtung as Governor, but he was given two advisers of equal rank. One of these was none other than Lin Tse-hsü, who though disgraced was ordered to remain in Canton. The other was the Governor before him, Têng Ting-chên, now Governor of Fukien. Since both these men had been removed for reasons of personal inadequacy from the office to which Kishen was now appointed, the amount of advice he might expect from them requires no comment. It was rather worse than this, however. Lin Tse-hsü and Têng Ting-chên became united in a desire to bring about Kishen's downfall at the earliest moment.

III: ELLIOT AND KISHEN—PRELIMINARIES OF A TREATY—THE BRITISH OCCUPATION OF HONGKONG

Thus when the two principal antagonists faced one another again, in the Pearl River in November 1840, there was a peculiar similarity in their positions. Kishen and Elliot were both moderate and level-headed men with some understanding (more than that in Elliot's case) of the forces confronting them. Kishen was under pressure from all the most responsible opinion in South China to exterminate the foreigners and drive them away for ever, rather than let them occupy Chusan and dictate terms to China. On his side Elliot found his countrymen supercilious and unimpressed by the Peiho agreement. It seemed to most of them ridiculous to bring so great a force to China to be used for nothing more substantial than to obtain formally what before Napier's mission they already enjoyed informally: trading facilities at Macao and Lintin. They did not understand Elliot's method of proceeding by short but secure steps one at a time. Nor perhaps did the traders know that he was under orders to use the maximum restraint in the use of military force, which was what he was doing.

Early in December Admiral Elliot, who was seriously ill, was obliged to return to England, leaving his cousin in his former sole control, although now with wider powers. The reaction of the British merchants was a foregone conclusion. In letters home they fulminated against the weakness of Charles Elliot in handling the Chinese, and moved their friends in London to approach Palmerston to obtain his dismissal. Elliot and Kishen, both aware of the forces at work against them amongst their own people, reopened their negotiations in a state of personal uncertainty that gave to their decisions a quality of detachment and unreality.

Elliot made the first move by demanding, as laid down in his instructions, the cession of an island. By the Chinese this demand was considered a disgrace too shameful to be contemplated. This was the attitude which Lin and Têng were careful to put about as soon as Kishen, in accordance with his imperial orders, consulted them on the possibility of allowing the British, as a suggestion of his own, to occupy Amoy or Hongkong.

The discussions, maintained by correspondence or through intermediaries, proceeded slowly, until in January 1841, after six weeks, during which the reputations of Kishen and Elliot at Canton and Macao respectively fell to a freezing point of non-confidence, Elliot delivered an ultimatum that unless by eight o'clock the following morning the Chinese proposed a definite basis for agreement he would seize the Bocca Tigris forts.

No reply being received, the second Battle of Chuenpé took place (7th January) at which in less than two hours the forts were crippled and occupied, 18 Chinese war junks were sunk, 500 Chinese soldiers killed and 300 wounded. The British casualties were 38 wounded, none killed. The Chinese officers in charge of the forts further up the river sent urgent messages to Kishen asking for reinforcements; but the latter took no notice, spending the entire night drafting proposals for submission to Elliot. Admiral Kwan next appeared in the river flying a truce flag and asking for a few days' respite until the proposals arrived. When they did, they asked for the return of Chusan and offered Hongkong as a place of British trade, together with an indemnity for the seized opium.

Elliot promptly accepted this basis for discussion, and on 20th January 1841 preliminaries of a treaty were announced ceding Hongkong Island to the British Crown on condition that 'all just charges and dues to the empire upon the commerce carried on there' be paid 'as if the trade were conducted at Whampoa'. An indemnity of $6,000,000 was to be paid by the Chinese; official intercourse between Great Britain and China was henceforth to be conducted on a basis of equality; and Canton and Whampoa were to be opened to trade within ten days. In consequence, Elliot ordered the immediate evacuation of Chusan, while the Chinese undertook to dismantle the batteries on Kowloon peninsula.

In several respects these terms fell short of the royal instructions. Chusan should have been held till the treaty was ratified, and the imposition of Chinese commercial dues in Hongkong would be a sure source of trouble of the kind Macao had with the Chinese customs and the Casa Branca. By the British at Macao the treaty preliminaries were ridiculed, as was everything to do with Elliot by now, the points chiefly selected for criticism being the acquisition of Hongkong, a useless island with scarcely a square foot of flat land on it, and the low amount of the opium indemnity. The entire agreement was held up as the latest and most complete proof of Elliot's weakness as a leader and as a negotiator with the Chinese.

Elliot's decisions at the time were dictated by several factors not fully understood by others. In the first place he understood Kishen's precarious position in respect of Lin Tse-hsü and Têng Ting-chên and the extreme difficulty there must be in persuading Kishen in such circumstances to concede anything of the slightest importance. Elliot knew that Kishen was certain to be disgraced even for the little he had yielded. Elliot's bargaining position furthermore was not nearly so advantageous as the local British—and later Palmerston—imagined. The British hostilities in China had not proved to be the walkover anticipated. Although on Chusan the troops had captured Tinghai, the principal town, they had been unable to make themselves masters of the whole island; and the incidence of disease among the soldiers—unknown fevers (including malaria), dysentery and skin infections—at Tinghai and elsewhere had temporarily crippled the expedition as a fighting force, a fact which must in a matter of days be known in Canton. Elliot thus chose to obtain from Kishen the best terms he could at the moment, before the latter should be replaced by someone more intransigent and the British arms be more severely tested. Knowing how events usually progressed in China he was confident that the future would soon present opportunities for improving on the concessions, and with relief ordered the evacuation of Chusan to prevent further needless waste of life.

If British civilians ridiculed the acquisition of Hongkong, however, to the naval and military officers it was considered a cause for celebration and something to be taken advantage of immediately. On Monday, 25th January, a survey party landed on Hongkong and amid its rocky wastes drank the Queen's health. Next day, without waiting for anything more secure and binding than Elliot's preliminaries, Commodore Bremer entered Hongkong harbour with his squadron and formally took possession of the island.

IV: CANTON AT ELLIOT'S MERCY

Elliot's immediate order to the British forces to evacuate Chusan—indeed his general technique in negotiating—requires some further explanation. It must be remembered that Elliot's chief negotiations hitherto had been conducted with two outstanding men, Lin Tse-hsü and Kishen. Particularly with Lin, Elliot had seen for himself what John Robert Morrison must early have apprised him of: the value which the Chinese attach to their word. From the moment Lin Tse-hsü sensed that in Elliot he was dealing with an honest man his attitude was

throughout the siege of the factories one of integrity recipro-
cated. Never once, having agreed to something, did Lin fail
to keep his word. To a man of Lin's intellectual quality and
standing to break his word, even to a barbarian, was a disgraceful action and one which he would never contemplate.

In Chinese eyes Elliot was a barbarian headman, nothing
more. In the broadest issue the British purpose in China—
which if achieved would of itself resolve the lesser issues of
islands and indemnities—was to change the Chinese traditional
conception of foreigners as being barbarians, bringing the
Celestial Empire to the realization that it was not the only
civilized country in the world, and that people from other
civilized countries must be treated in China as equals.

Foremost among Chinese methods of assessing other people,
as Elliot by now knew well, is judgement according to outward
behaviour. If the Chinese were to be persuaded that it was not
barbarians they were dealing with in the British, at Elliot's
disposal the first and immediate means of demonstrating the
fact was by treating the Chinese as he himself had been dealt
with by Lin Tse-hsü—with scrupulous regard to the keeping
of promises. The Chinese had somehow to be taught, as a
preliminary to understanding far more, that they were not the
only race whose language contained the word 'honour', and
not the only race whose word was their bond. This could only
be explained to them in a convincing way by example—by
outward behaviour. Thus in addition to the urgent need to
have the British troops off Chusan, where they were dying of
disease, there is also in Elliot's action a motive quality of giving
immediate fulfilment to a promise made to Kishen, a line of
thinking which becomes increasingly plain in the steady and
quite remarkable line of promises fulfilled on Elliot's part in
the ensuing months. It also becomes apparent at this time that
Elliot was pursuing a course far beyond the comprehension of
the majority of his countrymen, both in China and in England,
sticking to the spirit of Palmerston's instructions more than
to their letter, for reasons which at that date could only be
grasped by foreigners literate in the Chinese language and
acquainted with Chinese traditions. To them his every action
made sense, but to practically no one else.

As it turned out, in the person of the Emperor Tao Kuang the British plenipotentiary was not dealing with a person of the calibre of Lin Tse-hsü or Kishen. The arrival at Tientsin of a barbarian naval armament of horrifying strength (as the Chinese saw it) had caused alarm in Peking. Its 'obedient' withdrawal further south was interpreted by the *fainéant* on the Dragon Throne as a victory. The British, intimidated by the might of China, were retreating; what was needed, in the Emperor's view, was a final show of force to drive them away for ever. Orders to this effect were issued, and on the very day that Bremer took possession of Hongkong they reached Kishen, authorizing him to assemble a large body of troops and make 'an awful display of Celestial vengeance'. Kishen kept the orders secret. Due to meet Elliot the next day at the Second Bar pagoda for the signing of the preliminaries, Kishen kept his appointment, met the British 'with beaming countenance and a pleasant smile on his lips', and entertained them to lunch in an atmosphere of cordiality and goodwill.

Twelve days later further orders were received from Peking. Kishen was not summarily dismissed; he was stigmatized as having failed in his mission, as Lin before him, but told that he might be spared a similar disgrace if by a supreme effort he could exterminate all the red barbarians. He accordingly repudiated his agreement with Elliot and instituted minor attacks on British shipping. The value of Elliot's head was raised to $30,000. If captured alive, Elliot, Bremer and John Morrison (as usual the interpreters were in special danger) would each fetch $50,000.

This led to the third Battle of Chuenpé (26th February 1841), at which a large number of Chinese were killed, including the valiant Admiral Kwan, and all the principal forts in the Bocca were occupied. After the battle Elliot directed that after surrendering their arms and burying the dead the thousand or so Chinese prisoners taken were to be released unconditionally. (Remembering the unfavourable attitude taken by the mandarins to Anson's seizure and retention of prisoners, another move on Elliot's part can here be observed toward stimulating Chinese respect for 'barbarian' behaviour and motives.) Pressing forward to Whampoa, the British force then overwhelmed the garrison, which consisted of professional soldiers from Hunan province, some of China's best fighting men, and after five days, having reduced all the defences placed in their way, advanced to within a few miles of Canton.

At this point the Chinese sent a plea for a truce, which Elliot conceded. But when it became evident that the Chinese intention was merely to stall over the negotiations while improving the defences of Canton, he ordered a further advance to the walls of the city, where from his flagship in the river he announced in a Chinese proclamation that the war was being fought against the Emperor's bad advisers (a classic argument in all internal rebellions of a patriotic kind in China), and that if trade were resumed the city and its inhabitants would be spared. This announcement, of a kind steeped in Chinese historical tradition, implied in a manner plain to every Chinese a threat to overthrow the dynasty if the British terms were not met.

The plenipotentiary demanded that trade be resumed. In a sense it already had been. As the British fleet advanced up the river, the traders and the opium ships followed. Within an hour or so of the capture of Whampoa the merchants were reinstalling themselves and the price of opium was rising.

Six days later, on 12th March, Kishen was disgraced by the Emperor and publicly led out of Canton in chains, for trial in the capital. Desperate attempts were made by the Chinese officers left in charge of the city to establish masked defences close to the British ships, while the Prefect of Canton, with outward appearance of earnest willingness to come to terms, tried to hold Elliot in parley. Fireships were prepared and new cannon struck on the Chinese side, while day by day the British improved their stranglehold by dismantling the remaining river defences. British troops entered the famous factories and on a word of command could have invested the city.

Elliot, firm but polite, as magnanimous as Lin had been with him when occasion demanded it, maintained his cool attitude of restraint. When another truce was agreed upon, subject to ratification by Peking, he ostentatiously, as a mark of goodwill, transferred his headquarters from Macao to the factories, bringing his wife with him. At the same time he kept himself daily abreast of what the Chinese authorities were reported to be doing. They might, he was aware, be foolish enough to offer resistance and oblige him to order the taking of Canton. If so, he was determined to leave the first move—and thus the entire responsibility—to them. By so doing he intended to make the Chinese nation appreciate the reason and justice of British demands.

Wells Williams, observing events from Macao, approved of Elliot's tactics. 'This instruction of the Chinese Government by degrees', he wrote, 'into a knowledge of the power, forbearance, and resoluteness of foreign nations will, I think, be, in the end, much more salutary and beneficial than an overwhelming attack and great slaughter.'

By mid-May the Chinese preparations for the total extermination of the British by surprise attack were nearing completion. On 20th May, as a deception, a prefectural notice was issued encouraging all Cantonese who wished to trade with foreigners to resume their business without fear. On the night of 21st–22nd May fireships were let loose on the British squadron, masked batteries opened fire from several sides, and a large armed force attacked the factories.

Though well-concerted, the Chinese action was a total failure. Elliot, having received prior information of what was afoot, warned everyone to leave the factories on that particular night and keep all crews on the alert. Due to his excellent intelligence the fireships were all destroyed without damaging a single British ship. The factories were admittedly looted, first by Chinese troops, then by the Canton mob; but no foreigners were found there. The gunfire of the masked batteries was as usual inaccurate. Their positions were pinpointed, and as soon as it was light they were assaulted and demolished, while the river was cleared of armed Chinese shipping, over a hundred war junks and fireships being sunk.

The British forces now moved into positions for a full assault on Canton. Within the city a critical deterioration of conditions took place. Thousands of Chinese began evacuating their families and possessions, while relations between Chinese soldiers and civilians, and between Chinese professional soldiers and volunteers, were so bad that there was a situation verging on civil war. Truly scared at last, the Chinese leaders once more begged to negotiate. Elliot peremptorily dictated his terms, and a few minutes before the general assault was due to commence, the British commanding officers, much to the chagrin of their troops, were informed of the conclusion of the Treaty of Canton.

V: TYPHOONS AND FEVER IN EARLY HONGKONG

Under this treaty well over $6,000,000 was paid for the ransom of Canton and as an indemnity for British losses; the Chinese troops and special commissioners sent by the Emperor to take charge of affairs were obliged to move at least sixty miles away from Canton; and an assurance was given that trade might proceed peacefully at Whampoa. The Chinese were warned that any attempt on their part to rearm the Bocca Tigris forts (threatening access to Whampoa from the sea) would bring another British invasion force into the river. After the Chinese commissioners and troops had left and the money was paid, the British withdrew to Hongkong harbour. Elliot, preferring to reside ashore, went down to Macao.

What at first sight seems a curious omission from the Treaty of Canton is that it makes no mention of Hongkong, the British acquisition of which had not yet been confirmed by the Chinese. Not to have rectified Hongkong's anomalous position while he had the chance—there was still nothing but the initialled preliminaries—has been variously ascribed to Elliot's weakness, oversight or presumption that British ownership of Hongkong was beyond dispute. This has to be examined more carefully, remembering that Charles Elliot was by this time an adept at dealing with the Chinese and obtaining what he wanted from them with extraordinarily little use of force. His methods were so successful that the British were no longer in any real danger, while among the Chinese he had very nearly produced a civil war.

At the moment of dictating his terms for the treaty Elliot was aware that among the Chinese special commissioners he was dealing with, the subject of Hongkong, if once raised, would produce uproar and consternation. Kishen had already been led away in chains for his part in that affair, and to have demanded from these lesser commissioners, his successors, that the cession of Hongkong be confirmed was pointless. Theirs and the Emperor's negative answer was inevitable, and nothing would change this short of the seizure and sack of Canton, an action Elliot was anxious to avoid.

Besides, he already had in his hand Kishen's initialled preliminaries which Elliot intended to treat as binding, and on the basis of which he now took the next step. Returned to Macao, he appointed Captain William Caine of the Cameronians as magistrate with jurisdiction covering the island of Hongkong, and announced the first Hongkong land sale. Once buildings started going up and Europeans moved in, argument about British ownership would with the military force at Elliot's disposal soon be settled without undue upset. It might even lead to the cession of some more islands, such being the infallibility of the step-by-step system when supported by force. By the same method, disregarding what was said in the treaty preliminaries about Chinese dues, Elliot announced that Hongkong would be a free port.

The announcement of the land sale produced another outburst of ridicule among the British traders in Macao, espressed both privately and in the pages of the *Canton Register*. Nevertheless, just as the criticizing merchants had been only too swift to bring their opium ships up-river in the wake of the British fleet, so on the day of the land sale did all the ridiculing merchants turn up, the principal firms purchasing by auction every one of the seafront lots where today, along Queen's Road Central, Hongkong, arise the banks and towering offices of half the nationalities of the world. A day or so later Alexander Johnston was appointed to be in charge of the government of Hongkong— with John Morrison as Chinese Secretary and a Macao Portuguese as chief clerk—and moved across from Macao to his new office and Hongkong's first secretariat—a tent on the edge of the beach.

Elliot's attitude to Hongkong and the exertions he now undertook to persuade the British to move there were coloured by an urgent personal hope that the settlement, to whose existence he was committed, would prove a success. A certain amount of construction was undertaken at Hongkong in the same month as the land sale (June 1841), but it fell short of

Elliot's expectations, the main deterrent to Europeans moving from Macao being a totally unforeseen eventuality—Hongkong's alarmingly high death-rate. Both European and Chinese settlers were being mortally stricken by what appears to have been a form of malaria, at that time still an unnamed disease, and which here became known as the Hongkong fever. Not even Elliot's declaration that Hongkong would be a free port was much inducement to move beside the disquieting report that the Hongkong fever 'arose wherever the ground, having been opened up for the first time, was exposed for some time to the heat of the sun and then to heavy rains'.[1] The first visible signs of British settlement in Hongkong were thus Matheson's Opium Store—proudly indicated in early pictures—and a cemetery.

On 21st July the full blast of a typhoon struck the island. The foundations and lower parts of the new houses were of stone; the upper parts, due to a temporary shortage of stonemasons, were of wood and thatch. As a result the roof of every building came off. The stricken settlers were just rebuilding when after five days the typhoon recurved and ripped all the roofs off a second time. Elliot and Bremer, on their way to the colony from Macao, were caught in the same typhoon and shipwrecked on one of the Ladrones south of Lantao, and, having by now a total of $150,000 on their heads as reward for their capture alive, only with difficulty and a very large gift managed to persuade some Chinese fishermen to bring them back to Macao, where Elliot arrived in 'a Manila hat, a jacket, no shirt and a pair of striped trousers and shoes'.[2]

The following day the newspaper reported that Captain Charles Elliot, R.N., had been superseded in his appointment. It was the first Elliot heard of it. Five days later the report was confirmed in a letter from Palmerston, and after a few more days, on 10th August 1841, Elliot's successor, Sir Henry Pottinger, reached Macao.

VI: ELLIOT'S DISMISSAL, HIS ATTAINMENTS AND CHARACTER

The brusque way in which this was handled will indicate without explanation that the forces pitched against Elliot in China

[1] E. J. Eitel: *Europe in China.*
[2] Newspaper report quoted by Eitel.

and in London had achieved their purpose. When Elliot's despatch announcing his treaty preliminaries with Kishen reached London, Lord Palmerston had been extremely dissatisfied. As he commented in a letter to the Queen:

'The amount of compensation for the opium surrendered falls short of the value of that opium, and nothing has been obtained for the expenses of the expedition. . . . The securities which the plenipotentiaries were expressly ordered to obtain for British residents in China have been abandoned; and the island of Chusan which they were specifically informed was to be retained till the whole of the pecuniary compensation should have been paid, has been hastily and discreditably evacuated. Even the cession of Hongkong has been coupled with a condition about the payment of duties, which would render that island not a possession of the British crown, but, like Macao, a settlement held on sufferance in the territory of the crown of China.'

In London the acquisition of Hongkong was, as it had been in Macao, generally ridiculed. Even the Queen expressed surprised amusement that her representative in China should have presented her with a scarcely-populated, barren granite rock. On 21st April 1841 Palmerston received Jardine and other merchants, and in a testy letter written immediately afterwards, in which he complained of everything Elliot had done, he informed the plenipotentiary that he was to be dismissed, and that his successor would shortly be arriving.

On 24th August 1841 Elliot and Bremer boarded their ship of departure at Macao. A Portuguese fort fired a thirteen-gun salute. The Portuguese had a good deal of sympathy with Elliot; both they and he, they considered, had received the same treatment from the general run of the British community. Pottinger was not in Macao when Elliot left, and none of the more consequential Britons in China were present to see him off; while when he arrived in London it was to find that everyone who mattered, from the Queen and Prime Minister downwards, believed that he had disobeyed his instructions and, in the Queen's words, '*tried* to obtain the *lowest* terms from the Chinese'.

Elliot's Misunderstood Course

Charles Elliot, a naval officer untrained in diplomacy, by comparative accident found himself called upon to conduct one of the most difficult diplomatic exchanges in modern history. Although according to the letter of Palmerston's instructions he was conciliatory with the Chinese to the point of weakness, there was a side of his character which was of great strength. His attitude towards the opium trade was of uncompromising condemnation. He called it a sin and a disgrace, indistinguishable from piracy. Placed in the morally impossible position of having to conduct a war to preserve that trade, and rightly foreseeing that aggression against the Chinese in the cause of opium could not possibly promote eventual harmonious relations between the two countries, he made the fullest use of that section of his instructions that authorized the use of force only in an extremity. At every critical juncture he deliberately took care to demonstrate to the Chinese that he resorted to arms only under provocation, and he never missed an opportunity to enter into peaceful negotiations. In so doing he steered a miraculous but misunderstood course between the conflicting orders of his conscience, his superiors and his exceptional insight into Chinese realities.

Having in many ways the principles of a missionary, he applied them, as no missionary was required to do, to the amoral situation prevailing in the Pearl River. The yielding of an inch from this position would have gained him what he so conspicuously lacked and perhaps in general underestimated—the goodwill of the British community. It would have given him at once his status as head of that community. More salient, it would have given his wife the status she should have enjoyed, but was denied, as wife of the Queen's representative. Much as it would have benefited him materially to have done so, Elliot never yielded that inch.

We have already taken the opinion of a distinguished neutral on-the-spot observer, that of the American sinologue and missionary Samuel Wells Williams. Let us now take another opinion closer to the bone, the opinion of Howqua. After Elliot's departure, whatever the views of the Queen of England or the Emperor of China might be, Howqua at the mere mention of Elliot's name would nod his head sagely and say,

'E-lut number one hones' man'—by which, apart from the compliment, he implied (but long after the event) that perhaps Elliot need not have surrendered *quite* so much opium.

Thus the founder of Hongkong.

The striking similarity between the positions of Elliot and Kishen has already been noted. It did not end there. Elliot was 'banished', first to Texas as British Consul-General, and subsequently to Bermuda, Trinidad and St. Helena successively as Governor. He knew nothing of what had become of Kishen, and when the latter's name came up Elliot would reflectively say in so many words, 'Poor fellow! I suppose they cut off his head.'

But Kishen too had been 'banished', and years later the Abbé Huc was received by him at Lhasa, where Kishen was the Emperor's representative. There the last strange similarity came out. Kishen, whose regard for Elliot was as Elliot's for him, with a sigh presumed that Queen Victoria must have had Elliot beheaded.

XIV

THE CRACKED MIRROR

I: SIR HENRY POTTINGER—HIS TACIT ACCEPTANCE OF HONGKONG

WHILE CHARLES ELLIOT WAS IN CHARGE there still existed a last chance—quite a good chance, one would be inclined to say—of Great Britain obtaining her demands without inflicting on China a psychological shock producing far-reaching adverse consequences foreseen in some measure by Elliot, John Robert Morrison and the missionary sinologues, but by few others at that time. With Palmerston's dismissal of Elliot that chance passed, and the Anglo-Chinese War entered a sterner phase.

Sir Henry Pottinger, a person of balanced judgement, was better selected than Elliot to carry out Palmerston's policy in the way the latter wished it to be carried out. This policy remained one of forbearance in the use of military force in the presentation of only very moderate demands. Pottinger's moderation and justice in fact within the short space of two years put him well in the way to becoming almost as unpopular with the opium merchants as Elliot had been—a revealing aspect of the situation. The truth is that no leader was acceptable to the opium traders in the grab and get-rich-quick atmosphere which had descended upon the China coast.

The new plenipotentiary was none the less a man of harder temper than Elliot. Having no direct knowledge of the Chinese he was not influenced by any of the special considerations with which Elliot, John Morrison and others, by their very understanding of China, found themselves confronted. To Pottinger the Chinese were the enemy in an eighteen-months-old war.

They were perfidious, treacherous, cowardly and cunning, and as such they had to be treated. To the merchants, once they had sized Pottinger up, he was a reassuring change.

Two days after his arrival—it was the sole word of public encouragement Elliot received before his ignominious departure from China—Pottinger announced that the arrangements made by his predecessor in regard to Hongkong would remain in force temporarily until Her Majesty's pleasure were known. The same day a fire broke out in the collection of shacks known as the bazaar, occupied by Cantonese retailers at Hongkong, burning the whole lot to the ground.

Pottinger next sent his private secretary to Canton to convey to the Chinese authorities formal intelligence of his appointment, warning them in tones of plain severity that if there were the slightest infringement of the truce terms war would be resumed in the province. His missive caused an uproar in educated circles in Canton, producing some unprecedented scenes. That a red barbarian should with impunity address the officers of the Celestial Empire in so commanding a manner was seen as an insult and disgrace, and the City Prefect was howled at as a traitor by the students when he came to preside at the annual classical examinations.

Leaving Alexander Johnston uninterfered with at Hongkong, Sir Henry Pottinger now proceeded directly with his first main task of bringing the war to a quick and satisfactory conclusion. Amid the approval of the opium merchants at the new plenipotentiary's firmness of attitude, the fleet sailed northward from Hongkong on 21st August 1841, quickly occupied Amoy, Chinhai and Ningpo, and reoccupied Chusan. But there, due to the high rate of sickness among the troops, the advance stopped, while the Chinese feverishly prepared measures of retaliation, including a plan to seize Hongkong and murder every European on it.

Having been sent to China to rectify Elliot's mistakes, Sir Henry Pottinger found himself at the beginning of 1842 in the very situation Elliot had experienced and been unwilling to reproduce—the stalemate of 1840—with his troops dispersed at various places on the coast, immobilized by disease and unable to strike a decisive blow. There being nothing for Pottinger to do at Chusan, he left the troops where they were and returned to Hongkong.

There the chaotic conditions which had prevailed from the start continued with little change. In September 1841 the bazaar was burnt down for the second time, while in the same month sickness among the troops became so serious that as a precaution none of them were allowed ashore. With the coming of cooler weather in November general health improved slightly, but disease still remained a serious threat to the settlement's continued existence.

Nevertheless, having by now seen more of the China coast and realized more of its problems, Pottinger was coming to the conclusion that provided all impediments to absolute sovereignty were removed, the acquisition of Hongkong was not as worthless as it was generally considered in London; and in February 1842, although making no policy announcement on the matter, he indicated the trend of his future intentions by transferring the Superintendency of Trade from Macao to Hongkong.

II: HOSTILITIES ALONG THE YANGTSE—THE TREATY OF NANKING—HONGKONG'S FIRST CRITICAL YEAR AS A BRITISH COLONY

By March 1842, the Chinese considering themselves now strong enough to take the field, hostilities recommenced with an attempt to recapture Ningpo and Chinhai from the British. During the cold months the health of the British troops had improved; the Chinese attacks were repelled; and in pursuit of retreating forces the British began to advance inland. The following month Wusung and Shanghai fell, causing the projected Chinese invasion of Hongkong to be cancelled, the troops for it being hastily diverted to Central China. In July the capture of Chinkiang on the Yangtse River, at the head of the great inland canal supplying North China—including Peking—with much of its food, produced alarm in the capital, from which orders were reluctantly sent to open negotiations. The British advance continued to Nanking, the southern capital of China, where on 11th August, the British fleet and troops

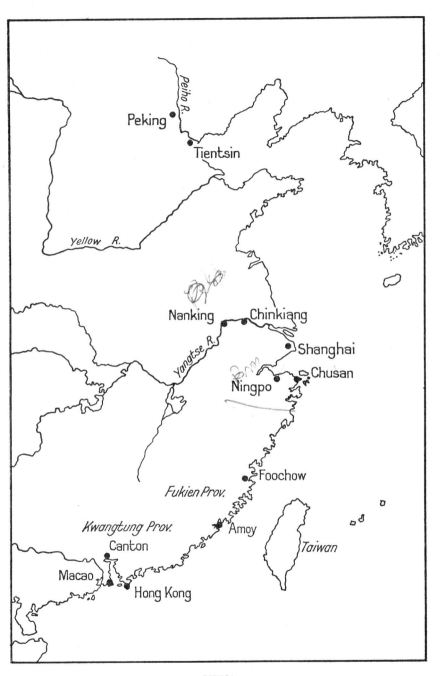

Peking

Peiho R.

Tientsin

Yellow R.

Nanking Chinkiang

Yangtse R.

Shanghai

Ningpo Chusan

Foochow

Fukien Prov.

Kwangtung Prov.

Amoy

Canton Taiwan

Macao

Hong Kong

CHINA

being on the point of assaulting the city, the Chinese sued for peace.

Pottinger's demands were forwarded at once to the Emperor. In Peking it was the story of the queen in the fairy tale whose mirror had always told her she was the fairest in the land. The queen's reaction when the mirror no longer spoke its comforting words was closely similar to that of the Emperor Tao Kuang faced with the British demands. With fear, hatred and feelings of revenge he signified his assent.

On 29th August 1842 the Treaty of Nanking was signed. By it Hongkong was ceded for ever 'to be governed by such laws and regulations as Her Majesty the Queen of Great Britain etc. shall see fit to direct'. No Chinese taxes or dues were to be paid on commerce conducted there. In addition, the ports of Canton, Amoy, Foochow, Ningpo and Shanghai were opened to foreign trade, permission being given for the British to reside there subject to their own laws, administered by such officials as Her Majesty's Government chose to appoint. Chinese export and import tariffs were regulated, and an indemnity of $21,000,000 was paid by the Chinese Government.

In geographical terms what the treaty conceded was slight— a barren island rock of which few if anyone in Peking had ever previously heard, and five patches of unwanted ground, which included mud flats and sandbars, adjacent to Canton and four remote ports. In a country so vast as China it seems at first hard to believe that such unprepossessing concessions could have caused the furore they did, arousing national hatred on a scale almost inconceivable in a country without newspapers and prior to the invention of radio. Here we have to remember the cosmology and the entire extraordinary realm of thought— the thinking of another planet—in which the Chinese lived. In these modest concessions—that Shanghai grew to be the fifth largest city in the world was a secret still hidden in mud— China's 'unchallengeable supremacy over all other nations' had been successfully challenged. An entire outlook on the universe had been threatened by the terrible message of its own unreality. A vision had been assailed and damaged. Like a cracked mirror it still possessed some virtue, but that virtue being no longer whole, its ultimate destruction was inevitable.

The Cracked Mirror

In June 1843 the Emperor's representative Kiying, a high-ranking Manchu official who had become what Kishen had originally been—the Emperor's cushion between himself and foreigners—proceeded in state to Hongkong to exchange the treaty ratifications. He was cordially received and entertained (at the new racecourse of all places for a mandarin, but no one seemed to consider this an odd choice) by Sir Henry Pottinger, anxious to impress him with the hope that future British relations with China would be friendly. Afterwards Pottinger was sworn in as the first Governor of Hongkong. He was concurrently the first permanent British Ambassador to China.

Within a month the Hongkong fever struck again and the number of deaths rose suddenly. One of the regiments lost a hundred men in six weeks. All those who were free to leave took part in a rapid exodus to Macao. By August the situation was considered so grave that even Pottinger himself crossed over to the healthier climate of the Portuguese settlement, where he remained several weeks. Among the many who died during September was Elliot's unassuming *éminence grise* John Robert Morrison, whose body was brought over to Macao for burial near the graves of his father and mother.

Nor was the outlook for the 'treaty' ports any too good. Amid the violent anti-foreign feeling which swept across China there were occasional pockets of moderation, one of which was providentially around Shanghai, where the new international settlement made a presentable start. Amoy, Foochow and Ningpo proved to be ports of little commercial importance, while at Canton popular hatred of foreigners was at such a pitch that it proved impossible for the terms of the treaty to be enforced there, foreign residence being still confined to the old factories.

Again as winter approached the health situation at Hongkong improved, and by the spring of 1844 there was an awareness among the settlers of all nationalities there that whatever the dangers and discomforts of the new colony, whatever the atmosphere of crisis and uncertainty, it was at this rate probably going to endure. Many of those hitherto undecided about leaving Macao now shifted their offices over to Hongkong, although retaining their cool and commodious old Macao homes for vacations or as an escape from the unhealthy heat of the Hongkong summer. Numbers of Macao Portuguese also came across to found their own firms and seek employment in government and commerce. Others went further north to the treaty ports, particularly to Shanghai.

As this movement of people took place, one aspect of the future became plain. Whatever future difficulties there might be with China—and that there would be more ahead was certain—there would be no large-scale return to Macao. The historic mission of the Portuguese settlement, to open and hold open for centuries a small door through which a mutual interchange of ideas, however fragmentary, between China and the West could be made, was accomplished. A new age in Sino-European relations had begun, and Macao was no longer the unique doorway for the West. Forty miles eastward, beyond the river and islands, the ticking of the mallets of a battalion of stonecutters was shaping the granite of Hongkong into stones for building—a sound that has hardly ceased.

BIBLIOGRAPHY

Much of the information in this book concerning internal conditions in Macao is derived from oral tradition. In describing the Anson episode I have availed myself of Chinese documents hitherto unpublished and in the possession of Mr. J. M. Braga, to whom I am also indebted for the Marquess Wellesley's letter quoted on page 93; the original of this letter is in the British Museum, and it here appears in print for the first time. Other background information comes from *The Canton Register* and *The Chinese Repository*, as well as from broadsheets and early newspapers published in Macao.

The principal books consulted are as follows:

Publications of Direct Relevance

HELEN AUGUR: *Tall Ships to Cathay*, Doubleday, New York, 1951.

E. W. BOVILL: *George Chinnery (1774–1852)*, Notes and Queries, New Series, Vol. I, Nos. 5 and 6, May–June 1954, London.

C. R. BOXER: *Fidalgos in the Far East, 1550–1770*, Martinus Nijhoff, The Hague, 1948.

J. M. BRAGA: *The Western Pioneers and their Discovery of Macao*, Imprensa Nacional, Macao, 1949.

WILLIAM WARDER CADBURY and MARY HOXIE JONES: *At the Point of a Lancet*, Kelly and Walsh, Shanghai, 1935.

MAURICE COLLIS: *The Great Within*, Faber, London, 1941; *Foreign Mud*, Faber, London, 1946.

E. J. EITEL: *Europe in China*, Kelly and Walsh, Hongkong, 1895.

G. B. ENDACOTT: *A History of Hong Kong*, Oxford, 1958.

SIR WILLIAM FOSTER, C.I.E.: *British Artists in India*, Journal of the Royal Society of Arts, London, May 1950.

MICHAEL GREENBERG: *British Trade and the Opening of China, 1800–42*, Cambridge, 1951.

Bibliography

WILLIAM HICKEY, *Memoirs of (1749–1775)*, edited by Alfred Spencer, Hurst and Blackett, London, 1919.

WILLIAM C. HUNTER: *Bits of Old China*, Kelly and Walsh, Shanghai, 1911 (first published Kegan Paul, London, 1885); *The 'Fan Kwae' at Canton Before Treaty Days, 1825–1844*, The Oriental Affairs, Shanghai, 1938 (first published 1882).

P. C. KUO, A.M., PH.D. (Harvard): *A Critical Study of the First Anglo-Chinese War*, Commercial Press, Shanghai, 1935.

ANDREW LJUNGSTEDT: *An Historical Sketch of the Portuguese Settlements in China*, James Munroe, Boston, 1836.

C. A. MONTALTO DE JESUS: *Historic Macao*, Salesian Printing Press, Macao, 1926 (first edition 1902).

ROBERT MORRISON, D.D., *Memoirs of*, compiled by his widow, Longman, Orme, Brown, Green, and Longmans, London, 1839.

HOSEA BALLOU MORSE, LL.D.: *The Chronicles of the East India Company trading to China, 1635–1834*, Oxford, 1926–9, 5 vols.; *The International Relations of the Chinese Empire*, Vol. I, Kelly and Walsh, Shanghai, 1910; Vol. II, Longmans Green, London, 1918.

PETER MUNDY, *The Travels of, in Europe and Asia, 1608–1667*, Vol. III, Parts I and II; edited by Lt.-Col. Sir Richard Carnac Temple, Bt., C.B., C.I.E., F.S.A., Hakluyt Society, London, 1919.

GIDEON NYE, JR.: *The Morning of My Life in China*, Canton, 1873.

G. R. SAYER: *Hong Kong, Birth, Adolescence, and Coming of Age*, Oxford, 1937.

SIR GEORGE STAUNTON, BT.: *An Authentic Account of an Embassy from the King of Great Britain to the Emperor of China*, London, 1797.

FREDERICK WELLS WILLIAMS: *The Life and Letters of Samuel Wells Williams*, Putnam, New York, 1889.

Publications of Contributory Relevance

C. R. BOXER: *The Christian Century in Japan, 1549–1650*, University of California Press, 1951.

The Cambridge History of India, edited by H. H. Dodwell, M.A., Vol. V, 'British India,' 1497–1858, Cambridge, 1929.

KEITH FEILING: *Warren Hastings*, Macmillan, London, 1954.

C. P. FITZGERALD: *China, A Short Cultural History*, The Cresset Press, London, 1935.

L. CARRINGTON GOODRICH: *A Short History of the Chinese People*, George Allen and Unwin, London, 1948.

DENNIS KINCAID: *British Social Life in India, 1608–1937*, George Routledge, London, 1938.

Bibliography

H. V. LIVERMORE: *A History of Portugal*, Cambridge, 1947.

FELIX ALFRED PLATTNER: *Jesuiten zur See*, translated from German by Lord Sudley and Oscar Blobel, as *Jesuits Go East*, Clonmore and Reynolds, Dublin, 1950.

ARNOLD H. ROWBOTHAM: *Missionary and Mandarin*, University of California Press, 1942.

G. B. SANSOM: *The Western World and Japan*, The Cresset Press, London, 1950.

C. R. WURTZBURG: *Raffles of the Eastern Isles*, Hodder and Stoughton, London, 1954.

GREGORIO F. ZAIDE: *The Philippines since Pre-Spanish Times*, R. P. Garcia Publishing Co., Manila, 1949.

INDEX

Index

Index

Index

Index